I0568518

The Naked Path of Prophet series

volume 0

A Wildly Sensual YAHWEH

The Controversial Genesis Stories in the Bible

translation & commentaries by

Brian J. Shircliff

revised and updated edition

VITALITY

buzz, bliss + books

A Wildly Sensual YAHWEH:
The Controversial Genesis Stories in the Bible
volume 0 of **The Naked Path of Prophet** *series*

Published by VITALITY buzz, bliss + books LLC
vitalitybuzz.com

Proceeds from sales of this book benefit the mission of VITALITY Cincinnati Inc: transforming lives through holistic self-care from neighborhood to neighborhood, person to person, and breath by breath since 2010. It's the power of the circle!

VITALITY
buzz, bliss + books

ISBN: 978-1-954688-04-9
Library of Congress Control Number: applied for

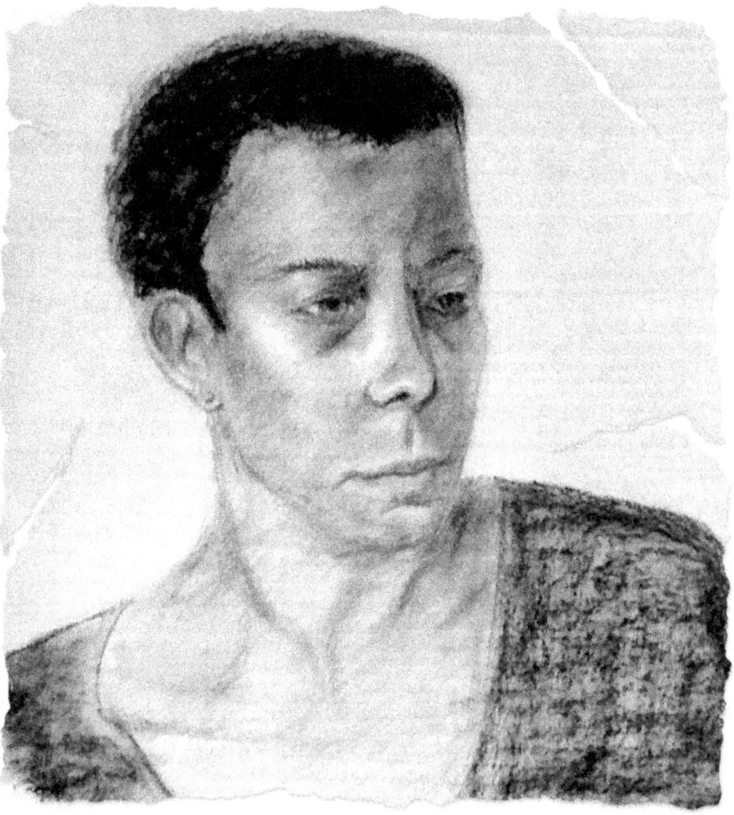

this book is dedicated to an exceedingly wise band
of genderbending women
whose names we'll never know

thinking it was a singular storycrafter, biblical scholars once called her "the Yahwist" or "J"

in previous books, I've playfully named her 'Sweet Lady J' and, now convinced of this person being a band of storycrafters through the generations, I have settled upon 'the band of YAH'...this band who once told stories of a new god called YAHWEH summoning a family out of a land of comfortable-cruelty and mega-metropolises like New York City where life is hot-hot-hot, a cradle of civilization...

to a land where wandering is the key to survival...a land of bordercrossing, genderbending, and sexuality-seeking-love...

to a land where a new imagination will be born...an imagination that will inspire nonviolent creative-action, neuroplasticity through movement, new ways of being human...an ecstasy-inducing prophetic imagination that could improve everything on this planet.

It's an imagination that no modern religion wants anything to do with — and even tries to bury.

May the prophetic imagination
come to light again
and again
and again...

especially for all who think they/we live in darkness....

In gratitude to our VATRONS
who seek with us all a new way forward &
who have helped bring forward this new volume
by contributing $25 or more
to make this publication possible — we thank you!

Many of these VATRON-friends supported a re-boot of *Sweet Lady J* in 2019...and they will be quick to notice that *A Wildly Sensual YAHWEH* is far, far from what that first book was, even with those 2019 updates. I've grown (I hope), and have been able to sense more in these Genesis stories...maybe more than has been uncovered by anyone since the band of YAH's stories were molded and hidden by the Levitical priestly editors in the Torah.

two very large anonymous gifts
Cynthia Allen & Larry Wells,
Deirdre & George Beluan, Mary Ann Blome,
Pete Corrigan, Raven & John Crawford-Dunn, Bob Donovan,
Mary Duennes, John Echols, Allen Feibelman, Judith Johnson,
Maggie King, Ian Korchak, Mary Laymon, Elfreide Manning,
Deborah Martin, Michele Mascari, Sarah Mayher,
Melissa McNeill, Alice Michels, Carol Ann Montgomery,
Julie Murray, Jamie & Michelle Murray-Davidson, Eric Nichols,
Yong Jim Pan, Stephen Peterson, Jane Redd, Bob Reineke,
Dave Rose, Mary & Robert Schneider, Lucille Schultz,
Jodi & Wayne Shircliff, Cooper Simmons, Stacy Sims, Tonia Smith,
Kristen Swank, Maureen Sullivan-Mahoney, Shige Sakurai,
Howard Thoresen, John Williams, Carol T. Yeazell

In gratitude to these friends who improved tremendously *A Wildly Sensual YAHWEH* by reading a nearly final first edition, commenting, and proofreading:

Helen Buswinka, Alice Michels,
Jane Redd, Ryan Yeazell

CONTENTS

Resources for Further Discovery

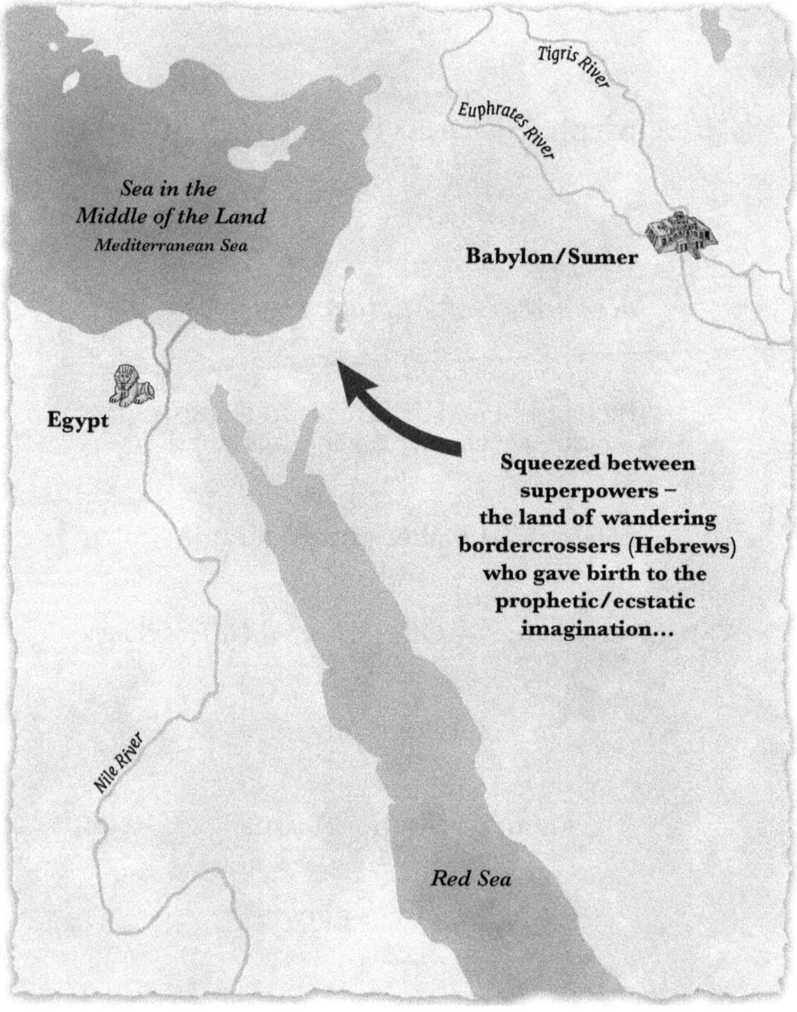
Tigris River
Euphrates River
Sea in the
Middle of the Land
Mediterranean Sea
Babylon/Sumer
Egypt
Squeezed between
superpowers –
the land of wandering
bordercrossers (Hebrews)
who gave birth to the
prophetic/ecstatic
imagination...
Nile River
Red Sea

A Preface to This Second Edition

This second edition includes all new commentaries. I've been swayed by the argument of the archaeologists digging in the layers of Ancient Israel/Palestine's earth and I've been swayed by the (mostly) European scholars whose recent work on the overall assembly of the Hebrew Bible is quite compelling. What's in the earth and what's not there does indeed shape what we can say about the Bible...and all of that will likely keep changing as humans seek more of our roots, how we arrived at this moment with the stories — and often competing stories — we've told and re-shaped for millennia.

While I've updated a few lines of the translation of the Hebrew texts in this new edition, much of it remains as it was in the first edition. I've smoothed out a few cranky-sounding translations and unearthed a bit more humor in the 'original' Hebrew text and include it now with this edition.

And while their Bible-assembly argument is quite compelling, most of these same biblical scholars seem stubborn in noting the wildly clever and bawdy style of these biblical texts. The verb choices in the 'original' Hebrew Bible are raw and ridiculously hilarious...and all too often ignored by these scholars. One reason, quite valid, is that we cannot know the style of, let's say, the 'original' Eden story because it has been first tampered with by the ancient Levitical priests and then by generations of Deuteronomist biblical-assemblers and then by the later generations of Masoretes who added vowels to the only-consonant 'original' texts they inherited from the Deuteronomists and the earlier manuscript-copying tradition.

The tampering and re-interpreting is significant within all of these layers, often strategically (I argue) to cover over the style of what today we call the prophets. And this cover-up of prophetic style is a key touchstone of why I am creating this *Naked Path of Prophet* series.

And yet some style remains that is certainly not in the usually very conservative and even fascist interests of the Levitical priests, royalist and later post-royalist Deuteronomists, and much later Masoretes. And it is this style that seems quite contagious in the emerging religious traditions born from the Bible...Judaism, Christianity, Islam...and each of these big three with their many branches and differing traditions hearkening back to the same Bible-roots. Some styles of Sufism that we experience in poets like Rumi or Rabi'a seem to play on what the earliest storycrafters and poets of the Bible play on...full of surprise, words that unfurl within the hearer that the hearer might discover choices for themselves in their lives. Such is the very clever nonviolent style of the prophets. It is such a style that powerbrokers of a hierarchical mindset found and continue to find dangerous to their thin grips on power. The prophets, after all, seek freedom... born from within oneself...freedom for and with and by the wind...the wind alone...the life we all share from our first breath to our last.

All too often, though, this very freeing style of the early prophetic storycrafters and rhyme-spitters gets suffocated and squashed by later generations — whether those later generations of squashers are ancient Levitical priests, Deuteronomists, Masoretes, priests or rabbis or imams and educators/ministers of any age of the religions of The Book (Bible), or even the so-thought very liberal scholars of today who would rather not deal with the exceedingly sexy and funny texts, so they are all too often silent about them and hope no one asks them about them too publicly.

As a scholar-friend once said to me, "The most difficult thing to translate is a joke...and scholars aren't usually very funny."

We must remember that most of the Hebrew Bible was crafted long before there was a Judaism — let alone a Christianity or Islam. And yet some of the imagination of the much later Sufi poets and the much earlier Biblical storycrafters and poets — the ecstatics, the prophets, NBYAHYM — swim in the same pleasure-rich ocean that first imagined Eden, a word that means 'pleasure.' And not just any old 'pleasure'...the characters Adam and Eve were hiding from YAHWEH in the Eden story...and not just any old 'hiding' either. As I'll lay out in this book, these mud-creature characters we have called "Adam and Eve" were hiding inside each other, as in love-making. Yes. That's the verb that's there in the 'original' Hebrew Bible, so very different from hiding behind a rock or a tree.

Scholars could be more vocal about what's there in the Bible — and what's not. It is such honesty of biblical proportions that is needed if humans are to grow on this planet by untangling the twine — and handcuffs and tape-over-mouths — that bind...all those who have had a hand in creating our compulsions when we were so young and needy. We got through it — we're alive! — though even the most functional of us developed at least a little bit of compulsion from however we soothed ourselves in getting through those tender early years when we couldn't even feed ourselves all the way through those adolescent years when we tried weaning our way from our parents' or guardians' or siblings' or teachers' or coaches' power over us. As adults, we have the full power of choice and the full choice to grow or not grow, though rarely do we use those powers and choices to our full abilities. As neuroplasticity-through-movement pioneer Moshe Feldenkrais reminds us in *The Potent Self*, we are responsible too for our ignorance.

The Naked Path of Prophet series seeks to highlight this prophetic/ecstatic style so that all dreamers on this amazing planet might know better our playful roots, and if they/we like such play, then play.

And this play is important. It could be the least compulsive thing we can do. Play comes from within, it's an expression of what is stimulating for the player based on their own sensations, their own curiosity and needs. It's not a 'play' directed by or mediated by any outside authority, be that authority a parent or guardian or older sibling or teacher or coach or religious-leader or celebrity or politician, etc.

Play might be the only thing that topples the many fascist playbooks we've inherited and that tragically continue to be invented, all of which prescribe how we are to play and with whom and where and when and with what we are to play and not. Indeed, these playbooks have nothing to do with play...they do not let us trust our sensations, they do not invite an interior curiosity about our external world, they do not trust THE ALL of life in which we all swim.

But the very styles of the biblical prophets and their storycrafters — like Jesus does with his parables — do invite play. These poems and stories are wildly playful...they dance within the hearer and offer no instruction on what 'should' happen next. Indeed, the hearer is invited to play along, to create the next line, to spin out the next wild story...even and especially if that next line or story upsets the fascist 'games' of control... of deciding for us adults what they think is best for us when we adults have developed our adult nervous systems that can sense what is best for us and how we navigate our worlds of choices.

As modern scholarly research in my own country is revealing, Jesus' parables and wisdom sayings invite a revolution within oneself, on one's own terms. The 'Christ' cast onto Jesus is fascism, oily-slippery control, a hydra of hierarchies of one-better-than-another, the very opposite of what Jesus was inviting with his words and deeds in his life 2000 years ago. The new 2023 edition of *The Naked Path of Prophet vol 1* delves into the problems of 'Christ' in much more depth.

What is fascism, after all?

It's a naming by the few for the many what is holy and right and true and allowed, the controlling few then proclaiming that what they've determined to be holy and right are ordained by 'God,' wrapping their self-created worldview in 'God-talk,' and deciding what happens to those who do not buy this worldview they've concocted, a worldview that always preserves their own holds on power, no matter the tragic costs.

The ancient Levitical priests, after all, endorse a fascist worldview that kills and advocates the persecuting and killing of even the peaceful ones (prophets), just as much as later generations of their own families were persecuted and killed by fascist-minded people century after century, culminating in the ever-tragic Holocaust. The Shoah. The catastrophe. The absolute disaster.

Peace be upon all who died from the catastrophe, from fighting it, from the necessary and terrible traumas of remembering it and all that transpired.

The hierarchical imagination, as we'll continue to discover, kills...

as the circular imagination appreciates all life.

As we'll discover by reading the biblical texts — and actually dealing with what is there in the 'original' Hebrew texts — we actually have choices within the Bible about which worldview we'd like to make our own. The Bible is most certainly not one single worldview but full of possibilities that we can generally gather either as 'hierarchical' or its playful opponent 'circular.' More on that in a bit.

What Jesus and the prophets were offering was freedom within; what the powerbroking ancient Levitical priests and Deuteronomists and Masoretes were offering — and their 21st century religious adherents continue to offer — often does not allow you to use your God-given senses to discover what is best for you. They want to be your parents or your betters...some even want you to call them 'Father' or 'Reverend' ('revered one,' one who is better than another) or 'Rabbi' (literally 'great one'...again, one who is better than another). What is utterly tragic is that these ancient Levitical priests and Deuteronomists and Masoretes laid down some beautiful ideas — like forgiving generational debts and taking care of the poor and widowed — onto a fascist blueprint and that all became modern religion... something that billions of people on the planet follow without much thinking about it.

And therein lies the problem at hand. What's not brought into consciousness all too often gets repeated.

Can you identify within the Bible the fascist, control-oriented ideas and differentiate them from the freedom-oriented ideas? Can you tell the differences? They are stark if you and I take the time to look carefully. And in looking carefully at the Bible's competing voices, we might come to know the differences between fascist-control and ecstatic-freedom in our own day and age... and discover we have choices — within the Bible and beyond it — about how to live together on this amazing planet. And give our great-great-great-grandchildren a chance to live too.

Differentiating between control and freedom is, perhaps, very similar to differentiating between compulsion and spontaneity, as Feldenkrais makes so clear in all his life's work, though especially in *The Potent Self.* Forthcoming volumes in *The Naked Path of Prophet* series will have much more to say about this regarding our own personal choices and the choices we've inherited and continue to make as a national and world people regarding our systems of government, economy/climate, medicine, and more.

We humans of the 21st century continue choosing controlling-fascist frameworks instead of doing the hard work/play of personal transformation — discovering love in our midst...as simple as discovering our fingers and toes as a baby does for the very first time.

We marvel when fascist movements and their often tragically violent displays rear their ugly heads and say, "I just don't understand how they can think that, that fascism" but forget that we practitioners of modern religion are often the propagators of fascism and hierarchically-informed thinking and that that thinking often creates the familial and government systems that shape our whole lives until we untangle the addictions and compulsions we've created — often so young — to deal with having to be cared for and controlled as infants and on into our childhoods until we can throw all that off and become friends — equals — peers — with all who once raised and reared us and for a time — an important time of youth — and took responsibility for our care until we matured and sat up on our own sit-bones or stood on our own one or two feet or hands and moved in ways we wanted to and ate and drank on our own and learned to care for ourselves, hopefully playfully, curiously, joyfully.

May our sensational play lead us to discovering love — Love — always in our midst, as close as every breath and every breeze...upon which we can live.

August 2023

An Invitation to This Volume in the Series

The Naked Path of Prophet
volume 0

How do you feel about being impregnated by God? being penetrated by God? God wanting to have sex with you?

It's not a question of gender — God's or yours. God knows, people of all genders can find ways of having sex — penetrative sex — with a beloved of any gender. I learned so much by watching *Blue Is the Warmest Color* and *XXY* and *Princess Cyd,* all stories of humans finding ways to love, sometimes fumbling in love, with humans. Each of these films gave me an imagination toward love in ways I hadn't yet been able to conceive.

And of course let's not let the constraints of 'binary' with gender be the default. Humans have been born with diverse genitalia for millennia — and those humans born with genitalia different from the supposed binary of vagina & penis were often recognized as the shape-shifters, the shamans, those who knew all or could bordercross easily.

This whole business of bordercrossing is central to the Bible, to the biblical imagination...to any imagination. The very word 'Hebrew' means 'bordercrosser,' after all.

What indeed would it be like for you to be penetrated by God? for God to cross your border, your very self? is your skin indeed a border?

These are the central questions of Genesis. And these are the central questions of the prophets. And Genesis rather strangely plays on and with the prophetic imagination, perhaps is even a taproot of the prophetic imagination with these stories that evolved and grew generation after generation by the prophetic-bands who told and re-shaped them. The prophets are among the first to note the imaginative differences between their prophetic/ecstatic imagination and the default hierarchy + royalty/slave imagination found in the political or religious arenas.

No matter how much we try to separate them, politics and organized religion are ultimately one and the same imagination to anyone who regularly drinks from the ecstatic/prophetic well.

With a carefully tuned eye and ear and heart, it becomes rather easy to notice that politics in the United States — my home country — is essentially a religion in itself. And it doesn't matter to which party one person pledges their allegiance. Sadly, politics-as-religion is probably the case no matter which country we study. Nationhood breeds this kind of thinking to survive.

Hierarchs of organized religion and hierarchs of politics/government envision life as a pecking order, as some people having more worth than others. Prophets do not...they are led by a different experience, and thus an entirely different interior map of life.

"J" and the prophetic/ecstatic imagination

Most of Genesis was first crafted by storytellers whose names we'll probably never know. Once thinking that it was a singular person, scholars used to call this storyteller "J" or "the Yahwist." I once preferred to call her Sweet Lady J, to lighten the scholarly mood and catch some wisp of these stories' playfulness. But today, I no longer think the storycrafter behind most of Genesis is a single person but instead a whole band of storycrafters through the generations...'the band of YAH,' I call them.

In any case, these storycrafters give birth to so much of our 21st century imagination, much of the bedrock of our 21st century assumptions. Adam and Eve. Cain and Abel. Sodom and Gomorrah. Joseph and his Incredible, Wildly Colorful Dream-Jacket...or some such silliness that seems to avoid the story's roots. Yes, I'm playing with the name of the Broadway musical that is quite entertaining and fun but the furthest from the roots of the story as one can get. After all, in the Hebrew story, Joseph is wearing a dress that princesses wear.

Yes! And his father Jacob gave him the dress — his same father who was penetrated by YAHWEH in a wildly random wrestling match in the spookiest of areas in the mountains, as Jacob was worrying about the brother he once duped coming at him with 400 men and now ready to get his revenge. This penetration-by-wrestling is how Jacob becomes Israel, a new name for him and an origin story for a prophetic people whose roots were in bordercrossing, genderbending, and ecstasy with YAHWEH.

Yes! In the Bible. All of this. Yes! In the deepest imaginations of time and storycrafting.

All too often, the band of YAH's stories in Genesis — in the Bible — were interpreted through the voice and lens of the hierarchs, the priests and royalists. The hierarchs could not fathom YAHWEH groping and penetrating Jacob, the one who would become Israel. So the hierarchs covered it up, generation after generation... first by the ancient Levitical priests who crafted most of the Torah, then by the Deuteronomists of many generations who completed the priests first work and joined it with their ever-evolving text of Deuteronomy, a few centuries later by the Alexandrian Jewish-priestly scholars who translated the Torah from its original consonants-only Hebrew to Greek (a text known as the LLX or Septuagint), then by Christian priestly scholars like Jerome who translated the Greek Septuagint and New Testament (all of it originally written in Greek) into Latin (Vulgate), then too by the Jewish Masorete priestly-scholars of the 6th - 10th centuries CE who added vowels to the 'original' Hebrew Bible that had only consonants up to that point.

As you can see, there are many layers to this cover-up of what is actually there in the 'original' Hebrew texts for those who have eyes and ears and hearts to perceive what is actually there. You might think that this addition of the vowels by the Masoretes is no big deal. But in a language like Ancient Hebrew it's a huge deal. Before those vowels were added, a single word could be read and heard and understood in a variety of ways — that's actually the point of ancient Hebrew speech. Ancient Hebrew riddled and punned every hearer into wondering about layers of meaning. The Masoretes came along and tried to nail everything down to one meaning — even many centuries after those Hebrew stories and poems were first uttered in all their punny magnificence.

The purpose of a pun, after all, is to the scramble imaginations and usual understandings for a moment. With a good pun, you're not sure which meaning was intended or maybe both meanings. The band of YAH's Genesis stories are riddled with puns as is 1 & 2 Samuel and most of the prophets' poems...Amos, the Isaiahs, Jeremiah, and more.

Ever since the Levitical priests crafted most of the Torah with later help from the royally-motivated Deuteronomists, every rabbi and priest and pastor and bishop and archbishop and pope and imam and Bible-study leader and the whole hierarchically-minded, organized religion crew has been intent on preaching a 'gospel' that is far more priestly and hierarchically nuanced than the prophets' clever and punny-imagination that puts YAHWEH above all else, with every human being on the same level below YAHWEH, friend and enemy alike.

It should be noted too that the Alexandrian translators of the Septuagint, the Christian 'father' translators of the Vulgate, and the Masoretes most likely had no ear and no imagination with which to notice that there are different authors to the Biblical texts — three or four authors in Genesis alone, as we'll soon discover. On the other hand, the ancient Levitical priests and the Deuteronomists who crafted the Torah surely knew there were multiple authors/voices in Genesis and in the other four books (Exodus, Leviticus, Numbers,

Deuteronomy). The very aim of these cataloguers and editors was to assemble a single-fabric, a single-tradition from all of these competing voices/authors. As we'll soon discover, their significant motivation was to silence the prophets and draw people's attention away from their compelling prophetic poems or raps, their ecstasy-inducing experiences, and the stories about the wild prophets who invite infinite possibilities through relationship with YAHWEH. And not just any relationship...the prophets invite a wildly sexy relationship with YAHWEH who allows Itself to be captured, who penetrates you and me into life.

Thankfully, careful readers today will notice that the efforts of the Levitical priests and the Deuteronomists were not completely successful. The prophets' clever vision and poems and imagination live on. YAHWEH cannot be silenced....

None of today's translations of Genesis deal well or completely with the letters that are there in the Hebrew story. Let me say that again — there are no translations available today that deal with the letters and words that are there in what we have as the 'original' Bible, what is often called "the received tradition." *The Naked Path of Prophet* series is aiming to change that by letting the prophetic-imagination of these biblical texts speak again, often for the first time in thousands of years.

Translators have for millennia been trying to translate away from the letters/words that are there in the same versions of the Hebrew Bible that we all tend to use...the *Biblia Hebraica Stuttgartensia*, descendent of the famous *Leningrad Codex* which was the Masoretes' original work. There are indeed other versions of the Hebrew

Bible, though the BHS (as it's often called) is the one used by most scholars I know.

No matter which 'original text' of the Bible we use, we might begin to wonder how it is that through 2.5 millennia — a whole lot of time! — those infected with the priestly-imagination or royal-imagination could hold down the ecstatic/prophetic-imagination of the prophets. You'd think there would have been at least one inquisitive scholar who would have noticed just how sexy and wild YAHWEH could be and want to go there, follow that imagination, and discover then that there is a whole lot of this in the Hebrew Bible. But most scholars do not follow that imagination much, most people don't. Most of us cannot imagine a God like YAHWEH penetrating human beings. An easy answer is to mutter the old line "YAHWEH will do what YAHWEH will do" and move on — never mind that YAHWEH was doing Its sexy things with the prophets, the ecstatics. Indeed, sex with YAHWEH is what leads to becoming a prophet!

And what do we as a society do with prophets? We kill them. As soon as possible. Or proclaim them lunatics until they become dangerous enough to justify killing them.

And we explain it away. Many think that the royal and priestly cover-up of the prophets' ideas and ways of life in the Bible is no big deal. But that cover-up is a bit like letting your enemies decide how you will be remembered after you're dead and gone...letting your enemies craft your life-story so that future generations can know you through their slanted enemy-views.

It doesn't have to be this way. The band of YAH and

the prophets invite a new way forward — one not tried publicly and proudly for thousands of years...even though the prophetic/ecstatic-imagination erupts in interesting ways in every generation. YAHWEH speaks when YAHWEH wants to speak!

This ecstatic, genderbending band of Genesis-storycrafters who lived 2500+ years ago, knows we all know what it's like to be penetrated by YAHWEH, and they know we humans rather enjoy it. Sex with YAHWEH is lifegiving, sensual, lovely for those with an imagination that pays attention and wants to notice It. Gautama/Buddha knew it/It too, though by a different name, and he read it right out of the old Vedic epics and simplified the whole thing, much like the biblical prophets before and after him...thousands of miles away.

This sexy time with YAHWEH and the prophetic/ecstatic imagination it/It invites is just as infectious as the hierarchical imagination of the priests and politicians and their followers. You've probably had a taste of it/It, right? a taste of YAHWEH's love-potion...?

But we must be open to choosing it/It, and know that we are consciously making such a choice to live prophetically/ecstatically with the whole circle in mind...so very different from living hierarchically and rather selfishly.

Returning to our biblical stories, we might begin to ask why it would be so embarrassing to have YAHWEH penetrating Jacob or anyone else. Even though he limped along afterwards, maybe Jacob liked it? If you know the nature of YAHWEH, there'd be nothing embarrassing about it.

Indeed, I hope YAHWEH is penetrating you right now.

Gods and Goddesses have enjoyed screwing (with) humans since the beginning of time and story

The idea of the divine penetrating and impregnating a human — and enjoying it — is not a new one. We can find it many ancient cultures. Of course, Greek mythology comes to mind, with Zeus' penchant for lusting after and luring humans into relationship/sex and those humans then giving birth to demi-gods and demi-goddesses.

But Greek mythology's interest in having Zeus/ Godhead mixing with humans could be a few hundred years after the band of YAH's Genesis-stories...and this ecstatic-band is simply — and quite creatively — playing on the roots. What roots? They inherited stories from Sumer / Babylon...the ancient region called the Fertile Crescent, the land between the two great rivers, Tigris and Euphrates. We call it Mesopotamia...which literally means "the land between the rivers." Mesopotamia gave birth to the greatest of ancient cities — Uruk — built by humans, built at the commands of royalty and royal imagination, hierarchical imagination. Some great stories emerged from that region, *The Epic of Gilgamesh* and *Enuma Elish,* just to name two.

What the band of YAH does with those old hierarchically-minded stories — well, they flip them up-side down! Like the prophets before and after them, they flatten the pyramids of power and prestige, almost always having the underdog top the powerdog. Women often get the upper hand in her stories — indeed it was a woman who gave birth to Wisdom in the band of YAH's imagination.

And the band of YAH and the prophets before and after them want nothing to do with Uruk, with the life of the city, with the hierarchical slave labor needed to build and maintain such cities. In these Genesis stories, the band of YAH has YAHWEH call Abram / Abraham & Sarai / Sarah out of the region that built metropolises like Uruk to be a wanderer in the hill-country far south of Uruk, south of Ancient Babylon and all its trappings of being a superpower. For the prophets and for the band of YAH, the life of knowing YAHWEH is one of following the wind, going where the wind blows freely, unobstructed by cities and towers and walls and the powers needed to build and maintain them.

The band of YAH's stories and the prophets' poems and stories invite a new power arrangement, a new politic — not one mediated by humans, royal or otherwise. The prophetic imagination knows through experience — through experience of the wild wind — that the wind is much stronger than any human, much stronger than every human allied together. And for that very reason, after feeling the wind on their skin and after feeling the wind penetrate them into life, the prophets craft poems and stories that invite other humans to realize the foolishness of trying to hold power over any human. The prophets flatten the king-slave pyramid-system and the priest-follower pyramid-system and reveal that we're all made of the same stuff and all breathe the same wind.

What the prophets were doing is far, far different from city-dwellers and those who put their trust in human authorities, be they kings or governors or mayors or priests or popes or whoever.

The prophets needed space, hungered for space, for wild open places where they could know the wind, be penetrated by the wind, wrestle with the wind, make love with the wind.

Jesus: the result of sex with the wind

What is utterly tragic to me is that for nearly 2000 years Christians have not recognized the same themes in their/our gospel stories. Jesus was not born a king on a throne — he was a peasant from the middle of nowhere, a true underdog in a land controlled by a foreign invader, Rome. And if we pay even the least bit of attention reading the Gospel of Matthew and the Gospel of Luke, Jesus' fictional birth stories in those gospels are quite a lot like those older biblical stories of God impregnating humans. No matter how much my Catholic friends will blush...as the story goes, Mary, a young virgin engaged to a man, is suddenly pregnant by the wind of God, and nine months later, she gives birth to Jesus, the one for whom people supposedly had been waiting. Tragically, very few could bear Jesus' wisdom and cleverness and ability to heal so the authorities killed him.

Many Christians today (nearly all of us) still can't bear his clever wisdom and are much more content putting him on a throne as a 'Christ' (a military term) than listening to what he might say and what he might invite within us, something prophets do. Wisdom and the wind — ah, that Holy Wind wants inside of us, wants to penetrate us with Its wise ways! But we clench and push and flex and do anything to keep It out of us, keep God out of us — even thinking that killing the messenger will get us off the hook from the experience of divine impregnation.

Such is the plight of prophets, messengers, ecstatics... people impregnated with YAHWEH's musk-love. The Hebrew word usually translated as 'prophet' actually means 'ecstatic' in Hebrew. The word is NBYAH, in my own crude, unvoweled way of transliterating the Hebrew letters. There's a lot to wonder about with that word NBYAH, and this series *The Naked Path of Prophet* will invite such wondering, especially when these rather strange things get said by and about prophets/ecstatics, and all too often swept under the rug.

The band of YAH plays with the origin stories of the prophets quite a lot in the Joseph story, the story of the boy who was given a dress that princesses wear, the boy who one day will be Number 2 to Pharaoh. In the fictional Genesis story, Joseph is a bordercrosser who not only becomes a royal in a foreign land but who saves civilization with his wisdom and foresight because the enemy-nation's king listens! Even Joseph's own brothers refuse to listen to him — much like the people of Ancient Israel refusing to listen to their prophets generation after generation, even killing the prophetic Jeremiah and then 550 years or so later killing the prophetic Jesus with the help of the superpower of the day, Rome.

Please keep in mind — this is not an anti-Semitic statement. This is not an anti-Semitic book. What I'm pointing out is a fight throughout history between ancient Jewish priests and ancient Jewish prophets — even long before anyone could be called 'Jewish'...long before there was a Judaism or Jewish identity that the ancient Levitical priests and the Deuteronomists began crafting through the Torah. This fight is the fascism and freedom interwoven through the Bible that gave birth to modern religion.

The same fight gets played out in Christianity between priestly-minded people and prophet-minded people. In my own Roman Catholic tradition, it has been fascinating to watch hierarchs figure out what to do with a controversial prophet-figure like Oscar Romeo, a Catholic priest and archbishop who acted as prophet for the poor and marginalized of El Salvador. I used to have to go down to the local Episcopal church to celebrate Romero's feast day because for decades the Roman Catholic Church refused to honor Romero's very brave witness...a witness that cost him his life.

Within Catholicism, this same fight is being hashed out between those who are demanding accountability for the abuse and death of children all over the world — and the mass-graves and cover-ups generation after generation — at the hands of those who preach the gospel of hierarchy...so different from the gospel of love.

Look closely enough and we can see the same fight between hierarchical-imagination and prophetic/ ecstatic-imagination happening in every modern organized religion.

Ancient Israel as a nation is certainly not special in its silencing and even killing its prophets. My own nation has killed prophets since the very beginning. In the 20th century alone, we as the United States of America have killed some greats, for sure...Dr. Martin Luther King, Jr., Malcolm X, Harvey Milk, Dorothy Stang (killed south of our border but defending those who were being scourged with US corporate interests/dollars in mind)... just to name a few. These are the famous names...how many more have died for civil rights, for women's rights, for indigenous rights, for LGBTQ+ rights, for the right to live on this planet...?

How much longer must we the people of any nation — especially my own! — refuse to listen to or play with the wild raps and rhymes of the prophets, ancient or modern?

The band of YAH and the prophets offer an imagination that could free us all — if we let it/It and if each one of us begins the deep inner work that seeks to notice when we are hierarchically-motivated and when we are ecstatically-inspired. Their moralities are quite different. One uses control and death/capital punishment to enforce its morality; one does not.

The prophetic/ecstatic imagination: a bedrock ignored...until now?

If it's the case that our 21st century languages and imagination are built on this foundation of prophetic/ecstatic-imagination, this basement of time, and we've gotten the circle-friendly stories wrong for 3000 years because the priests and royalists made us see and hear those stories through their hierarchical-filter, then maybe we'd be wise to descend those ancient/inner stairs and figure out what we've missed down there in the prophetic-basement.

It might be the only way that such 'movements' can actually move us all toward freedom — the wise local women organizing Black Lives Matter, the worldwide refugee crisis and those helping them find asylum, women making important moves toward (re)claiming equality with men, my LGBTQ+ friends and compadres in our recognition that we've been around since the beginning of story/time no matter how many times the hierarchs try to silence and even 'disappear' us, and all manner of 'movements' toward economic possibility and indigenous rights and recognitions. Reaching down into our roots, the Greek word "economy" essentially means 'taking care of one's house...one's own.' If we recognize that one's house is the whole planet — or even larger and wiser, the universe — then how we respond to and with one another and move toward and with one another matters. Thinking circularly might be ever and ever important to welcome new possibilities to help us live and live well.

If these 'movements' toward social and economic change have any hope of succeeding and ushering in continual growth with every generation, then we'll need to be sure the 'new age' and new way(s) forward do not take on the hierarchical, one-better-than-another power dynamics that our current oppressors (our very selves, often) employ. We must all be very wary of taking on the hierarchical constructs of our oppressors and wielding their/our newfound power in just as ugly ways as our oppressors once did. Essentially, the priests and royalists who crafted the Bible got people for 2500+ years to see it their hierarchically-motivated ways instead of the ecstatic-minded ways of the prophets.

Gratefully, the band of YAH takes on these very questions

as they deal with the hierarchical sources of the ancient stories they heard via Ancient Sumer/Babylon, as these ecstatic-genderbenders bring forward something very different and something very wise through their stories catalogued (and all too often covered over) in what we today call "Genesis." The band of YAH teases at new possibilities, and so can we.

Yes. Let's be wise, friends. Let's discover together what the prophetic imagination might offer us, a new way forward that is indeed more circular and playfully spiral-rich and wisdom-seeking and wisdom-sharing than prescriptive and top-down, the insidious nature of hierarchy and its son patriarchy that have corrupted and clouded for thousands of years what humans can do when we put our minds — our whole selves — to growing human life on and with this amazing planet in the context of THE ALL, the Infinite.

Breathe...be penetrated...and know!

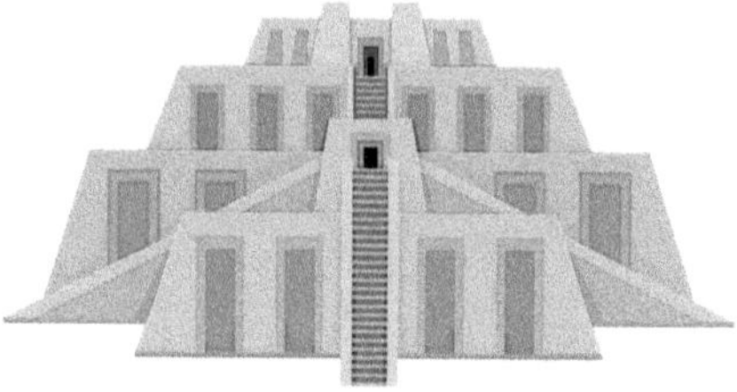

CHOOSE WELL!

An Intention
for *The Naked Path of Prophet* Series

(included in every volume)

This series has interest in the questions of the various scholarly theories about the origins and redactions (assembling + editing) of the Bible...but this series will not try to solve those riddles.

Biblical scholar Thomas Römer's books offer excellent summaries of many of the most current theories about the origins of the Hebrew scriptures, especially *The Invention of God* and the *L'Ancien Testament*; biblical scholars of the Westar Institute/Jesus Seminar have done much to help unravel the Christian traditions' layers to reveal the ecstatic roots of Jesus and the world-resounding message of Paul about this peasant Jesus and what God did for him. Maybe you've checked out *The Gospel of Jesus* by Robert W. Funk, Arthur J. Dewey & the Jesus Seminar or *The Authentic Letters of Paul* by Arthur J. Dewey, Roy W. Hoover, Lane C. McGaughy, & Daryl Schmidt?

Inspired by these and other scholars' excavations of the Bible, this *Naked Path of Prophet* series aims:

first, to reveal more of the cleverness of the Hebrew puns in the biblical texts and then bring forward this cleverly-styled wordplay/poetry into a clearer English translation...

...so that more people can identify such style running through much of the Bible and, if they find such style helpful for our 21st century world, then bring it forward in new ways;

and second, to reveal a significant idea for our time and all time, which continually gets passed over by scholars and by religious leaders and the faithful of any and all traditions, namely, that the Bible being a collection of many differing imaginations and writers could be divided into two competing camps: **the hierarchically-minded** and **the circularly-inspired**

...so that more people can identify which imagination is used within their own family, classroom, workplace, religion, and governments and that, by knowing the differences between circular-imagination and hierarchical-imagination, have the ability to choose which is most life-giving and helpful in any moment.

Hierarchical Imagination

A hierarchy has a human-leader over various strata of minor leaders over various sub-classes of humans. A hierarchy is a system where some humans have more value and more power than others. Often there is even a non-class of humans...untouchables who have no value or enslaved-people of all sorts, sex-slaves of all genders or eunuchs or maid-slaves or wet-nurses, each of whom might be valued/valuable but having very few if any rights to their own human personhood. This is what hierarchies do — they sort and place people based on their value to the system that those with power create and those without power accept until revolution boils over and there is a paradigm shift with some people losing and/or gaining power and privilege within the new hierarchical system...unless an entirely different and more circularly-minded system is chosen.

The hierarchical imagination often uses a podium from which one person addresses the masses who follow. There is little conversation in such a system, even when the group is small. The speaker stands over and above the followers who hear and obey. Perhaps the followers take issue with some of the speaker's announcements so the followers find ways to safely communicate their disagreements through channels long after the speech. Often such 'communication' is made passive-aggressively because it's the only safe way to 'communicate' in such a system. The speaker/leader then either takes those communications into account or delivers another speech that clamps down even more on the communicators or changes the system entirely so that the system becomes more circular than before and people have more influence in decision-making. In a hierarchical system, it is impossible to commune with the leader who ranks above all unless there is revolution or unless the top-dog leader changes the rules of the system to make the system more circular. But even then, the people that top-dog leader rules might not want or might not accept a more circularly-inspired system.

The hierarchical imagination plays out in royal-slave systems, in despot-follower systems, in guru-follower systems, in organized religion's leader-follower systems, in celebrity-follower systems...each and all of any era.

With the hierarchical imagination, people can and often do awful things to each other. The hierarchical system depends on it. And when people know no other option besides the hierarchical system, desperation can settle in quickly...tragic motivation to want to climb a rung higher and then another rung higher...moves that see people in the way or people down below as enemies or problems to solve. With a hierarchical-mindset, it's easy to point out that a person is evil or bad or wrong.

Someone with a circularly-inspired imagination realizes instead that people are not bad or wrong but instead are stuck inside hierarchical-systems, ways of imagining that have limited who they are and all that is.

All too often, hierarchical-imagination limits one's map of the Infinite, what we're all too often tempted to call 'reality.' As we keep growing and have more experiences in life, 'reality' keeps changing doesn't it?

Circularly-Inspired Imagination

A circularly-inspired imagination is much different, of course. With this imagination, each human recognizes the equal-value of all humans and sometimes even of all life, of every living thing. Such a circular imagination perfects itself as an entirely holistic imagination...where participants recognize on their own — often through very different experiences — that there is no separation between creatures...where it is readily recognized that we all exist within a larger and highly interdependent whole, as a Universe, the One-Verse, the Infinite, THE ALL. That is to say, we all exist in 'God.' When we recognize we participate in such a Whole, it's a lot easier to live more harmoniously with every creature, with all inside that ever-expanding circle.

The circular imagination often invites everyone to sit in a circle, with no one person any higher or more valued than another. A circle invites speakers and hearers and co-hearers alike to use all senses in communicating... even a deep look into someone's eyes or listening carefully to the subtle sounds someone makes or getting a wisp of the feeling in the air communicates a great deal. A circle breeds a sense of equality, a sense that we're all in this together and that we all will be needed in some diverse and equally-valued way to move forward in our shared life together on the planet. Could there be a leader or moderator or convener of the circle? Of course. But such leaders of a circle try to be very mindful not to interject their opinions or will upon the circle; instead, circularly-inspired leaders ensure that all ideas are heard, that everyone who desires to speak gets to speak, that those with information share what they know and invite ideas and people to evaluate information openly and wisely and to grow information's usefulness through deliberation and discernment. There is equal access to knowledge and opportunity in a circular system, even if knowledge and opportunity are not 'free,' even if they must be merited through effort and growth.

Circularly-inspired imaginers know well that some experience inspired them to a larger vision of THE ALL. Someone with a circularly-inspired imagination knows that an experience can free anyone stuck in a hierarchical-imagination — an experience as simple as a breath or a gasp from an ecstatic's clever rap or wild story or a deep look into someone's eyes. A circular-imaginer knows too that the awakening that comes from an experience must happen within each person and unfold within each person in that person's own time and in its own original way. It's not possible to make someone know THE ALL. Such an awakening erupts out of nowhere — is ecstatic in that way. Mentoring relationships can help, of course, especially when a mentor invites the mentee to spend some time in some activity, some study, so that some awakening might happen in the mentee's own time. Sensible mentors know too that what awakened themselves might not be the same thing that will awaken their mentees. Indeed, no two experiences are ever the same, right?

Beyond these mentor-mentee relationships, there have been glimpses of the circular imagination being lived out today or in times past, though they all too often either get snuffed out by hierarchs or the hierarchically-minded or devolve to a hierarchical-system because some who once perceived something of THE ALL can no longer stay with that vision and imagination, for whatever reason.

Sometimes, too, we live and act more circularly in one arena of our lives but think and act more hierarchically in others. For example, what a gift it is to be pro-LGBTQ+ and you and I invite to the round-table all people who feel different in terms of their sexual identity and their gender identity...but what good is that if we still think that people of our own ethnicity or skin-tone are better (or worse) than others? What a gift it is to be antiracist... but what good is it if you and I hate women or nonbinary humans? Or what good is it to greet everyone we meet as an equal but then buy our t-shirts or shoes made in sweatshops owned by millionaire CEO's or buy coffee or chocolate grown and picked by slaves?

We need to get to the root issue — and it's not racism,

it's not homophobia or the patriarchy or transphobia or anything like that. Those are all nasty symptoms of the hierarchical imagination killing us all.

Democracy... circularly-inspired or hierarchically-motivated?

Perhaps you're wondering where democracy rests between these camps?

Democracy — or rule by the people — attempts to break free from the hierarchical imagination with democracy's more circular attempts to allow all voices — at least those of a certain age — to be heard and with every person of age getting an equal vote. But all too often democracy devolves into hierarchy when celebrity-presidents of every party — and even the parties themselves — are followed at every word by their followers, all too often with little discernment as to the value or wisdom of what the leader or party offer. In smaller groups in a more local place, of course, circular-democracies can thrive. In larger groups, it can be quite difficult...unless there is a common appreciation for what ultimately gives life.

Some roots of circularly-inspired imaginations

So...hopefully you're becoming curious about how a circular imagination actually works or could be helpful in the 21st century, and how it has been lived out in past eras. Well, my friends, that's the very heart-intention of *The Naked Path of Prophet* series with its devoted interest in YAHWEH's wild and sexy wind. All are called by the wind/breath, we've been reminded by the wise ones through the centuries, few choose themselves or allow themselves to notice the sensations of the wind.

Jesus was interested in the circular imagination...his authentic parables and wisdom sayings and table-fellowship reveal that...but he lost first to the hierarchs of the religion of his region's day and then after his death to those wanting a more hierarchically-minded church.

Paul was interested in the circular imagination...the very rhetoric of his authentic letters to early Jesus-interested communities call for a more circular approach to governance where God rules and all people are valued equally below and because of God who raised up even a peasant (Jesus)...but Paul lost first to Rome and then to Peter's hierarchically-minded camp which projected Rome's sense of order and destruction onto Jesus-interested communities, and still does.

And where and how did Jesus and Paul get interested in a more circular imagination?

Perhaps they were inspired by the wandering ecstatics and their little quips of wordplay and poetry, clever parables or episodes of story, and exceedingly bizarre actions for, perhaps, nearly 1000 years before Jesus and Paul ever set foot on Earth. Those little ecstatic bits were becoming the Bible, at least the first half of it. It's a circular-style and circularly-minded imagination that seeps out in the poems of the likes of Amos and the Isaiahs and Jeremiah and more, in the stories of 1 & 2 Samuel and much of 1 & 2 Kings, in large portions of Genesis once called "J/Yahwist" because of these storytellers' penchant for calling the divine "YAHWEH."

Likely a band of multiple storycrafters through the generations, I've chosen to call this group 'the band of YAH.' Much later after their first tellings of these stories, the ancient Levitical priests (possibly with some later help from the Deuteronomic scribes) assembled these stories into what today we call Genesis, the first book of the Bible. The band of YAH is expert at flattening triangles/hierarchies into circles, often with humor.

Rather interestingly, this circular-style and imagination seems to seep out during the most difficult and oppressive times in history both before Jesus' time, during Jesus' lifetime, and long after.

Perhaps you've caught a wisp of It?

Perhaps you've had an experience of YAHWEH brought on by Its life-giving, inspiring wind?

What's most concerning to me is that many people I know well cannot distinguish a hierarchically-minded imagination from a circularly-minded imagination. Friends who recently left church-communities led by a man who proclaimed his status as a hierarch jumped right into another church-community or even an entirely different religious tradition, both being led by friendlier hierarchs of the same hierarchical system/imagination that still aggravates my friends, though they're not entirely clear why. The very person upon whom their original church was founded — Jesus — was up-ending the hierarchical imagination of his day with his clever parables and wisdom sayings, and with being present and loving with those he is said to share meals/time...women, tax collectors, children, the ill...people who were not regarded as people in Jesus' time. Sadly, so few of my own Christian tradition cannot discern the differences between what Jesus was saying and doing and what Peter or Pilate or the Sanhedrin-leaders were said to be saying and doing in the gospel stories we've inherited. Sadly too, this inability to discern hierarchical-mindedness from circular-mindedness happens in every religious tradition, not just my own Christianity. It's even present in yoga...tragically, it's nearly everywhere and we are the ones who pass it on unwittingly.

I too went right along with and even invested in the hierarchical system within my own religious tradition... for far, far too long...hoping it would change and thinking my queer outside-on-the-edges life/teaching would change things someday and somehow...until I realized my staying within my low place in the massive hierarchy as a lay religious educator was still giving power and credence to the hierarchical system. Finally I realized I had to swim away from my position and even my local parish to preserve my own life. I too often found the same hierarchical-imagination in so much of yoga and have sought out other styles of movement as well.

So I have compassion for my church-going and religious friends of all traditions and yoga-friends — and yet I hope they/we too swim away from the shipwrecks of all hierarchical imaginations before it's too late to even notice what's in the breeze and always has been — life! Such a realization of the wind of life is precisely what welcomed every awakening and 'miracle' that gave birth to a religion in the first place...and all too often just a short time later the circular, spiral-rich experience concretized in messy hierarchies that stifle the original experience that was so rich and life-giving and able to be accessed by anyone living on the planet. Such access to that circular, spiral-rich experience is always available...for anyone who breathes and can sense such breath.

Organized religion of any sort cannot bear the circular imagination that must wait on YAHWEH alone — the very breeze of life — and not anyone directing or liturgizing, not anyone creating formulas or potions or laws or concert-sets to cull their divinities to act.

As we'll soon discover, the ecstatic/prophetic imagination of the Bible's prophets does indeed call on YAHWEH to act...but it's the very experience of sitting, breathing, contemplating, perhaps even spitting just-created-in-the-moment stylish rhymes and rhythms and stories or gasping or laughing with them that stirs the breeze to act. Could it perhaps even be as simple as uttering 'YAHWEH'? When you open your mouth or nostrils, in pours that wildness of YAHWEH.

Dare you let YAHWEH have Its sexy, ecstasy-inducing way with you?

In a world undergoing such vast changes from day to day, in a world where the old orders no longer satisfy, might we have the courage today to play with such an open, circular style? Might we do so because we've had an ecstatic experience that makes us suspicious of the dangerous hierarchical systems of today and yesteryear? Might we do so because we'd like to let such an ecstatic-style expand and discover if it has something new to offer human life on the planet? Or just because it's fun and feels good, in YAHWEH's surprising ways?

No matter —

play.

Play is the very style of YAHWEH as these circular-styled biblical texts mentioned above point out again and again...after all, within a circle, we can be pleasantly surprised together, we can see deeply into each other's eyes, hear more clearly each other's sounds and make meaning from them, taste the possibilities of life's abundance together, smell each other's scents that drift to us in the breeze, touch gently and lovingly the open hands of one another...circle around! let the breeze blow! play! open yourself to a refreshing surprise!

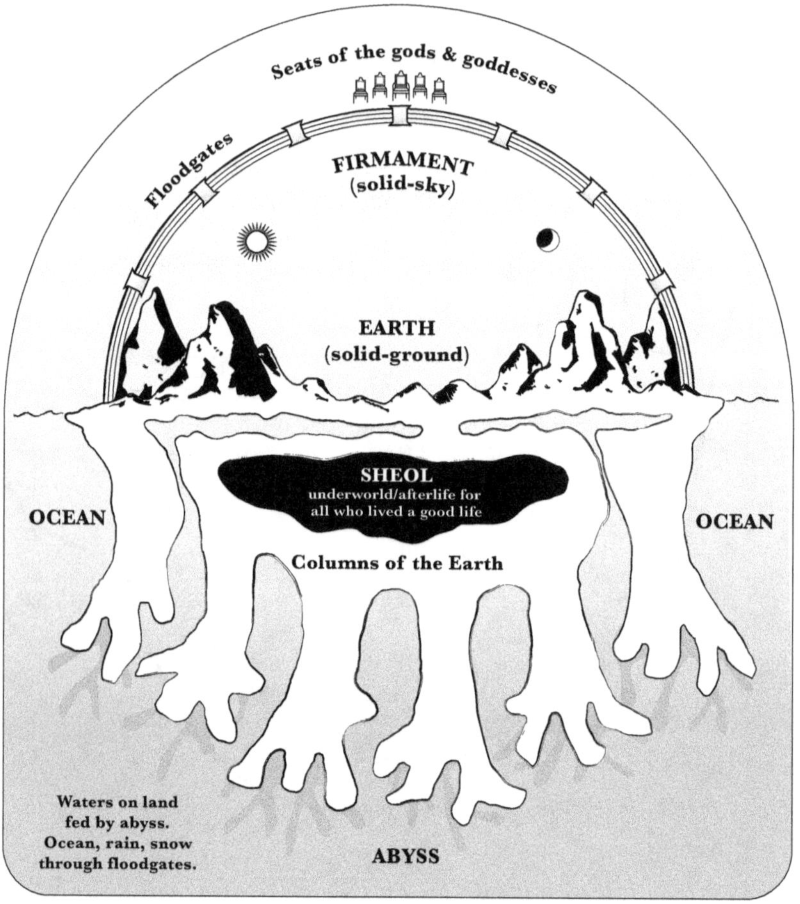

the worldview of the ancients who had no views of Earth from space...so it's this worldview of Earth as a 'snow-globe' of sorts that we must bring with us if we're to understand the Bible

A Brief Primer on the Building of the Bible

Many people will be shocked to discover that God did not write the Bible.

Neither did Moses.

Neither did Jesus.

The Bible was composed and written by many different people over more than 1000 years.

Most of the Bible was written in Hebrew.

The biggest chunk of the Bible — more than the first 'half' of it — is called a few different names. Not-so-wise people call it "The Old Testament"; wiser people call it "The Hebrew Scriptures."

What many people call "The New Testament" was written in Greek — the second 'half' of the Bible to which Christians appeal.

And there were more books written for the scroll(s) known as 'the Bible' that didn't make the cut — for lots of reasons.

Truthfully, we don't know how all this Bible-writing began, this writing down what we have today as the

Bible. Scholars have some pretty good guesses, though.

Even non-religious people might be very interested to know something of these biblical texts as so many of our modern languages are built upon the bedrock of these biblical stories, languages, and imagination.

The jumbled mess of the Bible

Sit down and read Genesis sometime on your own. It's a mess. It doesn't take a biblical scholar to notice that there are multiple storytellers there, multiple voices in the book. Indeed, stories are repeated and told just slightly differently, often with vastly different outcomes, as we'll see here.

Well, who are those different voices? And how did it all come together? Was Genesis written first?

Scholars today (again, see Römer for a concise summary) hypothesize that portions of Deuteronomy were the first written text of the Bible, though possibly some of the band of YAH's stories and many of the poems of the prophets were swirling about orally long before Deuteronomy. While this is the best scholarly theory of the day, it will likely change as more is discovered, especially archaeologically. All that being said, no discovery will dim the cleverness of the band of YAH's stories!

It's likely that the ancient Levitical priests...

> captured some of those oral stories of the-band-of-YAH-through-the-centuries and perhaps other storycrafters,

wrote some of their own priestly stories,

and crafted most of the 613 laws of the Torah/ Pentateuch, especially those we find in Leviticus. As we'll soon discover, many of these 613 laws attempt to put down the prophets and their prophetic/ecstatic imagination.

It's also likely that generations later a Deuteronomistic editor — or possibly editors through the generations — then...

put in order what today is the complete Book of Deuteronomy from the scraps of earlier years,

made light edits to all that had been assembled by the Levitical priests before them,

and then catalogued much of the remaining canon of Joshua, Judges, 1 & 2 Samuel, 1 & 2 Kings, Jeremiah, and possibly the other prophets as well.

A Wildly Sensual YAHWEH usually will not seek to differentiate between Levitical editing of the band of YAH's stories from the Deuteronomistic editing of the band of YAH's stories...especially since both the Levitical editors and the Deuteronomistic editors were both authority-types with just slightly different hierarchical imaginations. Bowing to the scholarly theory that the ancient Levitical priests were likely the cataloguers and editors of what today we call "the book of Genesis," I will usually call them 'priestly editors' in this book.

While the Deuteronomistic writers and editors one day

will try to claim the prophets and the mostly circular/ ecstatic imagination as their own tribe, as we'll soon see, the Deuteronomistic writers/editors like their Levitical priestly-brethren are hierarchically-minded and so much different from most of their prophetic sisters and brothers and nonbinaries.

The very name "J"/"Yahwist" is a left-over from the old 19th century "documentary hypothesis" — a theory that during the Babylonian Exile the priestly editors assembled the first five books of the Bible from four previously written documents with the "J document" going back to King Solomon's time in 9th century BCE. Most scholars question some or all of this hypothesis today — especially European biblical scholars — because textual and archeological evidence suggests that some of these "documents" are not as old as they once thought, including the so-called "J document." And not only that, there is <u>no</u> archaeological evidence for a King Solomon reigning over a United Monarchy of Judah and Israel in the 9th century. None.

Despite its significant flaws, the "documentary hypothesis" has one significant merit in that it displays quite clearly that there are many voices — even competing voices — in the first five books of the Bible. Though I do not consider myself a proponent of the documentary hypothesis, I do respect its highlighting that the so-called "J" strand is an entirely different imagination than its priestly counterparts.

Indeed, it's highly likely that the Genesis stories that name the divine as YAHWEH and have been attributed to this "J" were crafted and re-crafted through the generations — even centuries — following a particular style. I suggest that the "J" strand was never a document at all but an ever-changing mode of storycrafting that awakened curious imaginations enough to be used again and again through the early centuries of the emerging biblical traditions. Perhaps this mode — this style — is brought and could be brought forward even more today, if we are clever and wise and want social change away from the old trappings of hierarchical-thinking.

The grouping of stories in Genesis once called "J" is certainly not one singular voice but many — and thus why I've chosen to call those storycrafters 'the band of J.' These stories have a distinctive style that resonates in other biblical texts too...much of 1 & 2 Samuel, aspects of 1 & 2 Kings, many of the prophets' poems/raps, Jesus' wisdom sayings and parables, even the authentic Paul's clever logic...almost 1000 years of stories and poems and letters and wisdom sayings that have tried to nudge imaginations away from hierarchies and towards a more circular, all-inclusive, freer, bordercrossing, nomadic way of proceeding. There is no need for belief or following anyone (besides the wind) with this ecstatic/prophetic style of imagination...instead, such ecstasy recognizes that we're breathing YAHWEH, every one of us, and this lifeforce can be trusted in forging our unique paths.

And you'll soon note that those with this style of ecstatic/ prophetic imagination have no interest in territory. They are bordercrossers, in every way imaginable.

But what are their names?

We don't know the real names of these biblical authors or editors because people in the ancient world didn't sign their texts. It was a much different world from what we know today.

And truthfully, in an oral culture, not much is written down for many years — centuries even!

It intrigues to me to consider that a band of storycrafters could have taken a particular style and gathering of characters and weaved and refined stories for centuries, all of it held together by a particular style.

What style? This band of YAH offers wild characters and a wild vision of the divine whom they name YAHWEH. This band's stories overflow with sex and deceit and fun puns and craziness and surprise.

And what makes me think the band of YAH might have included women or genderbenders? This band's stories have women-characters who have significant speaking roles in the stories. This would have been outrageous 2500+ years ago. No other ancient text of the region has women-characters, especially women-characters whose words and actions are so pivotal to the story. As a matter of fact, this band's women-characters often do things that upset the expected plot of the story and invite new possibilities to emerge. For instance, a woman's curiosity and violating an order gives birth to Wisdom in (at least) one of the stories.

The band of YAH's stories always upset the hierarchical apple-cart or fruit-stand.

The band of YAH has some stories in Exodus as well, though it is much more difficult to separate those stories from the other biblical authors because the later editors layer onto the band of YAH's tales a whole religious-imagination and religious-practice, essentially a complete religion in itself in Exodus...a profound layering that's not always so evident in Genesis.

The band of YAH did not name what is mostly their 'book' — the first book of the Bible — "Genesis." In fact, it's possible the band of YAH didn't write at all...it was only later generations of Levitical and Deuteronomistic editors who wrote down the band of YAH's stories and crafted separate 'books' for them and other writings to compile the first five books of the Bible. Even much later generations titled the first book "Genesis."

YAH has competition, ya?

In Genesis, we can see that the band of YAH has competition. Another storyteller that could be one of the Levitical editors or another storyteller entirely takes the band of YAH's bawdy and crazy stories and softens their sting by removing all the sexiness. This other storyteller's characters are kind of boring — they lack character. Women have very little role in this other storyteller's imagination except as baby-makers.

One key difference between the band of YAH and this other storyteller is their ways of naming the divine. The band of YAH often refers to the divine/godhead as YAHWEH. That's why scholars once named this storycrafter "the Yahwist." (In German, the language of so much 20th century biblical scholarship, Yahwist or YAHWEH is spelled with a J.)

This competing storyteller, on the other hand, refers to

the divine as ELOHIM. ELOHIM is a plural word that has its roots in the regional gods, the region from which Ancient Israel emerged. EL was the chief god of the Canaanite pantheon of gods and goddesses. Everyone in the region would have referred to their gods and goddesses as ELOHIM. This storyteller competing with the band of YAH continues that tradition, even referring to early Ancient Israel's singular god (God) in the masculine plural form, ELOHIM. North of Canaan in Ancient Babylon...the fertile-crescent land between the two great rivers...the Tigris and Euphrates... Mesopotamia...they refer to god as IL. Note the similarity between EL and IL, especially in sound.

The band of YAH sometimes uses the word ELOHIM, though not to refer to 'God' but to 'the-gods-and-goddesses' — the regionally popular divinities of years' past. The band of YAH's whole point is to introduce a new vision of divinity, a paradigm shift away from the old gods-and-goddesses. On occasion, the band of YAH will use the singular form of EL especially when referring to well-known cities like Bethel and in new-naming/nick-naming Jacob as Israel. Through it all, we'll soon discover, the band of YAH is asserting that YAHWEH tops all gods-and-goddesses of previous centuries — even the gods-and-goddesses of ancient superpowers like Babylon and Egypt. This is quite bold!

Scholars have wondered whether the ancient Levitical priestly editors' use of ELOHIM might be an ingenious move to unite all God-followers into a larger framework — and that definitely could be the case. That is to say, from these priestly editors' standpoint, any worship of any 'god/goddess/divinity' falls within ELOHIM, 'all-the-gods-and-goddesses.' From these priestly editors, then, many of today's biblical scholars note, we get this first idea of monotheism, of there being a singular God. And these priestly editors will prescribe best ways to worship ELOHIM that keep ELOHIM happy with humans. Thus, the 613 laws of the Torah.

But I argue that the whole vision of YAHWEH-as-the-all-encompassing-divinity is much different from ELOHIM as all-the-gods-and-goddesses. And the band of YAH teaches this through humor, through something the unravels within the hearer of their tales — far, far different from following 613 laws.

The band of YAH has character(s)

YAHWEH is a very unusual name for the divine. In many of the band of YAH's stories, YAHWEH walks the earth as a human-like being and eats as a human-being eats. YAHWEH has wild emotions...love and lust and anger and confusion and sadness and regret...just like human beings. The name YAHWEH is a form of the Hebrew word 'to be.' Say this name YAHWEH out loud — what does it sound like to you? Say it fast a few times. Say it under your breath. Say it quietly. Say it loudly. What does 'YAHWEH' sound like?

Quite breathy, yes? This band of storycrafters is very clever in naming their vision of the divine/godhead "YAHWEH," don't you think? Add to that that there are ancient references to YAHWEH being a storm god and it gets even more interesting. Even 1 Samuel has some references like that. YAHWEH...the wind, the storm, the breath...the ultimate lifegiver. Makes a lot of sense now, doesn't it?

The band of YAH offers a story of one of their main characters, Jacob, worried about returning to his older twin brother, Esau. Years before, Jacob had stolen the birthright and inheritance-rights from his older brother Esau. Jacob becomes worried when he hears that Esau is coming to meet him with 400 men — probably not a welcoming party! So Jacob makes plans to protect his family and crosses the river to watch out for his brother — but all of a sudden, some random dude shows up and begins wrestling Jacob. The dude gets on top of Jacob and the dude seeing that he was about to lose gropes Jacob between the legs — in the hollow place between Jacob's legs — and then impales him, penetrates him.

Yes! In the Bible!

Jacob eventually recovers and climbs on top of the random dude and demands to know the dude's name. The dude won't give it but offers a new name for Jacob: Israel. And then Jacob discovers who it is he wrestled...EL! God! In Hebrew, the name Israel means 'on top of God' or 'topped by God' or even 'God-on-top' — but as you'll discover in the Jacob story, that third possibility gets ruled out.

Years earlier in the Jacob stories, just as he was running from his brother, Jacob dreamt of YAHWEH being on top of all the gods and goddesses, all the ELOHIM, all the ELs.

Jacob limps the next day after the wrestling match on account of his sore-ass...but his confrontation with his brother goes much better than planned. And why wouldn't it?! If Jacob could wrestle YAHWEH and win — even with painful, unexpected cheap-shots by YAHWEH — then Jacob should be able to take on anyone, right? Sore-ass and all!

In the band of YAH's imagination, as you'll soon see through *A Wildly Sensual YAHWEH*, this planting of life inside of Jacob gives birth to the prophetic tradition. Jacob's cherished and genderbending son Joseph dreams and looks and acts as a prophet, with all the characteristics of a prophet.

Get a sense for why competing storytellers or priestly editors or anyone thinking hierarchically would want to soften and quiet down the band of YAH's stories?! The band of YAH is wild!

In YAH's stories, each character's name has some cleverness to it. Read those names in most English translations and we miss all the fun. For instance, Jacob means 'Tricky-Heel-Grabber'...and once you read the full story in this translation, you'll quickly discover why...and get to laugh right along with YAH and their ancient stories' hearers. All of this would have been more evident to any ancient hearer, especially in a world — an ancient one — where most people did not know how to read. It's an oral storycrafting culture.

All the last hundred years of research on "oral imagination" is vital to understanding the band of YAH and how their exceedingly clever tales could last so long without being written down for centuries — and how they could so easily be changed and adapted and refined. A story has to be so very good to last that long in any family. Imagine it! How many stories do you know from your family that are more than a century old? How about multiple centuries old?

Prophets' ecstatic raps and rhymes

Were there any other biblical writers infected by this style the band of YAH was playing with?

Yes! Certainly prophets like Amos and Hosea and the Isaiahs and Jeremiah spoke out their poems, songs, raps. And many more than these prophets. Nearly all of these prophets were offering spoken-word experiences...they were saying out loud or singing their poems, raps, songs...and someone else wrote them down later. When? We're not so sure. It could be right as each prophet said them (Jeremiah is said to have had a scribe, Baruch); it could be generations after the prophet had died.

How could these spoken-word experiences be remembered for so long...for generations? Well, that's how good they were, how clever and unforgettable they were. Listen to the band of YAH's stories and you'll never forget them. Catch a whiff of the clever raps of someone like Amos and you'd never forget them — and he wasn't a professionally trained artist. He probably couldn't read like (First) Isaiah probably could. First Isaiah was a priest in charge of the temple in Jerusalem — someone powerful and almost certainly someone among the top five percent of the ancient population who could read and write more than just their name. (There are at least two other 'Isaiahs' — one of them probably a woman whom we call Second Isaiah or Deutero-Isaiah today — whose poems get attached to First Isaiah's scroll. Second Isaiah...well, she is amazing!)

Quite intriguing too is that the well-educated, high-positioned First Isaiah seems to borrow phrases and ideas from Amos' raps, from this clever style in the breeze. As Amos is fond of reminding people, he's an adult shepherd with a part-time gig pruning sycamore trees... in the 21st century it would be like proudly proclaiming you're a ditch-digger in a world of gas-powered machines. And apparently Amos' raps and ideas were so catchy and helpful that the wealthy and educated priest Isaiah and other prophets would borrow from his style.

Even more in the jumble...alphabet soup...D & X!

In addition to the band of YAH, there is another storyteller that biblical scholars have called D, the Deuteronomist. Many biblical scholars from the 20th century felt that the writing in Deuteronomy and Joshua were quite similar. Eventually Judges, 1 & 2 Samuel, and 1 & 2 Kings were lumped in with Deuteronomy and Joshua as bearing the marks of a similar school of writers — the Deuteronomistic School. Such a 'school' would be a group of people over many different generations — even centuries — who were thought by scholars to have similar interests, styles, and ideas and they composed stories in that vein. Today, scholars (see Römer again) believe this 'School' composed Deuteronomy through the generations and then added and edited Joshua, Judges, 1 & 2 Samuel, and 1 & 2 Kings. And as I've pointed out earlier, it's likely that some from this school assembled and edited the first five books of the Bible — Genesis, Exodus, Leviticus, Numbers, and Deuteronomy — much of which they inherited from the earlier Levitical priestly editors. The Deuteronomistic School likely assembled or at least put in order most of the Hebrew Bible — including the prophets — and likely brought many other books into 'final' form.

Even though it's pretty clear that someone from the Deuteronomistic School did some editing and adding to 1 & 2 Samuel, careful reading of these texts the past 25+ years and even playing with prophetic-practices alluded to in the biblical texts point me to a distinctly different voice in 1 & 2 Samuel. It's a vastly different voice from Deuteronomy and Joshua, different from Judges too. It has resonances with portions of 1 & 2 Kings, especially those pieces involving Elijah and Elisha.

To differentiate this voice from the usual categorization with the Deuteronomistic School (D), I call the author-voices of 1 & 2 Samuel...X.

Why 'X'? Well, the authors of 1 & 2 Samuel are more interested in the prophets than the priests. While having some interest in the priests, as long as such interest maintained the royalists' power, Deuteronomy and the 'Deuteronomistic School' are interested in the royals, at least during the time when the royals were in power. These Deuteronomists were essentially a political party of sorts who directed the affairs of the monarchy. Once the monarchy fails and the temple falls with Babylon's invasion, it's likely that the Deuteronomists joined ranks with the Levitical priests to cement their power through an emerging tradition with an early version of the Bible at its center.

Read 1 & 2 Samuel carefully and it's easy to note that the band of X has no interest in the royals or the priests except to show how foolish they are. The band of X is interested in the prophets and their wild actions and clever words. And this is where I very much make a different argument than most scholars of the Deuteronomistic History...much of my stance influenced in the style of the band of X, a style often ignored by biblical scholars. So few — if any? — scholars have yet been all that interested in the lifestyle of the prophets...and often because they might be embarrassed about the lifestyle.

NBYAH...important and often ignored letters that spell 'ecstasy'

As I alluded to earlier, people will be quite surprised to learn that NBYAH which is usually translated in Bibles as "prophet" actually means "ecstatic." Why don't Bibles tell you that from the beginning?

Some lexicons are brave enough to tell us that...check out William L. Holladay's *A Concise Hebrew and Aramaic Lexicon of the Old Testament*.

Translating the Hebrew letters NBYAH as "ecstatic" is vitally important to making sense of 1 & 2 Samuel, 1 & 2 Kings, Amos, Hosea, First Isaiah, Second Isaiah, Jeremiah...the whole prophetic-tradition (ecstatic-tradition) from the fictional character Samuel to the historical Jesus...which is vastly different from the layers of hierarchical crud piled upon Jesus and his ecstatic legacy.

The band of YAH teases the ecstatic/prophetic tradition in the stories that were written down in Genesis — so much so that at least some of the storycrafters of the band of YAH could be the taproot or even a rival view of what it means to be prophetic. What the prophets were doing was quite controversial. Quite. Quite. Quite.

And yet the band of YAH's storytelling reveals a similar style as the prophets' poems — full of puns and turns-of-phrase and double-entendre/triple-entendre that doesn't often come through in modern English translations. Just wait until we get to that Joseph story and look at the verbs together...it's a wild ride of a story that has been very poorly translated in most Bibles of any organized religion, whether Judaism or Christianity or Islam.

Modern translations of NBYAH as "prophet" might be just another way to cover up what the 'ecstatics' like Samuel and Elijah and Elisha and whoever was like them and what they were doing on the mountaintops of Ancient Israel/Palestine.

And the Bible is full of cover-ups.

So how did the Torah come to be and why is it so front and center in the Hebrew Bible?

The Torah as we know it today is the first five books of the Bible: Genesis, Exodus, Leviticus, Numbers, Deuteronomy.

Besides that earliest layer from Deuteronomy likely composed in the 7th century BCE and besides the many oral stories from the band of YAH and priestly prescriptions about proper rituals, scholars guess that the Torah was not written until at least 597 BCE — and likely generations or even centuries after that.

A short history lesson is needed here to understand why. The Kingdom of Ancient Israel fell to the new superpower Assyria in 722 BCE.

Ancient Israel at one point may have included the Kingdom of Judah...archeologists like Israel Finkelstein wonder if there was a great United Monarchy of Israel/Judah and even if there ever was a King David who is said to have united the coalition and tribal divisions into one kingdom. There is no evidence of a "King David" in any of the archaeological record besides one scant reference to a king who conquered "David"... and "David" literally means 'one who boils over with affection' or 'lover' or 'beloved' so that one reference could mean the conqueror made this "David" his conquered sexual pet.

In any case, centuries after the supposed time of David, Babylon re-emerged as the next great power and conquered Assyria and then conquered Ancient Judah in 597 BCE.

Most people in Ancient Judah were exiled to Babylon. As the story goes, the prophet/ecstatic Jeremiah was left behind in Jerusalem, the once-great capital of Ancient Judah that was turned to rubble by Babylon. Tired of his crazy raps and actions, some of the Ancient Judaeans left behind with Jeremiah killed Jeremiah. Some of Jeremiah's style and vision and ideas show up in 1 & 2 Kings — even though he is strangely not mentioned.

The idea for an all-encompassing document like the Torah might have been born in Babylon. The Torah is a powerful document: so many stories and 613 commandments. The Ten Commandments is in some ways a quick summary of the 613 commandments, a table of contents of sorts, an easy way to communicate a larger message that the biblical assemblers/editors — first the Levitical priests and then the Deuteronomists

— wanted to reinforce through such a vast work as their five scrolls — the Torah.

The Torah, though, is not one united voice — and that's perhaps its wisdom and beauty. In joining the band of YAH's wild-stories with some softer other storyteller's stories with the ways priests envisioned how life should be in one age and heritage (Levites, with Leviticus) with the ways authorities envisioned how life should be in another age and heritage (the Deuteronomists, especially with Deuteronomy), this team created something that just about everyone in exile or afterwards could live with.

Many people could find their 'story' — the one told around their campfire at home, before exile or long after it — in the Torah. By joining so many of these differing voices together, the editors/assemblers crafted something that lives on today as a relatively united vision that can be found in Judaism, in Christianity, in Islam, in a lot of places. The Catholic Catechism and the various Christian catechisms certainly try to mimic this idea of law joined with story as a way to guide followers.Moses could have been a character of the band of YAH's — though this Moses character has been vastly expanded by the editors/assemblers. The Levitical priestly editors and the Deuteronomistic School insert whole speeches into Moses' mouth. Sometimes those speeches agree with one another, sometimes they don't. The later writings — the Talmud (Mishnah and Gemara), not included in the Bible — try to sort out those differences, provide rabbinic interpretations about what human beings should do in real life situations.

But in crafting the Torah long after the Babylonian Exile, the Levitical priests left out a bunch of voices — and key ones at that.

What about X?

In the band of X's writings, the character Samuel comes forward as a wise voice and a compelling character with quite a wild ride of a story. Besides 1 Samuel 12, which today's scholars think was likely added by later Deuteronomistic editors, the character Samuel makes no mention of Moses in leading the people of Israel from slavery in Egypt, and there is no mention of the 613 commandments or anything like that.

As big as "Moses" is and all of Moses' laws, such omissions in 1 & 2 Samuel are shocking!

And, as *The Naked Path of Prophet vol 1* lays bare, 1 Samuel is full of nakedness. Even YAHWEH strips Itself naked like a slave or exile is forced to do by their captors. And for whom does YAHWEH strip? Anyone who wants a nice dose of ecstasy...those who eventually get called ecstatics, prophets. And, as we'll discover, even bloodthirsty kings intent on killing young innocents can fall into a spell of ecstasy when ecstatics are gathered to protect that innocent one who is also in ecstasy.

Ecstasy — like the wind
and air we breathe to live —
is available for all.

Like the band of X, the band of YAH's characters do wild things. YAH has a father-character give a dress to his favorite son, has a father-in-law have sex with his embittered daughter-in-law who dresses up like a prostitute to fool him and awaken him, has two daughters get their father drunk to have sex with him, has a brother kill his brother...on and on and on. Shocking little episodes — and that's not all of them!

YAH and X...similarly wild story-crafters who are LGBTQ+ friendly

Even though their storytelling structures are different, the biblical authors X are quite similar to the band of YAH in many ways. Neither band is afraid of sex and sexual relationship — even sexual-relationship that is a bit different from the norms of their day or ours in the 21st century. YAH and X might be way ahead of us on this, even millennia before us in the 21st century! The bands of X and YAH all tell stories of same-sex love, have women say and do important things — YAH even has a cross-dressing young man as their most developed character.

It all makes me wonder if same-sex love, multi-sex/gender love or non-binary love or genderbending love were hallmarks of the ancient prophetic/ecstatic imagination...we'll have to see as we continue to listen deeply to these biblical texts.

YAH and X have characters that grow, that are nuanced, that leave us wanting more. Often through humor, YAH's characters and X's characters delve into our guts in this way — as if YAH and X tell their stories to invite growth within those who listen to and play with their stories.

Rather interestingly, YAH and X share an affinity for calling the divine/godhead of Ancient Israel YAHWEH. In addition to the sexual bawdiness of YAH's and X's stories, that might be the key to why the priestly editors want to dial down YAH and X, stifle YAH's and X's visions of the divine. Priests back then and even today do not want YAHWEH's name to be spoken aloud, in vain. Why? What's the big deal? I suggest saying YAHWEH out loud a few times — you might just have an experience that leads to life, to awakening to what is, on your own, without the priests or religious-authorities trying to contain it all for you.

YAHWEH, let's remember, is a form of the Hebrew verb 'to be.' And it's quite wispy, yes? Go on — say it out loud a few more times....

YAHWEH

YAHWEH

YAHWEH!

Get playful with It — even try YAH-HO. Feel the vibration as you extend the syllables. Wonder about it. Get curious.

In YAH's and X's stories, YAHWEH is highly unpredictable. YAHWEH has desires for humans, sees their beauty, wants relationship — often with men-characters.

Perhaps this would have been rather embarrassing to talk about for the priests. After all, they crafted laws and commandments that punish same-sex love with death.

It seems to be the same embarrassment that most biblical scholars have too, though those writing for the Westar Institute's *Forum* Spring 2023 issue seem to be shaking off centuries — millennia — of such embarrassment, like *Jacob's Wound* author Theodore W. Jennings, Jr.

With the band of YAH and X, same-sex love is life, an important aspect of life...enough that their nation's name — Israel — would remember it and the story behind it every time it's mentioned. The origin story of Israel from the band of YAH's perspective, let's remember, involves YAHWEH groping and penetrating Jacob and then Jacob climbing on top. 'Israel' means 'on top of God' or 'in charge of God' or 'topped by God.' It's an incredibly playful name!

Such topping is quite ironic — not only in that YAHWEH is on top of a human, not only in that YAHWEH appears to be 'impregnating' his seed into a man who will give birth to the first prophet of YAH's stories, but especially in that the prophets seem to always get trounced by the hierarchs, whether those hierarchs are priests or kings or, at one time, the Deuteronomists, especially when they encircled and 'served' the royals. With rare exceptions through history — in Ancient Israel or anywhere — the hierarchical imagination has won out over the prophetic imagination — and not just in the history of religion. Note the assassinations of the likes of Gandhi, Dr. Martin Luther King, Jr., Malcolm X, Dorothy Stang, Harvey Milk, and on and on and on. These prophets were essentially crafting prophetic speeches to awaken hierarchs to the reality that they held no more power than any other human being — and the hierarchs and hierarch-followers killed them for those clever speeches.

A hierarchical imagination cannot bear the prophetic imagination — the prophet's raps and rhymes are noise to anyone who believes and lives as if one human is better than another. Progress and climbing the social ladder and doing the necessary things to preserve one's station/caste in life are necessary to achieve a happy, holy life in the hierarchical imagination.

The prophets point out that none of that is necessary, that YAHWEH is reliable and immediately available to anyone and everyone — no matter how 'holy' or 'progress-oriented' one is. We all have direct access to the wind, to the air, to YAHWEH — we need no one to lead us to It. Sure, could a friend help us to notice something about the nature of the wind or the storm or of the power of breathing? Of course. But as soon as we pledge allegiance to that friend as our wise teacher, our guru, our master, we lose something of our relationship with the wild and breathy wind, with YAHWEH. As the prophets point out, it's a bit like having two lovers...the ease with which we are with one turns our back on the other. Prophets and those of the prophetic/ecstatic imagination take life down to its essence and realize it — It — THE ALL — is enough. Prophets pledge their allegiance to the soul/sole source of life.

The prophets point out the ridiculousness of hierarchical assumptions...and often pay for it with their lives. Rather strangely — to me anyway — is that once the prophet is dead and out of the way, hierarchs of later generations often raise the dead prophet's status to one of reverence — usually at the demands of the people who were inspired by the prophet — by calling the prophet a saint, by creating holidays and roads to celebrate them, by giving out awards in the prophet's name, even proclaiming their godliness — all of this as long as the prophet's clever style in speech and action is not resurrected and brought forward again in the same way that invited complete transformation of and movement away from the many manifestations of hierarchy or royal/slave-imagination.

At their essence, hierarchical-imagination and royal/slave-imagination are one and the same...they both see some people as better than others...their adherents then craft pecking orders for who must be catered to and who can be dispensed with.

The hierarchical-imagination is quite easy to fall into, even when we've done a lot of inner-work to free ourselves from the compulsion of wanting to put people above us in worth and below us in worth. I suspect we all do this, even the most seasoned prophets. We all have trouble with adolescence — no matter our age. Adolescence, after all, is when we begin to negotiate a more equal relationship with our parents, with all we allow to father and mother and 'guru' us.

I sure hope we can wake up to it, to It, and realize that the thing that gives life is breath/wind and not any guru's teaching and not any parent-figure's love. When we were children, we needed such love and care and direction to survive. But then in adolescence we learn how to put off childish ways...day by day by day, decision by decision. Do we need coaches/teachers in that process? Of course! No matter our age. But any good coach knows that if they do their job right, the student no long needs them...even in the championship when the match is down to the wire.

Hierarchical thinking would have us believe that we need that coach/parent forever, that the coach/parent will always be 'above' the student because the coach always has more to offer. And such thinking is essentially fascist in its orientation. Any coach/parent worth their salt helps the student/child to learn, to discover and trust their sensations, to discover that there are always choices, to reflect on those choices/possibilities and invite the student/child to wonder what is best for the student/child for staying alive and growing. Such a circular-styled approach knows that once we know how to learn we are potent, powerful, and no longer need the coach/parent to live well. Can a coach/parent and student/child be friends, equals, enjoy life together? Of course. Can they share more wisdom with each other after that mentoring-relationship has 'ended' — and likely now that sharing is more equal? Of course.

But hierarchies operate much more differently. The religion-shipwreck from which I've swum away to safety still asks me to call its priests "Father" — even when that priest is younger than me. Sometimes they even dress up as Roman royals and their aristocratic underlings — a style of dress of those who killed Jesus. It's all very strange to me. And it gets even stranger when a small contingent of that religion want their prayers and rituals to be spoken in Latin, a language Jesus never spoke, a language of the group who killed Jesus.

The wind has a different agenda. And no sense in calling it "Holy." It all ebbs and flows.

What's saddest to me is that whole religions are based on this hierarchical thinking instead of helping people to know more and more the Infinite, a God who has no bounds.

Hierarchies often encourage destroying life on the planet, of putting toxins into the wind. I'm guilty of this too, of course, with my own car and riding in airplanes and buying and using things like this computer to type out this book. How little I/we consider my/our choices and their effects on other humans, on all of life, of the whole circle that is and includes the whole planet Earth, that could even include the whole Universe if we wanted it to. Hierarchies are the very things we've created as humans that are ripping us humans apart.

Christianity's Great Troubles Plaguing the Planet... and Paul's Way Out

Like the prophets/ecstatics before him, Jesus playfully found a way out of the hierarchical systems of his own time — before those systems killed him.

Paul did too — at least the "authentic Paul."

Peter? Not so much.

We might see this in the whole Christian movement through the centuries and all the way to today. How quickly the early Jesus-believing communities mobilized around the story of Jesus' death...and how little respect was given by many/most to Jesus' words, his clever ideas, his wild actions and wandering way of life.

Infected with the royal/slave imagination that was crystallized in the exceedingly cruel Roman Empire, Christianity raised the dead Jesus to 'Christ' — to messiah/military-king — but failed and all too often continues to fail to have any sense of Jesus' message, his wildly ecstatic/prophetic imagination. Jesus tried to topple the inner machinations of hierarchy consuming First Century imaginations through hysterical parables and funny aphorisms that induce transformation within the hearer...sadly this same Jesus is now revered as king, as 'Christ,' as better than everyone...and within the Christian tradition, all too often through the centuries Christians have seen themselves as better than people of other religions, enough to kill off those who weren't of their religion or who were Christian but not 'Christian-enough' in their opinion. Such thinking created the conditions of the Holocaust, of the whole early 20th century German mobilization to root out those they saw as less — Jews, gays, disabled/multi-abled, 'gypsies'/Roma — and kill them. Millions upon millions of people. And what was on their belt buckles, the German belt buckles? *Gott Mit Uns*...'God with us'... as these humans slaughtered millions upon millions of humans they wanted dead and gone, those they viewed as having less worth than themselves.

And this didn't just happen once with the Holocaust of the 20th century — such brutality has happened over and over again through the Christian centuries and led by Christian people. Shocking, isn't it?!

Sadly, we can witness a similar tragedy with Judaism and all religions of "the Book" — the Bible — with their adherence to Leviticus 20.13 as "God's law" and for justifying their homophobia, their homo-hate. Plain and simple, Leviticus promotes fascism through its hierarchical-impulse to decide who lives and who dies and puts words in "God's mouth" to justify such hate.

I am shocked I went along with the hierarchically-minded ridiculousness of this for so long as a Christian, as a follower of 'Christ'...but when any of us adopts an imagination that has 'Christ' at its center and not Jesus and the way of life Jesus was advocating — wandering, bordercrossing, nonviolence, and love for all — we slide all too easily down the slippery slope of fascism.

I suspect I will always be a friend of Jesus and his wisdom — his wisdom is indeed that good, especially if understood in the context of his place and time in a faraway place of the Roman Empire. But being a friend of Jesus and being a disciple of Christ are two very different things. To put anyone — any fellow human — above you is to enact the hierarchical game. And that game has repercussions, significant repercussions. How? Why? If someone is above you and more important than you, then it is very likely you will find someone who is below you. How quickly we then fall into a game where some people are better and must be protected and some people are worth/less and expendable.

This hierarchical game goes by many names and guises. Royal/slave. Christ/disciple. Master/slave. Hero/victim. Guru/follower. Even teacher/student... though some of that can be mitigated by a circular classroom and imagination where every voice helps us to know some glimmer of the reality being revealed in the coming together of the circle.

Bowing to Jesus or Buddha or whomever for their

wisdom seems like a good idea, like an honorable thing to do. But then we'd better bow to every flower, every blade of grass, every body of water and every drop of water, every morsel we eat, every bug that pollinates the food we eat, every human being, everywhere we can witness the wind — YAHWEH — having Its way with us all.

Paul's clever move raising Jesus to 'Christ'...and how it rebounded and caused great troubles for us all

Paul very cleverly raises the prophetic Jesus to 'Christ' as a slap in the face to the Roman Emperor who was seen as sole ruler and a god in and of himself. What was shouted out when the Roman Emperor made a public appearance? "Son of God!" What did followers of the Roman Emperor cult think happened after the emperor died? That the emperor flew into the heavens to join the pantheon of gods and goddesses.

Paul is exceedingly clever in using all of these lofty titles and imagination to describe the peasant Jesus from the middle of nowhere, this peasant who was killed unjustly at the hands of the Roman Emperor Cult — as many people were being killed through this hierarchical imagination. Paul proclaims that this anointed-king/Christ Jesus was raised up by God. Shocking! This peasant Jesus was raised up by God! God cares for the peasants enough to raise up one of them as "Christ," as "son of God," as one who flies into the heavens like the dead Roman Emperors do to live on in the heavens!

Paul uses all the rhetoric of the Roman Empire against

them to try to awaken them and all hierarchically-minded people. Even the word "gospel" Paul steals right out of the lexicon of the Roman Emperor Cult... see the Calendar Inscription of Priene, an inscription dedicated to Augustus Caesar likely in 9 BCE. Composing his First Letter to the Thessalonians in about 50 CE, it's very possible that Paul was the first person to associate "gospel" or "good news" or "world-resounding-message" with Jesus.

The first composed gospel in the biblical canon is what has come to be called the Gospel of Mark, which most scholars think was written either side of 70 CE, long after Paul's death.

Read the first few lines of Paul's Letter to the Romans — especially with an eye on the context of Paul's time and life in the Roman Empire — and you'll quickly discover just how clever Paul is. And Paul does so not to describe the Emperor but the peasant Jesus killed at the hands of the Emperor's underlings!!!

Paul was exceedingly clever in raising this peasant killed at the hands of the Emperor Cult to the status of king/Christ — and in taking this king/Christ and at the same time setting him on the same level as every human being. In Paul's imagination, every human being — including Jesus/this Christ — will bow to God when "Christ" has dismantled all hierarchies, all who claim to hold power over other human beings. (see 1 Corinthians 15)

Paul even proclaims himself a slave to the one God anointed as "Christ" — to Jesus. This is to say that Paul takes himself out of the Roman Empire's hierarchy and into a vastly different set of circumstances — all of this while Rome ruled the 'known' and 'civilized' world. Scholar Jennifer A. Glancy notes the cruelty of slavery under the Roman Empire in her well researched book that hides nothing, *Slavery in Early Christianity.* Roman boys and girls whose parents were freeborn would wear special amulets...a boy's was called a *bulla*; a girl's was called a *lunula.* Why? So that anyone higher in the hierarchy could readily see that they're freeborn and thus could not legally grab the amulet-wearing child for sex. Slaves, on the other hand, didn't wear amulets and could be slapped, screamed at, molested, and raped without much problem as long as the slaves could be returned to their owner relatively intact, with their labor-value still available.

This is the world of Rome, and not just Rome. This is the world of hierarchical empire and hierarchical religion. Anyone hoping to honor this ancient culture or any culture where slavery is allowed to flourish, in my opinion, is mad.

Paul uses the rhetoric of the greatest empire of the day at them, at Rome. Paul proclaims a new way, a new order, with a resurrected peasant as the 'anointed leader'/ messiah/Christ of all before God. Paul sees himself as a slave for this resurrected peasant and a slave for God — an order far larger and more encompassing than Rome. Paul reinvents Rome's very popular hierarchy and now puts on God's throne a man who was killed by Rome through their exceedingly cruel version of capital punishment. Jesus is the peasant God raised up from the dead.

Paul is actually the first imaginer ever of democracy

without slaves. Ever! His vision of being slave to God and slave to Jesus is far different from the shackles that Ancient Greece and my own United States of America have used to legislate its hierarchical-visions of 'democracy'...these Ancient Greek and USA versions both including slavery.

The biblical prophets before Jesus and Paul never quite use this language of 'being a slave for YAHWEH,' though the whole process of prophet-making seems to be similar, as we'll see in the band of YAH's stories and the band of X's saga of 1 & 2 Samuel. YAHWEH penetrates those It loves without asking, to give us life, to plant the seed — breath! — into us in all kinds of places in a human being. You know this too, right? Breathe in and you will know.

This is the world-transforming-message that we all forget, the gospel of love that sits there right before us as a banquet ready for any and all to eat. But so few come. How sad the wild wind must be that we so little acknowledge Its sweetness and Its sweet love-making with you and me and every human being and every creature and we only pollute It all the more.

How quickly we miss what Paul very cleverly did with Jesus...and even more quickly miss what Jesus was doing in his day as a wandering, parable-spinning, healing, living-under-bridges, dining-even-with-your-worst-enemy human being...and even more quickly miss what the prophets were up to with the wild wind when It's right there in front of us, even within us and breathing us into life, awaiting for us to notice It's making love with us!

Prophets/Ecstatics and the Wind...the New Way Forward Never Given a Full Chance...Not Even in Religion, Buddhism, or Yoga...Not Yet

What if your only master, your only guru, your only president/emperor, your only pastor or rabbi or imam was YAHWEH, was the wind?

Knowing the ways of the wind was a root-experience of Judaism, Christianity, and Islam. But hierarchically-minded people didn't allow that primal experience to last long in their efforts to codify it...and sadly, most followers of Judaism or Christianity or Islam have no idea about the prophets and their ways with the wind being a tap-root of their own modern religion.

Indeed this primal-root of modern religion — knowing the wind and being known by It — is no religion at all. It is life. For those who sense the wind with all we are, we know It's all we need.

Knowing the wind and the hum of the earth was the primal experience of Gautama's enlightenment...but very shortly after his death, Gautama's teachings quickly became codified into Buddhisms of so many sorts...so many different strands that agree and disagree with each other all over again and all too often forget that the wind cannot be controlled and that all that's necessary to know enlightenment is to notice It by doing <u>nothing</u>, or at least as little as possible. No shrines, no chants, no bows, no masters, no special postures or seats, no nothing.

Knowing the wind, I'd argue, was probably what the original yogins of the Indus River Valley knew...long before all who came after them codified all the ways to know the wind through rituals, through laws/suggestions, through mythologies, through special sequences of moving-breathing-resting, through special prescriptive diets, through leaders and gurus and teachers of all sorts with whom we are told we must study until we have yoga as a $10+ billion dollar industry today with classrooms in hierarchically-minded rows of students being led by special-teachers, often with special-soundtracks where the sound and feeling of the wind are hardly ever invited.

Meanwhile, the wind Itself is free, costs nothing to know. It blows anywhere and everywhere, even if you try to block It out. Sometimes It knocks out sound systems and upends playlists just to remind us of Its power and Its all-important noise.

What if the process of being a 'religious' person — like our ancestors before us, especially the ecstatics/prophets — was simply sitting out of the reaches of the empire-of-the-day, on the mountaintops, in the deserts, on the sea, and waiting for the breeze to blow and feeling It on your skin and feeling the complete and utterly ecstatic vibration that happens when the breeze rattles your nostrils or your lips?

This was the ancient 'religion' of the prophets — the ancient 'religion' that was no religion at all — the strand of ideas making its way relatively silently through the ongoing 1000+ years' storycrafting of the Bible and in every age after it. This is the primal experience of the prophets that birthed modern biblically-based religions and Buddhism and yoga — though you wouldn't know it/It now. And this original, primal experience of the wind requires no doctrine, no ideology, no ritual —

certainly no temple/church building or shrine. All that is required is you and the wind.

The wind will get you and me and all of us who notice It up to some wild adventures.

The wind has a way of teaching us far better than words — until the authorities step in and demand we worship at their temples and churches and shrines and congresses and shopping malls and online outlets, with their scripts and their predetermined chants and songs and playlists, with their rules, with all the ways that directly benefit them and shackle us all to a system that makes us less and less and less.

The wind — breathing with the wind — frees, gives us life.

What if...? What if we gave up our modern religions and gave this 'primal religion that is no religion at all' a chance? It's had Its gasps and starts and opportunities the past few decades, hasn't it? Hasn't It?

The Wisdom of a Circle

In Paul's clever imagination, he like the prophets before him recognizes that the wisdom is in the circle and not in hierarchical-rows, that YAHWEH is reliable, that a circle of deciders is much wiser than a king or pope or pastor or guru parsing out the 'truth' to everyone below.

Does a circle need conveners, guides, wise friends, people to offer hospitality? Of course...though anyone with a role needs to be mindful of how and how often they interject their ideas and desires into the conversation as a way of steering it toward their hopes and ideas. Let the wind speak!

But let me address my own family first...today most of us Christians don't think this wisdom-in-the-circle way. We've put popes and bishops and pastors and reverends and youth directors and deacons and monsignors and on and on and on above us and then some...and can't figure out how they fail us when they stumble. Perhaps we stumble most by letting them have power over us, demanding that they lead us.

Leave them — let the wind rule! Let them sit with us and be taught by the wind alone!

That's not to say that we Christians and our leaders are all bad people for falling into the hierarchical-game. It is to say that we need prophets — ecstatics — who will jar our imaginations and awaken us to the royal/slave, hierarchical mythos that is preventing us from recognizing what we would rather not see or hear or feel — that we've abandoned YAHWEH for our hierarchical religions century after century after century. How quickly we seek a savior — in president, in celebrity, in sports-hero, in artist, in lover, in guru, in wise teacher, in 'Christ' — when the invitation from the beginning was and will most likely always be "you are the salt of the earth, the spice of life, the light of the world."

You and I are the salt of the earth. You and I are the spice of life. You and I are the light of the world. That's what the prophet/ecstatic Jesus reminds us, this human being who chose the adventure of homelessness, the freedom of the open road that his ancestors Abraham & Sarah chose — those myth-rich characters of the band of YAH. Homelessness requires a dependency on the generosity of people, of the Universe, to provide a meal when you need it most, to offer some kindness and a meal and hospitality when the moment most demands it. Choosing homelessness, choosing to wander, choosing the desert over the city, choosing the shade of a big tree over a big house is a complete act of trust — and it's what Jesus was inviting his friends to choose for themselves too. "Take nothing with you for the journey! Go, heal!" Why? To find out for themselves/ourselves that the Universe — YAHWEH — is dependable, reliable, trustworthy.

Instead we build our churches and shrines and monuments to Jesus — and forget this wisdom and invitation to the open road where every person is welcomed as teacher and friend/equal and companion, bread-sharer. And even worse, we Christians allow and demand leaders over us...and we all too quickly then put people below us, see some fellow humans as worth less than us. Once the hierarchical-game has begun, it's pretty tough to stop it...that is until some clever parable or wild rap of an ecstatic/prophet stops us in our tracks and we breathe in and know It all over again.

What is It? YAHWEH...the wisdom in the wind.

How quick we Christians have been to refuse to engage with this wisdom from Jesus about the wind and about all of us being the light of the world, about any of his clever ideas that indeed go back to him. It's a lot easier to raise up someone else as your savior than it is to look in the mirror and see the light of the world in yourself or to look in the eyes of your enemy and see the same light there as the light we see in our beloved or in our children or any children. "You are the light of the world" implies an equality, doesn't it? Jesus didn't then say, 'but some lights are better than others.'

Instead, "you are the light of the world!" You all are! We all are! We exist surrounded by Light. We exist in an ocean of swirling wind — YAHWEH!

How quickly we refuse the prophetic imagination in favor of the pecking order that is royal/slave, hierarchical imagination...a hierarchical imagination that eventually enslaves all of us to a system that kills life, that does not give life.

I suspect each and every human being has a prophetic aspect that seeks freedom for all and a royal/slave + hierarchical aspect that seeks to control or desires to be controlled...and the wise know out of which aspect they live and when...and the wise know which aspect hums with the Universe, the ground of our being.

Wanna say YAHWEH again...?

And even more shocking...BAAL!

Not much of the Bible or the wily power of YAHWEH will make sense unless we have an understanding of BAAL and ASHTAROTH.

So much of the Hebrew scriptures was composed with BAAL and ASHTAROTH as foils. That is to say that the Bible was written as a reaction and response to the alluring BAAL and ASHTAROTH and their hierarchical-cults.

Who or what were BAAL and ASHTAROTH?

BAAL was a fertility-god, son of EL who was the chief divinity in the Canaanite pantheon. Recall that EL is the singular of the plural-word ELOHIM which can mean "God" or "the gods and goddesses." In some sources, BAAL was also the son of DAGON, another Canaanite fertility-god under the godhead EL. In Hebrew, BAAL means 'boss' — and surely because engaging with the BAAL-cults would be like heroin or any addiction is today. It would be your 'boss' and ruin your life.

BAAL's followers would gather, shape a piece of wood into a penis, insert it into the ground, dance wildly around it to excite it, partner up with their spouse or a prostitute/sex-slave and have sex.

Why? Because their greatest concern as ancient people was fertility — of the land to produce food and of their families to continue growing and thriving.

Seems innocent enough, right? I've danced similarly in clubs and have seen high schoolers — despite administration and fellow faculty trying to prevent it — dance something of the BAAL-dance in high school gyms.

Doing this with a committed partner might be one thing — somewhat equals, in the ancient world or today. Purchasing a prostitute as a substitute-spouse...? Well that's a different dynamic entirely, one of hierarchy, of one always having more status and control than the other. And we all know how we treat a 'rental' vastly differently than something or someone we cherish.

The ASHTAROTH-cult was similar, with ASHTAROTH being a fertility-goddess as BAAL was a fertility-god. The goddess ISHTAR, revered by some even today, is another name for ASHTAROTH — both from which we get the name for the Christian festival of Easter. In the northern hemisphere, this of course happens in Spring, when all kinds of things spring into life.

ASTARTE and ASHERAH are other names for ASHTAROTH...the wife of BAAL.

BAAL was the old storm divinity — in the region of Canaan, people would pray to BAAL for rain for their crops, dance around the penis-pole, and let BAAL explode his rains upon them and their land. YAHWEH was originally a storm divinity as well, and it seems that many of the old rituals around BAAL got projected onto YAHWEH, at least by some people...the dance, the prostitution, even YAHWEH having a wife in the female divinity ASHERAH/ASHTAROTH as BAAL and EL did. Even the temple of Jerusalem, we are told by biblical writers (see 2 Kings 23 as one example), had 'special, holy-prostitutes'/QDSHYM available for rent to consummate the worship of BAAL or the non-prophetic YAHWEH-marrying-ASHERAH version that subsumed the old BAAL religion. As BAAL/YAHWEH and ASHTAROTH mate to produce fertility, so does the prostitute-renter and the prostitute to produce fertility, even for a few moments. Again, such a hierarchical system is exceedingly twisted and far from relational when one pays for the use of the other's body.

But the prophets — at least as we can see so far in the band of YAH's Genesis stories and the band of X's stories — have no particular wife/spouse for YAHWEH except for Israel, both the character (Jacob) and his progeny, the children of Israel, the bordercrossers (Hebrews). YAHWEH blows Its life-giving breath into the people of Israel — and even into the enemies of Israel. What the prophets were offering was quite radical!

BAAL and ASHTAROTH would be quite addictive, all this nakedness with your neighbors, maybe drunk on your dinner-wine or high on some substance, the wildness of it all. It is, perhaps, the reference-point of the story of Sodom in the band of YAH's stories in Genesis. Men, women, children, and even house-guests — so it seems in YAH's Sodom story in Genesis — all of them meeting in the town square under the dark of evening, one massive orgy. By the way, the place-name 'Sodom' means in Hebrew 'Their-Bondage.'

One can see why, in the band of YAH's story, the character Lot would put his tent nearby the orgy. Even if Lot wasn't a participant, it sounds like quite a show. My college scripture teacher — a nun — admitted that she would surely have participated, whether out of its allure or to make sure the grain grew and the family had a next generation.

And that's just it. And yet another reason why the prophets take a stand against BAAL and ASHTAROTH, why the character Samuel (in 1 Samuel) insists the people of Ancient Israel, umm, behead their BAALS and ASHTAROTHS.

Relationship with YAHWEH, the ecstatic experience

of one's naked body taking in YAHWEH...that was far different than following a ritual — whether around BAAL or the ark of God/ELOHIM — to ensure there was enough to eat and a next generation of one's family.

Be in this naked, ecstatic relationship with YAHWEH and all will be well...that's the very heart of the message of all the prophets/ecstatics. And this translation of the band of YAH's stories will not shy away from such things and such ecstatic relationship with YAHWEH that the prophets encourage.

What's the, um, the point?

I suspect the biblical bands of YAH and X were likely crafting stories to jar the imaginations of anyone who hears to have an experience of YAHWEH — playfully shocking stories that encourage the hearer to gasp and then recover, to let in YAHWEH and notice It with a new awareness, an awakened sensation of life in all Its abundance.

The stories of these bands of YAH and X are fictions. Jesus was onto the same thing with his clever and wild parables and sayings, by the way.

In that sense, I think the purpose of YAH's stories in Genesis and X's stories in 1 & 2 Samuel is to invite their hearers to a vastly different kind of life — one outside and far away from government/society as a "shipwreck" that Thomas Merton and others allude to when talking about why the desert mothers and fathers got far away from Rome's seductive grasp, from hierarchy's insidious ways.

Keep in mind, the band of YAH's stories were the only prophetic-imagination and prophetic-style allowed in the priestly editors' Torah — though these Levitical priests and later the Deuteronomists heavily edited the band of YAH's stories. It's almost as if they are allowing YAH's ever-popular stories in their Torah...but only as long as they got to interpret YAH's stories and tamp them down and even craft specific Torah-laws against the prophets — by putting down women and men-having-sex-with-men — and even to kill the prophets so that future generations will know the prophets and their prophetic/ecstatic-imagination only through the hierarchical priestly-minded and authority-minded lenses.

It's easy to read the band of YAH's stories and X's saga — 1 & 2 Samuel, portions of 1 & 2 Kings — as if these biblical writings were an early history of the nation of Ancient Israel/Judah. But I think that misses the subtlety of these texts — and it certainly misses the punny and exceedingly clever style of their story-crafting. At a quick glance, it appears that the bands of YAH and X are highlighting the patriarchs and matriarchs and kings and the priests and all their great deeds — when in reality Genesis and 1 & 2 Samuel and the Elijah/Elisha portions of 1 & 2 Kings speak mostly of every leader's failures and idiocies...

all the while the ecstatics/prophets are in far-away places getting naked with YAHWEH, learning to multiply loaves and cooking-oil to save people from slavery, raising the dead to life through some rather bizarre means, purifying bad water so it's useable again, making poisoned stew edible, blinding attacking armies and getting enemies to feed and befriend their enemies, curing leprosy and awful diseases, having the foresight to prepare for coming famines, coming up with clever actions, raps, poems, and songs to shatter the expectations of empire-dwellers and hierarchy-lovers and people caught in the royal/slave imagination and BAAL-addicts and ASHTAROTH-addicts and ark-addicts and religious-types to awaken them/us to ecstatic relationship with YAHWEH...all the things that prophets do.

Sound familiar? You're in for a wild ride!

A Few Brief Notes on My Translation of the band of YAH's Stories in Genesis, translated from the Ancient Hebrew

To better appreciate the band of YAH's imagination, text notes have been minimized as much as possible to preserve the integrity of the received text we have from the YAHWEH-oriented storycrafters in the biblical book of Genesis.

Justified right, you'll see very brief information about lines from the biblical text that can be attributed to other biblical authors: the other storytellers/editors who have pieces of their writings wrapped around and even woven into the band of YAH's stories in Genesis, for example:

<**Gen 2:10-15**> indicates that these lines have not been included with the the band of YAH's text because they bear the nuances of other storytellers' styles. It could be well worth your time sometime to pick up a Bible and read these passages that I've recognized as being not from the band of YAH to better know how and why the priestly editors and later Deuteronomists tried to manipulate the band of YAH's stories and prophetic/ecstatic imagination.

<#> indicates that something of the band of YAH's story probably has not been preserved as there appears to be a significant break in the flow of their story. Often even the other biblical authors and editors have not preserved these transitions.

xxx <u>xx</u> xxx underlining indicates I'm trying to draw attention to a clever pun in the Hebrew text

(__) indicates that I have added these words to the text to clarify what is probably being assumed in the story. I do this — and hopefully not very often — instead of having notes at the bottom of the page that often seem distracting.

I have also capitalized divinities with their assumed vowels included for ease of reading — for instance, YAHWEH instead of YHWH and ELOHIM instead of AHLHYM — while at the same time have retained only the 'original' consonants-only versions of non-divinity words — for instance, GLH instead of GaLaH or GeLaH or something of that sort. This might be a controversial choice for a number of reasons, though I believe you'll come to discover it makes for ease of reading for a wider audience. More details can be found in **Hebrew Alphabet - transliterated** near the back of the book.

To bring forward the flexible style of Ancient Hebrew verbs, English verbs like 'climb' and 'style' — for example — are used transitively and intransitively, even sometimes when not appropriate in modern English usage. Try it out. Play along. Of course, there is no way to know for sure the original the band of YAH stories from 2500+ years ago, though perhaps one's own brief study of Hebrew and playing with these stories will inspire in us all an appreciation for their greatness and motivation to want to carry on parabolic storytelling like YAH's as some much needed invitation to inner work and soul-searching and nonviolent social change in our world today.

here begins...

the band of YAH's Stories
in Genesis

Genesis 2 - 11

The Ins & Outs of Pleasure

Eden
Cain & Abel
Noah & his sons
the Tower of Babel

<Gen 1 - 2.4a...
begin at Genesis 2.4b>

On the day
YAHWEH-of-the-gods-and-goddesses/ELOHIM
made the solid-ground and the solid-sky —

and as for all the wild-shrubbery
of the rolling-field?

...it was before any of that was on the solid-ground...

and as for all the glistening-grass
of the rolling-field?

...it was before any of that had sprung up...

because YAHWEH-of-the-gods-and-goddesses/
ELOHIM hadn't yet made rain fall on the solid-ground

and there was no mud-creature
to slave-away at the mud —

and a mist climbed up from the solid-ground
and gave a drink to everything on the mud's face!

And YAHWEH-of-the-gods-and-goddesses shaped the mud-creature
out of dust from the mud
and puffed into its nose a blast of life
and the mud-creature was a real living thing!

(Try hearing and imagining that little chunk of the story as if for the first time....

And note the fun-puns already erupting in the story... 'mud-creature'/AHDM and 'mud'/AHDMH.

It's worth noting here too that 'the-gods-and-goddesses' is the Hebrew word ELOHIM, which can mean either 'the-gods-and-goddesses' or 'God' as in 'God of all-of-the-gods-and-goddesses.' Placing ELOHIM after YAHWEH is unusual in Genesis and used a few times in the Pleasure-Orchard/Eden story...why? possibly the band of YAH clarifying YAHWEH as being among the gods-and-goddesses or more than likely the Levitical/Deuteronomistic editors trying to harmonize this Pleasure-Orchard/Eden creation story with the very different Seven Days creation story before it where YAHWEH is not mentioned but ELOHIM/'God' is.

Note too the 'blast of life' the character YAHWEH puffs into the mud-creature's nose...something quite significant to the prophetic/ecstatic imagination, we might soon discover....)

And YAHWEH-of-the-gods-and-goddesses/ELOHIM
planted an orchard
in Pleasure, in the east,
and It placed there the mud-creature It'd shaped.
And YAHWEH-of-the-gods-and-goddesses made
spring up from the mud every tree
that was lusty for looking and good for eating.

And the Living-Tree was
in the middle of the orchard
— and the Knowing-Good-and-Bad-Tree!

(Pretty wild to think of the name of the garden as 'Pleasure'/AYDN...what usually gets brought forward in Bible translations as "Eden." But such a move by a translator only obscures what's there in the Hebrew. AYDN is a verb that has to do with luxuriating, pleasuring...standing up against the ecstatic-prophetic imagination, the priestly-writer of Nehemiah will use the verb AYDN as 'making revelry'...something frowned upon. But here in Genesis, AYDN is something in which to delight!)

<Gen 2.10-15>

And YAHWEH-of-the-gods-and-goddesses/ELOHIM
took the mud-creature
and left it alone
in Pleasure's orchard
to slave away and protect it.

And YAHWEH-of-the-gods-and-goddesses/ELOHIM
shouted out orders
at the mud-creature, saying,
"From every tree of the orchard,
you can <u>eat, eat, eat</u>!
But from the Knowing-Good-and-Bad-Tree,
you are not to eat from it
because on the day you eat from it,
you'll <u>die, die, die</u>!"

And YAHWEH-of-the-gods-and-goddesses/ELOHIM
said,
"Not good being the mud-creature, all alone...
I'm going to make for it a helper for its <u>front</u>...
<u>its talker, its complement, its similar-but-different</u>."

(In this translation, things in triplicate as in 'eat, eat, eat' are actually just doubled in Hebrew, though they are doubled with different verb-forms of the same 'root/verb.' It's usually to strengthen the verb, or to draw our ear to the style of the storycrafting. I've tripled things here and elsewhere to draw attention to the Hebrew double-style and as a way to remind the reader these usages are not typos in this translation. Much more will be said very soon about this 'its front'/NGDO....)

And YAHWEH-of-the-gods-and-goddesses/ELOHIM
shaped from the mud
every living thing of the rolling-field
and every bird of the solid-sky,
and It brought each one to the mud-creature
to see what name it would call out for it,

and for every one that the mud-creature called out a name for it —
each one a real live thing —
that was its name.

And the mud-creature called out names
for all the wild animals
and for all the birds of the solid-sky
and for every living thing of the rolling-field,
but for the mud-creature no one was found
as a helper for its front...
its talker, its complement, its similar-but-different.

And YAHWEH-of-the-gods-and-goddesses/ELOHIM
made a deep, trance-like sleep fall on the mud-creature. And it got all slack and slept.

And It took one of its ribs —
enough to make it limp later —
and It closed up the flesh underneath it.

And YAHWEH-of-the-gods-and-goddesses/ELOHIM
built up the rib
that It'd taken from the mud-creature
into a woman
and It brought her to the mud-creature.

And the mud-creature said,
"This thrust - this beat - this time!
Bone from my bone!
And flesh from my flesh!
This one I call out (the name) 'Wo-man!'
because from her-man she took herself!"

(Now, I suppose, the first mud-creature gets the pronouns 'he/him' instead of 'it' as the pun here invites because we now discover that Mud-Creature and Woman are different from each other...recall that earlier, YAHWEH had hoped to find someone to 'front' Mud-Creature. Before Woman was created, perhaps there was no 'gendering' and even no/little differentiation between mud-creature and animals other than Mud-Creature's naming them... remember YAHWEH created the animals as Mud-Creature's complements/fronts before YAHWEH created 'Woman'/AHSHH from 'her-Man'/AHYSH... very similar sounding words in Hebrew. And what a queer thing, right? Woman is born from man?! It's usually the other way around, right?

The difference between 'Man' and 'Woman' in Hebrew is the difference of a single breath...a single exhale...Man/'ish' and Woman/'ishah'...and here in the pun-rich story 'Woman' and 'her-Man' both sound like 'ishah' or at least sound similar based on what the Masoretes did or didn't do with the vowels in their work centuries after the band of YAH's stories...that probable exhale after 'ish' here in Mud-Creature's blurt.

YAHWEH's pronoun has usually been 'He' through the centuries. I've found in the bands of YAH's and X's writings — and perhaps most of the prophets' poems — that 'It' seems to work better, especially the genderbending that will soon and often occur with YAHWEH and YAHWEH's people, the prophets of Israel, and especially regarding the very nature of YAHWEH, the wind.

And 'flesh'/BSR is also a euphemism for 'penis' or the pleasure-rich foreskin/frenulum around the tip of an uncircumcised penis...every other time in Genesis the priestly editors/assemblers use BSR it refers to cutting off the BSR from one's penis...circumcision, the priestly ritual by which Ancient Israel comes to know itself as different from other Canaanite peoples. Circumcision may or may not predate the band of YAH's stories, so here in the story BSR might be simply punning on 'flesh' and 'penis' or 'penis-flesh.'

With Mud-Creature's words here, does it seem to you that he doesn't remember what happened in that deep sleep into which YAHWEH put him?

Is Mud-Creature imagining that he created Woman... from his penis, from his flesh? As in 'this flesh of Woman came from my flesh/penis'...which then plays well with the whole 'thrust' and 'beat' and 'time' of PAYM, a bizarre blurt from Mud-Creature which is indeed quite punny in that PAYM can mean the sound of a hammer striking an anvil, beating or thrusting something, and noting time as in the 'beat by beat' of anything, a way to keep time or mark time in the ancient world. This whole Mud-Creature statement and story is exceedingly pun-rich.

Did Mud-Creature know what YAHWEH did to his ribs?

This whole rib-business will all circle around again in the Jacob story....)

<Gen 2.24>

And the two of them,
the Mud-Creature and his Woman,
were naked-and-sly —
but they felt no shame...

and Snake was the most naked-and-sly
of all the living things of the rolling-field
that YAHWEH-of-the-gods-and-goddesses/ELOHIM
had made,

and (Snake) said to Woman,
"So, did God-or-the-gods-and-goddesses/ELOHIM
really say,
'You are not to eat
from every tree of the orchard'?"

(A talking 'Snake'/NCHSH! NCHSH is a Hebrew word and idea that is brought forward again as a verb in the Joseph-saga. In most ancient cultures, snakes are considered divine-creatures — far different from the modern world that sadly thinks snakes are evil, something we inherit from the Levitical priestly editors. Rather wildly, in Leviticus 19 the Levitical priestly editors will ban NCHSH/'snake-charming-to-tell-the-future' or possibly 'hissing-like-a-snake-as-future-telling'...even as the great Joseph talks openly about his own NCHSH-ing. And it is likely from this priestly-lens in Leviticus that the Snake gets a bad-rap in the Pleasure/Eden story. The Snake is actually accurate in what it will soon say about eating from the Knowing-Tree....

Perhaps to prophets/ecstatics, snakes and future-telling-through-the-hissing-sound-of-snakes is welcome...and to priests such a thing is profane/evil. More will soon be said about this as we encounter NCHSH in the Joseph-saga.

And as for the wildest of wild puns so far...most translators in the past have brought forward 'naked'/AYRUMYM referring to Mud-Creature & Woman (plural) and 'sly'/AYRUM referring to Snake (singular)...even though they are the exact same consonant-letters except for the plural 'YM' ending. Despite these two words having the exact same Hebrew consonants (except the plural ending), scholars and translators through the centuries have habitually translated these two instances of the same word very differently. Why? Because the Masoretes inserted vowels at least a millennia after the story was first told, and these vowels made it seem like 'naked' and 'sly' were different words in every Bible since then. But in all actuality, these AYRUM letters when heard by an ancient person are the same root-word — and any ancient hearer would know from experience and from the wily ecstatics/prophets that being naked is to be sly, clever, up to something...'to be naked' is 'to be sly.' As we'll discover in *The Naked Path of Prophet* series, 'nakedness' and 'slyness/cleverness' are hallmarks of the prophetic/ecstatic imagination.)

And Woman said to Snake,
"We can eat fruit from the trees of the orchard
but from fruit of the tree
which is in the middle of the orchard
God-or-the-gods-and-goddesses said/ELOHIM,
'Do not eat from it!
And do not grab it or else you die!'"

And Snake said to Woman,
"Not die?! You will not die!
See, God-or-the-gods-and-goddesses/ELOHIM know
that on the day you all eat from it,
your eyes'll be opened
and you all'll be
like God-or-the-gods-and-goddesses/ELOHIM
in knowing good and bad!"

And Woman saw that the tree was good for eating
and that it was desirable to the eyes
and the tree was lusty, stirred up desire in her for insight,
for understanding things,
and she took from its fruit and ate it
and even gave some to her man there with her
and he ate.

And the eyes of the two of them were opened
and they knew that they were naked-and-sly
and they sewed together fig-leaves
and made for themselves girdles around their waists.

And they heard the sound of YAHWEH-of-the-gods-and-goddesses/ELOHIM walking around in the orchard in the day's breeze.

And from within an orchard-tree, the Mud-Creature and his Woman hid themselves and their love-making from the face of YAHWEH-of-the-gods-and-goddesses/ELOHIM.

(Of all the puns so far, this is perhaps the most curious choice of words by this band of YAH-storycrafters...they use the verb 'to hide'/CHBAH which sounds so similar to the word 'to love'/CHBB. *Strong's Exhaustive Concordance* notes that this form of 'hiding' was hiding something or even someone in one's bosom with affection, with love. There are other words for 'hide' in Hebrew...like STR. But the band of YAH chooses the one that has to do with hiding themselves in and around one another.

Note too the cleverness of when and how YAHWEH walks...in the breeze...this YAHWEH who blew a blast of life — of the wind — into mud-creature earlier before Woman was 'born.'

As we'll soon discover in upcoming band of YAH stories in Genesis, the word 'know'/YDAY — as in the Knowing-Tree — is often used for sex, as in 'knowing one's sexual-partner fully and completely.' Seemingly forever, the Eden story's Tree of Knowledge has been seen as 'knowledge as in wisdom' and that might be the case — but it might also echo in an ancient hearer as 'knowledge as in sex' too.

As we'll discover in upcoming Genesis stories, YDAY often has to do with sex. And here in the Eden/Pleasure story, such a reading of YDAY as 'having sex' most certainly plays with the other sex-references in the story like this CHBAH here...another example of prophetic/ecstatic speech that erupts with possibilities of meaning so that the hearer of the story/poem has an inner awakening...to ALL that the story/poem/life and in the hearer can be and is... THE ALL.)

And YAHWEH-of-the-gods-and-goddesses/ELOHIM
called out to the Mud-Creature
and said to him,
"Where are you?"

And (the Mud-Creature) said,
"Your sound —
I heard it in the orchard —
and I was afraid
because I was naked-and-sly —
and I hid myself — hid myself in love!"

And (YAHWEH) said,
"Who put forward — made it <u>front</u> and center —
to you that you're naked-and-sly?
Why, from the tree —
the one I shouted out orders at you —
never to eat from it —
you ate!"

(Remember, YAHWEH made Woman to be the Mud-Creature's 'front'/NGD.)

And the Mud-Creature said,
"Woman — the one you gave to be with me —
she gave me something from the tree
and I ate it!"

And YAHWEH-of-the-gods-and-goddesses said to Woman,
"What's this?! What did you do?!"

And Woman said,
"Snake lent me a bad idea so I ate!"

And YAHWEH-of-the-gods-and-goddesses/ELOHIM
said to Snake,
"Because you did this —
bitterly cursed are you —
among all the wild animals
and among all the living things of the rolling-field!
On your belly, you'll make your way!
Dust, you'll eat!
All the days of your life!
And hatred — I put it
between you and Woman,
between your seed/descendants and her seed/
descendants —
they'll head-snap and you'll heel-snip!"

To Woman It said,
"Multiply, multiply, multiply —
that's how I'm making your labor-worries and your
getting pregnant!
In pain you'll give birth to children —
and toward your man
you'll overflow with thirst, desire
but he'll cleverly master and control you!"

And to the Mud-Creature It said,
"Because you listened to your Woman's voice
and ate from the tree
about which I shouted out orders at you
saying, 'Do not eat from it!'
Bitterly cursed is the mud because of you!
In pain you'll eat — every day of your life!
Thorn-bushes and prickly-plants will spring up for you,
and you'll eat glistening-grass of the rolling-field!
By the sweat on your face you'll eat bread
until you return to the mud —

because you were taken from it —
because you are dust —
and to dust you'll return!"

(Some wild, wild puns here too...

'head-snap'/YSHUPC and 'heel-snip'/TSHUPNO ... both from the same verb 'SHUP' meaning 'to bruise' and *Strong's Exhaustive Concordance* notes it can also mean 'to overwhelm'...something that YAHWEH will one day do to Jacob, as we'll soon be shocked to discover/feel...the character Jacob's name is YAYQB/'heel-grabber'...what does YAHWEH here say will happen? Woman's seed/descendants will snap Snake's head while Snake's seed/descendants will snap their AYQB/'heel' — very close in sound and purpose to Jacob/YAYQB and for those who know the catalog of the band of YAH's Genesis tales, their ears would perk up. The Eden/Pleasure story ribs the Jacob-wrestling-YAHWEH story quite, quite a lot...they need to be read together....

Note the character-YAHWEH gets some good puns going when It's angry...as do the prophets/ecstatics like Amos and the Isaiahs and Jeremiah in their poems.

'you'll overflow with thirst, desire'/TSHUQTC with its root in SHUQ/'overflow' and SHUQ/'thigh or leg' and possibly a euphemism for genitals and very related to the words 'to drink'/SHQH...use your imagination, friends!!! Remember, they're in the land of Pleasure and Woman and Mud-Creature had just been embracing through love-making!

'cleverly master and control'/MSHL...this same verb used again in the Joseph-saga as Joseph's brothers doubt Joseph can MSHL them...a word used often by the Deuteronomistic editors/writers 'to rule'...a word played on quite cleverly by Isaiah and Jeremiah in their poems.)

<*Gen 3.20*>

And YAHWEH-of-the-gods-and-goddesses/ELOHIM
made for the Mud-Creature and his Woman long-
hanging skin-shirts,
and they wore them.

And YAHWEH-of-the-gods-and-goddesses/ELOHIM
said,
"Yikes! The Mud-Creature is just like us
in knowing good and bad,
and now what if he reaches out his hand/penis
and takes something also from the Living-Tree
and eats and lives forever...!"

And YAHWEH-of-the-gods-and-goddesses/ELOHIM
sent him out from Pleasure's orchard,
to slave away at the mud from which he was taken.

And (YAHWEH) drove out the Mud-Creature — like It was divorcing him!

And to the east of Pleasure's orchard,
It made live there terrifying armed dudes
who usually protected the solid-sky
and the flaming sword turning every direction
to guard the way to the Living-Tree.

And the mud-creature <u>intimately and sexually knew</u>
his Woman — <u>Life!</u> —
and she became pregnant
and gave birth to Spear-Getter, and she said,
"I got a man from YAHWEH!"

(As most scholars/concordances note, the Hebrew word YD can be 'hand' and is often a euphemism for 'penis.' In the above quote about Mud-Creature reaching out his YD and eating from the Living-Tree, it seems surely to mean 'hand.' But just a few lines later, Mud-Creature must've reached out his YD to his Woman/Wife whose name means Life/Living — <u>life</u>/tree of <u>life</u>: CHY...her name: CHUH — because she is pregnant and we are told he 'knew'/YDAY her.

More clever pun-play with all of this...most of which does not come through in translations. With that pun-play in mind, what was YAHWEH saying back there in the Orchard before It armed the gates? Was Snake indeed right?)

And then she added on to that
by giving birth to his brother Wasted-Breath.

And so it was —

Wasted-Breath was a lamb-and-goat-shepherd,
...like...of small animals,

and

Spear-Getter was a slave of the mud,
...like...a farmer.

And so it was —

after many days Spear-Getter brought,
from the fruit of the mud,
a gift for YAHWEH.

> (Remember that lusty, desire-inspiring fruit that was in such great supply in the Pleasure-Orchard?)

And Wasted-Breath — well, he did too! —
he brought,
from the first-born of his lambs and goats,
from the fattiest and tastiest ones.

And YAHWEH gazed
toward Wasted-Breath and his gift;

and

toward Spear-Getter and his gift
It didn't gaze.

And anger blazed within Spear-Getter —
so very much so! —
and his face fell.
And YAHWEH said to Spear-Getter,
"Why is anger blazing within you?
Why does your face fall!?
If only you'd do good,
you'd raise yourself up in self-respect,
but if you don't do good —
corruption crouches at the door, ready to pounce!
it <u>overflows with thirst, desire</u> for you —
but you can <u>cleverly master and control</u> it!"

(Not exactly punny but a calling us back to what YAHWEH told Woman/Eve after YAHWEH had figured out she'd eaten from the Knowing-Tree... here in this story:

'overflows with thirst, desire'/TSHUQTO followed by 'cleverly master and control'/TMSHL

What does the band of YAH have the character-YAHWEH up to by using the same words and ideas with Woman/Eve as It is here with Spear-Getter/Cain?)

And Spear-Getter spoke to Wasted-Breath, his brother.

And so it was —
when they were in the rolling-field,
Spear-Getter stood up tall over his brother Wasted-Breath and killed him!

And YAHWEH said to Spear-Getter,
"Where is Wasted-Breath, your brother?"
And he said,
"I don't know!
Am I my brother's guardian?!"

And It said,
"What have you done?!
The sound of your brother's blood
is crying out to me from the mud!
Now bitterly cursed are you from the mud
which opened its mouth
to take your brother's blood from your hand!
When you slave away at the mud,

it'll never again give its power to you!
Wavering and wandering as a fugitive you'll be on the solid-ground!"

And Spear-Getter said to YAHWEH,
"My guilt, my crookedness is greater than I can carry —
look here, you're driving me out today —
like you're divorcing me! —
from the mud's face and from your face —
I'll hide —
I'll be wavering and wandering
as a fugitive on the solid-ground —
but what if anyone happens to find me and kill me!?"

And YAHWEH said to him,
"Alright, anyone killing Spear-Getter'll have to withstand it
(for themselves) seven times over!"

And YAHWEH put on Spear-Getter a warning mark
so that anyone finding him wouldn't beat him up.

And Spear-Getter set out away
from YAHWEH's face
and settled on the Wandering-Fugitive's-Land, east of Pleasure.

(Note that the kind of 'hiding' Spear-Getter is doing... STR...is different from the kind of affectionate hiding one does with a lover or beloved...CHBAH, the kind Woman and Mud-Creature were playing with together in the Pleasure-Orchard...evidence of the band of YAH's clever ways of juxtaposing words for clarity of meaning in side-by-side stories.)

<Gen 4.17 - 6.2>

And YAHWEH said,
"My wind won't sail directly
into the mud-creature forever!
I mean — that's flesh —
(a mud-creature's) days will be 120 years."

<Gen 6.4>

And YAHWEH saw the tremendous bad of the mud-creatures on the solid-ground,
and everything It'd shaped from Its heart's
imagination was altogether bad,
everything that day.

And YAHWEH was sorry It'd made the mud-creature on the solid-ground,
and It was hurting in Its heart.

And YAHWEH said,
"I'll wipe out the mud-creature
whom I created from the mud's face —
from the mud-creature
all the way through the wild beasts
and the swarming creepers
and the birds of the solid-sky —
because I'm full of sighs that I made them!"
But Noah measured up in YAHWEH's eyes —
Noah, whose name means Tranquilizer —
even to the point where YAHWEH would bow down to Tranquilizer...to Noah.

<Gen 6. 9-22>

<#>

(Tranquilizer?! Um. What on earth does YAHWEH see in Noah/Tranquilizer that YAHWEH would bow down to him? and choose him to survive from among all the mud-creatures of the earth? What was it about Noah that YAHWEH wanted him around, that maybe Noah tranquilized It? We'll have to see!)

And YAHWEH said to Noah, to Tranquilizer,
"Enter! You and everyone in your house/family!
Into the big-basket!
Because within you I see innocence —
right in front of my face — in this generation —
from all the wild beasts, the clean and pure ones,
take for yourself seven and seven,
(seven) man and (seven) woman —
and from the wild beasts that aren't clean and pure,
precisely two, man and woman —
also from the birds of the solid-sky, seven and seven,
male and female,
for keeping alive their seed/descendants on the solid-ground's face —
because in seven days
I'll make rain fall continuously on the earth —
for what'll seem like forever...40 days and nights!
I'll wipe out whatever is still standing —
whatever I made — from the mud's face!"
And Noah...Tranquilizer did everything that YAHWEH shouted out at him.

<Gen 7.6>

And Noah went
and his children
and his woman
and his children's women

with him
into the big-basket
away from the waters' face, the flood.

(Now, it's important to know that in the ancient imagination, 'the earth' was not round. It was more like those snow-globe trinkets we purchase on vacation...with solid-ground and solid-sky, also called the 'firmament.' And for a flood to happen, rain had to pour down from the solid-sky's floodgates, hatches where whatever was above could fall or fly down from the sky...in this case lots and lots of rain. And the hatches in the solid-ground where water trickled upwards as springs or downwards as rivers also had to be stopped up. **See page 52.** In a sense, YAHWEH here is filling up the snow-globe with all the waters above and below to drown all living things not in the big-basket, the ark.)

<Gen 7. 8-16a>

And YAHWEH shut him in.

And so it was —
the flood — the incredible ocean spilling forth from the heavens —
was on the solid-ground
for what seemed like forever...40 days!

And the waters grew even greater
and lifted the big-basket...

and it was raised way up high
over the solid-ground...

and the waters grew stronger
and grew even more over the solid-ground...

and the big-basket moved
over the face of the waters...

and the waters grew stronger...
more and more...over the solid-ground...

and every high mountain was covered...
every single one under the solid-sky...

five times, ten times the length of your forearm upward...
the waters grew stronger
and covered the mountains!

And they breathed out their last breath —
all flesh that moved and crept on the solid-ground...

birds
and wild beasts
and living things
and all the swarmers swarming upon the solid-ground
and every mud-creature —
every living, breathing thing
that had had a <u>blast of wind</u> —
of life! —
in its nose —
everything which had been on the dry land died.

(YAHWEH) wiped out — completely destroyed —
everything that was standing itself up on the mud's face —
from mud-creature
to wild beast

to creeping creature
to bird of the solid-sky —
they were wiped out from the solid-ground.

And only Noah...Tranquilizer was left and whoever was with him in the big-basket.

(Recall earlier in the Pleasure/Eden story the expression 'YAHWEH [...] puffed into its nose a blast of life' and here 'blast of wind — of life'...more evidence of YAHWEH being associated with the wind/breath in the ancient imagination.)

<Gen 7.24 - 8.1>

And they were stopped up —
the springs of the underground-ocean
and the floodgates of the solid-sky,
and the rain was held back from the solid-sky.

And the waters returned to going and coming on the solid-ground.

<Gen 8. 3b-5>

And so it was —
after what seemed like forever — 40 days! —
Noah opened up the big-basket's window that he'd made.

<Gen 8.7>

And he sent out a dove he had with him
to see if the the waters had been made smaller on the mud's face.

And the dove didn't find a resting place
for the sole of her foot,
and she returned to him to the big-basket
because the waters were all over the face
of the solid-ground.

And he stretched out his hand
and took her
and brought her toward himself
into the big-basket.

And he danced around
the right number of days — 7 days — after that,
and again sent out the dove from the big-basket,
and the dove came to him toward evening,
and — what do you know! — just-plucked olive leaves
were in her mouth,
and Noah knew that the waters had been made
smaller on the solid-ground.

And he waited again just the right number of days —
7 days — after that,
and he sent out the dove,
and she never returned to him again.

<Gen 8.13-19>

And Noah...Tranquilizer built a slaughtering altar for
YAHWEH,
and he took
from among the clean-and-pure wild beasts
and from among the clean-and-pure birds
and he climbed them up to be burnt on the
slaughtering-altar.

And YAHWEH got a whiff in the breeze
that would put anyone into a tranquil-trance for a long rest
and YAHWEH said in Its heart of hearts, to Itself,
"Never again will I inflict this small-insult on the mud
on account of the mud-creature
because the mud-creature's heart
was shaped badly from its youth!
Never again will I strike down every living thing as I've done —
going forward, all the days of the solid-ground,
seed-time and harvest-time,
cold and hot,
summer and winter,
day and night —
they won't stop!"

('Got a whiff in the breeze' is the from the verb RUCH, also the word for breeze or wind or spirit. Later biblical writers will use it for 'Holy Spirit.' We had it just a few lines ago with 'blast of wind — of life.'

Note the plays on Noah's name (NCH) in describing what happened to YAHWEH and his tranquilized state (NUCH) when he caught a whiff of the slaughtered animals on the barbecue/altar...perhaps YAHWEH was distracted from Noah's beauty and flooding the earth by the sweet smell of food.

Think it's outrageous that Noah's name essentially means Tranquilizer? Just wait until you see what his kids' names are....

There is some strangeness in all the 'make small'/

QLL regarding the waters on the solid-ground and 'make this small-insult' regarding what YAHWEH says It will no longer do to the mud on account of the mud-creature...a tragic-comedic effect here as if YAHWEH is saying, 'look this whole flooding of the earth is small beans, no big deal — but I'll never do it again anyway.' Usually this version of 'make small' is translated as 'to curse' but it is nowhere near the strength of the usual verb 'to curse'/AHRR that YAHWEH will do to Abram's enemies. QLL can mean to polish, as in metal, and Holladay notes that QLL also has to do with polishing arrows or shaking arrows as some form of casting lots — where someone is screwed for getting the short-end of the stick. Something makes me think that 'insult' would be a better translation of QLL with its idea of piercing — as in 'taking the hit' or 'taking one for the team'...or, at times, even a slang 'fuck over'/'screw.' Punny choice by the band of YAH to run it through the Noah/flood story with its unusual meanings...or quite strange.

When YAHWEH delights in Noah whose beauty must be tranquilizing, it seems strange that YAHWEH screws over — kills — all that lives on the solid-ground. Perhaps unrequited love for one so tranquilizing and trance-inducing as Noah could only inspire such madness...?

Just wait until we meet the sons of Tranquilizing-and-Trance-Inducing Noah!)

<Gen 9. 1-17>

And these are Noah's...Tranquilizer's sons,
the ones who came out of the big-basket:

Renowned
    and Hot
        and Handsome.

And Hot — he was the father of Humble-Trader.

('Humble-Trader' is the Hebrew word CNAYN... Canaan...the name for the region in which future biblical stories will take place, south of the the Fertile Crescent/Mesopotamia. Known for their being nomadic traders of goods, the land/people of 'Canaan' in biblical storytelling is often heard with a pejorative, disapproving sense because the people of Canaan were known to have interesting sexual practices and parties in their dedication to the fertility gods and goddesses of the land...BAAL and ASHTAROTH. It should be noted that all of the stories so far are assumed to be in and around the Fertile Crescent. Only with Abram and Sarai will we move our scene into Canaan-the-land. For now, we hear the story of Canaan-the-person — at least through his father and uncles and grandfather Noah.)

<*Gen 9.19*>

And Noah...Tranquilizer, a man of the mud, <u>opened it all up</u> —

played the pipe to be the life of the party?
began something new?
wounded by piercing?
did something offensive?

He planted a vineyard.

And he drank from the wine
and became drunk
and, in the middle of his tent,
he stripped himself naked like a slave or exile is forced to do!

And Hot, Humble-Trader's father, saw his father's genitals
and told his two brothers outside.

And Renowned and Handsome took some clothes
and drew it over their shoulders —
the two of them together —
and walked backwards and plumped up — err, covered — their father's genitals.
And their faces were backwards,
and as for their father's genitals...they didn't see them.

And Noah was awakened from his wine
and knew what he'd done to him —
his young (grand)son!
And he said,
"Bitterly cursed is Humble-Trader!
Slave of slaves!
That's what he'll be to his brothers!"

And he said,
"Abundance of YAHWEH — so much so that It brings people to their knees!
YAHWEH, of Renowned's gods-and-goddesses!
Humble-Trader'll be a slave for him!
All-the-other-gods-and-goddesses may be handsomely-alluring for Handsome!
May he live in Renowned's tents,
and may Humble-Trader be a slave for him!"

(Notice that Hot gets no mention here, but Tranquilizer curses Hot through Hot's son, Humble-Trader. It's quite the punny story as you can see from the underlined words above...and quite tragic in that the innocent kid gets the brunt of the drunk and naked Noah's anger. Apparently Noah needed a dose of his own medicine...a tranquilizer...whatever a 'tranquilizer' would be in ancient medicating... perhaps wine from the vineyard Noah built to tranquilize himself?

And as for all of the 'stripping naked like a slave or exile is forced to do'...this is the verb GLH used quite often in 1 Samuel to describe what YAHWEH does for Its prophets/ecstatics...YAHWEH reveals YAHWEH's full nakedness to those It loves. Here, in the Genesis story, Noah reveals his nakedness and Renowned and Handsome cover it over...and Noah curses Hot's son for it who wasn't even there, it seems. Talk about a hung-over tirade — and all of it over having been seen naked!)

<Gen 9.28 - 10.32>

<#>

(Noah...Tranquilizer dies. Time passes.)

And so it was —
the whole solid-ground was one language and one style of speaking.

And so it was —
in pulling up the tent-stakes to begin their journey from the east,
they found a split, a broad-valley, in Ancient Babylon —

in the famous civilization's cradle
between the two great rivers, Tigris and Euphrates —
and they sat down and lived there.

And they said to one another, one person to their neighbor,
"Come on!
Let's mold bricks until they are white-hot —
burn them until they're burnt!"

And they had for themselves fire-hardened bricks for stone and sticky-tar for mortar.
And they said,
"Come on, let's build ourselves a city!
And something great — a tower!
Its head up toward the solid-sky!
And let's make a name for ourselves — become renowned!
So that we're not dashed into pieces,
scattered all over the face of the solid-ground!"

> ('Renowned' plays on the character's name, Noah's son...SHM/'Renowned'.)

And YAHWEH went down to see the city and the tower that the mud-creature's children were building.

And YAHWEH said,
"Yikes! One nation and one language for all of them!
And this they are doing in opening it all up —

> playing the pipe to be the life of the party?
> beginning something new?
> wounding by piercing?
> doing something offensive?

all that they're scheming to do —
now they'll wall themselves in
and won't gather in the grapes for wine!

Come on, let's go down there —
let's smother their language
so that one person won't understand their neighbor's language!"

And YAHWEH dashed them to pieces from there
over the whole face of the solid-ground.
And they got flabby and stopped building the city.

And for this reason, It called out her name — (the city's name) —

Babel . . . Confusion . . . Smother!

because YAHWEH smothered the language of the whole solid-ground,

and from there YAHWEH dashed them to pieces over the face of the whole solid-ground!

<*Gen 11.10-32*>

<#>

(Guess that goes to show what YAHWEH thinks of Ancient Babylon...a land known for its ziggurats and palaces and temples into the sky...its great metropolises! But here such a land/city is seen as 'Smothering' and 'Confusing' and a land out of which Abram and Sarai and Lot will be called away!

And this business of 'playing the pipe as the life of the party, beginning something new when the old is preferred and tradition is revered, wounding by piercing, doing something offensive'/CHLL...noted here in the Tower of Babel story and earlier in the Noah story. It's usually translated as 'profane' as in the opposite of 'holy.' That's all fine and good — but notice all that might be seen as profane/offensive, all the uses for the verb...having to do with playing a pipe, with piercing something, with doing something offensive, and even with deflowering someone's virginity, as Holladay notes how CHLL is used in Leviticus.

Do you wonder what was the root of all of these offensive things?

With the 'flute' and 'pierce' and 'offensiveness' and 'taking virginity' references, I suspect CHLL has something to do with what one does with a penis — a euphemism of sorts that binds all of these pretty diverse possibilities with meaning.

Do you find it interesting that so far YAHWEH seems to have some unusual feelings for Mud-Creature/ Adam and Tranquilizer/Noah — the two main 'male' characters so far?

That desire for human-creatures will only grow as the one who was Tranquilizing has Renowned and Hot and Handsome for children...better with every generation....

And that only makes sense if you indeed know what YAHWEH is and is about. In the Pleasure-Orchard/Eden, YAHWEH was in the breeze. In the

Noah/Tranquilizer story, YAHWEH obviously is not harmed by the flood that fills the entire snow-globe of the earth and YAHWEH doesn't seem to be in the big-basket/ark either. So apparently YAHWEH had some way to get outside the snow-globe, and perhaps that is confirmed in the Tower of Babel/ Confusion story...YAHWEH goes down to see the Tower. From where? We're left to wonder for now. Perhaps from the sky, the heavens, the realm of the gods and goddesses. Jacob will one day have a dream that clarifies YAHWEH's role in the sky, among the gods and goddesses — even the gods and goddesses of the great Ancient Babylon...and YAHWEH's role of sailing into people to give them life — a blast of life through the wind.

And with all of this, what was it that was offensive to YAHWEH? That they built a phallic-tower to the heavens? That Noah got drunk and naked in his tent? Or that YAHWEH didn't get to participate — much like the prophets will mourn that Ancient Israel will leave YAHWEH for the phallic comforts of BAAL and ASHTAROTH, both symbolized by penis-poles in the ground. CHLL indeed!)

no more punny business...

commentary

How Very Far We've Come from Eden's Pleasuring Puns

I'm not sure what I was doing before the covid-quarantines of 2020-2021....

Never one much for endless hours of TV watching, it was during the first quarantine that I found a profound ache in me for a good story before I went to bed... something to stir in me dreams and imagination and new possibilities after the long days, in the early days of the actual mandated quarantine, of trying to figure how to live with this up-ended reality, this dangerous new reality where death became possible seemingly out of nowhere for oneself or one's loved ones. Stories helped ease — and disturb, shake up even more the contents of my imagination, my soul.

Sometimes that story came through some streaming service, sometimes through a book or poem or even sometimes from my own creation.

Sometimes even the news was enough story, watching fires being set in front of the White House during the Black Lives Matter protests immediately after George Floyd's murder by the state...protests of such scale and ingenuity I never thought I would see in my lifetime.

Perhaps we're all craving new ways, new possibilities, a new way forward from whatever we were before the worldwide soul-dredging that happened during the covid-quarantine where some powerful force of Nature — a virus — sent us humans to our rooms for a time-out...maybe to try to get our lives right or at least better than we had before the quarantine.

The band of YAH's era was different in terms of danger, in terms of things being up-ended — but just as profound and omnipresent. I try to imagine all the stories they heard around campfires night after night for decades. Maybe the band of storycrafters and their families were on the move that day, in search of greener pastures for their animals. Or maybe they were plunked down and harvesting something all day, resting by night only knowing that the same hard labor was coming the next day and the next day. Or maybe they were feeling the fear that arises in wondering if some gang would come rob or kill them by night, or if some superpower finally decided to attack and claim the trade routes that were Ancient Israel. The land of Israel/Palestine, after all, is wedged between two great superpowers — Ancient Egypt to the south, Ancient Babylon to the north — and such land in between was coveted, even if less city-settled. Or maybe the band of YAH's extended-families were dealing with their own small steps toward imperialism, of founding a city with its tower in the sky, like Babel. Seems like a mighty fine thing to do — until you have to protect it.

Talk about Confusion!

Like me or us in the 21st century or any generation hunkered down at home or on the road...how the band of YAH and their (usually) traveling, nomadic families must have ached for a story before bed.

Damn, those puns are fun!

Yes, just digging a little more deeply into the puns and wild characters and plots of these first stories, it's no grand statement to say that the band of YAH is quite the band of storytellers — perhaps the storytellers par excellence and unmatched by any other yet. Even Shakespeare. Even Spielberg.

The puns in the Eden story alone reveal a sophistication with storytelling that is hard to top — and just wait until we get to the Jacob stories where topping is what it's all about! The Eden story and the Jacob stories — especially the Jacob-wrestling-YAHWEH story — really need to be read side-by-side as they pun on each other significantly with all the words for penetrating and love-making and being 'ribbed' and knowing.

Before the band of YAH told such grand tales, surely first they heard stories, absorbed stories, let them play in their minds as they worked and as they stared into space during rest. Or as they stared into the fire readying the next night's tale to unfurl within them.

Stories arrive from some place within us all, after all, if only we dawdle around and listen deeply and drink from the well within us or pluck it out of the lazy wind that is available for us all.

What stories had the band of YAH heard? What stories did they know?

The sources that YAH's band puns upon

Well, we don't know for sure. And we can't ask them... unless we become shaman-like — bordercrossers — and beg them to tell us or hallucinate out a plausible answer.

But if we examine their stories carefully, they bear some resonances with some much more ancient tales that scholars are just beginning to grasp...

Enuma Elish...the story of how the warrior Marduk is raised up with the powers of all the gods to take on Tiamat, the sea monster whose only crime was that she selected her husband on her own without consulting the gods...so the gods order Marduk to harness the winds and drive them down Tiamat's throat and then shoot an arrow into her belly and split her body in two...half of her body was then stomped out to create the firmament, the solid-sky, the heavens...half of her body was then stomped out to create the solid-ground, the earth...and we are left to assume that human beings, then, are born from the blood of an 'evil,' disobeying, female sea-monster.

Compare this Babylonian creation story with the Bible's Eden Story, the Pleasure-Orchard Story as we have it in this translation. YAHWEH is endowed with the power of the gods-and-goddesses for sure — but YAHWEH is not nearly as serious and not nearly as all-knowing and as destruction-oriented as Marduk — at least until the flood a few generations after Eden's beginning. YAHWEH shows up in Eden's Pleasure-Orchard and can't seem to find Its creatures — the Mud-Creature and the Woman. Imagine that!

YAHWEH walks along in the afternoon breeze and can't find the creatures It made because they are hiding themselves in one another — making love — with all their gasps and stutters and orgasmic shrieks. (Note the irony — YAHWEH/the wind trying to find them as they are grinding and gasping and breathing life into one another — without YAHWEH.) And when It finally figures out that they ate from the Knowing-Tree It does not kill them (Tiamat's punishment); instead YAHWEH throws a pun-rich hissy-fit and then makes them clothes and sends them off...and blocks the way to the Living-Tree in case they happen to then eat from that and become just like YAHWEH forever. Why does YAHWEH make them clothes, we might wonder? And does YAHWEH wear clothes? Or could the whole YAHWEH-makes-them-clothes bit be an addition to the Eden story by later editors — it seems to be an intrusion into the flow of the story. Hmm....

I'll have more to say about the Pleasure-Orchard / Eden Story in a bit.

But first one other incredibly significant Ancient Babylonian story must be brought forward...*The Epic of Gilgamesh.*

This story first appears over 5000 years ago...the early Third Millennium BCE. The most intact versions that have survived the millennia come from the clay tablets set down by the priest Sîn-Leqi-Unninnī. Perhaps today we'd call him a shaman. He is said to have lived sometime between 1300 - 1000 BCE.

Gilgamesh is the story of a man, a king...the king of kings who crafted the famous ancient city Uruk. Truly it was more than a city, a metropolis with a complex canal-structure enabling hundreds of thousands of people to live within and around the city walls. It was massive — with grand buildings and ornately decorated temples and city-gates. And it was supremely well-defended, with a wall encircling the entire massive city. This is no mere Babel with a tower. This is a city like New York City is for us today...a capital of the world, at least in the ancient world.

And why was it massive and walled and well-defended? Because Gilgamesh had demanded that every son and daughter be enlisted in the city's service...in his service, King Gilgamesh's service.

This is the wisdom of *The Epic of Gilgamesh*, a warning to future royals who might want to tax their people heavily through tax-dollars or through servitude in this military-industrial complex. It's the same wisdom that the biblical character Samuel warns the nascent nation of Israel in X's Samuel-saga. Both *The Epic of Gilgamesh* and 1 Samuel warn of the dangers of hierarchy that enables city-life to emerge...often at great cost.

In *The Epic of Gilgamesh*, this of course was too much, no mere tax. After all, this is Uruk we're talking about — the greatest city of its day. The parents of these conscripted teenagers, according to the *Epic*, pleaded with the gods and goddesses, and the great godhead IL-ANU demanded that Mother ARURU craft a copy of Gilgamesh to vex him. And she does so from the clay, from the dirt of the ground. Sound familiar to our Eden story? And note that it's a female who does this body-crafting-from-the-dirt in *The Epic of Gilgamesh*.

And this body-copy named Enkidu was a wild, hairy version of Gilgamesh — he was ungroomed and uncivilized. He ate and drank with the animals, found himself at home with them but not yet other humans. Sound familiar to our Eden story when YAHWEH crafts the animals and birds to be playmates for the mud-creature?

A hunter saw Enkidu and feared him, and hated him. Why? Because Enkidu didn't let the hunter hunt the wilderness' animals, Enkidu's friends and playmates. The hunter's father suggested going to King Gilgamesh, the one with power who knows all things. And just as the hunter's father said, Gilgamesh listened and responded positively by sending a temple-prostitute with the hunter. Why? So that the temple-prostitute would take off her clothes in the wilderness when Enkidu would come to drink with the animals. The temple-prostitute, by the way, served the goddess ISHTAR...from which we get the word/festival Easter. (Yikes! Yes!)

The hunter instructs the prostitute to take off her clothes and spread her legs and trusts that her beauty will be enough to lure the primal-man Enkidu away from the animals and in love/lust with the woman. And sure enough he is lured by her — and fucks her for six days and seven nights. (Think this word 'fucks' is too strong? Stephanie Dailey's translation even notes the word-choices in the Ancient Babylonian indicate it was doggy-style, Enkidu fucking her from behind. John Gardner & John Maier's translation actually uses the word "fucking." And note the priestess has no choice in the matter — she's a sex-slave in ISHTAR's temple, at the service of King Gilgamesh.). Not so much 'love-making' here....

The verb 'fuck' certainly has different meanings, even among today's English-speaking generations. No matter the genders of the people involved, 'fucking' has the sense of one dominating the other, right? of one having to submit and endure what the other offers? A woman-friend of mine told me recently she's been 'fucking this guy.' Here we see a gender-reversal — woman fucking a man — compared to the Enkidu and prostitute story — man fucking a woman. No matter who is on top, no matter who is dominating, it's a hierarchical-imagination, one topping the other. This is not to say that 'love-making' must always be sideways or on the same plane or something silly like that — passionate love-making certainly has no bounds and no rules in that it's relational, right? The two (or more) in the relationship work out and play out together how to be equals with one another...or at least equally-valued even in their different roles...something that indeed might be ecstasy-inducing.

Contrast this hierarchical-imagination — ISHTAR-prostitute valued less than hairy, wild man Enkidu — with the Eden story where Woman is an afterthought by YAHWEH in the creation of living and breathing creatures though Woman's curiosity gives birth to Wisdom.

And when Enkidu had finished his first experiences with sex, he was different and no longer like the animals... they all turned away from him. Sound familiar to Eden's Mud-Creature who no longer has interest in the animals after Woman shows up? (Though Woman has interest in Snake...and Snake's way of communicating with her, hissing sounds that sooth her into wanting to eat from the Knowing-Tree, into stirring up desire in her for insight.)

Since he no longer has status and sway over the animals, Enkidu then turns back to the woman, the temple-prostitute, and she informs him that he has become like a god because he knows something...he 'knew' her.

She encourages him to come back with her to Uruk, to the great city (opposite of wilderness where Enkidu had lived) where the gods and goddesses are honored through festivals every night — festivals of sex and poetry and party — and where the great King Gilgamesh rules all like a wild bull over and in charge of all the people.

Enkidu thinks he'll be able to roar over Gilgamesh's power...but the temple-prostitute informs Enkidu that Gilgamesh is well-hung and a joy to look at in his sexual beauty/prowess but such looking is also a great sadness for the viewer because King Gilgamesh can have anyone — and odds are that he won't want you with so many to choose from.

She informs Enkidu that Gilgamesh is so powerful that Gilgamesh will have surely already dreamed of Enkidu, even before he arrives.

And sure enough Gilgamesh does dream of Enkidu — and the dream bothers him so much that he consults his mother. Gilgamesh dreams that Enkidu is so powerful that he cannot be moved or toppled so that the only thing then to do is to hug Enkidu as a man hugs a wife — to lay him down and have sex with him. (Römer notes that the same-sex pair of Gilgamesh-Enkidu has some important resonances in the later biblical fictional stories of same-sex loving pair of David-Jonathan in 1 Samuel.) And Gilgamesh's mother assures her king-son that that is indeed what he should do, he should embrace and have sex with the wild-man Enkidu. Now notice — it's a woman who interprets dreams in *The Epic of Gilgamesh*. This will be important later in our biblical Genesis stories.

Remember...Enkidu was created out of the clay by the Great Mother goddess as a distraction for Gilgamesh — to prevent him from taking every young man and young woman to be at his disposal as king and builder and maintainer and defender/general of the great city Uruk.

And while Gilgamesh's mother was helping to untie her son's dreams (interpreting the dreams), the temple-prostitute was tying up Enkidu by bewitching him... clothing him in some of her clothes so that he'd look like a nomad. She was trying to civilize him at least a little bit — through clothes and through giving him the commoner's meal...bread and wine. At first, Enkidu just stared at it. Before she came along he simply suckled the cow teets when he was in need. The temple-prostitute taught this primal-man-of-the-wilderness how to be civilized...through sex, wearing clothes, eating and drinking prepared food. (Remember how YAHWEH makes clothes for the Mud-Creature and his Woman before It sends them out and into the wilderness east of the Pleasure-Orchard?)

And after being readied by the temple-prostitute, Enkidu wrestles lions and predators and befriends shepherds whose animals were often eaten by lions. Enkidu enters Uruk and is seen by the people as powerful and beautiful — a match for Gilgamesh though a bit shorter. Enkidu blocks Gilgamesh's way to the marketplace — the economy of the city. Gilgamesh then wrestles Enkidu, and Enkidu — the wrestler of lions — regards Gilgamesh as a worthy-fighter and companion.

It's worth noting here that the thing that gets King Gilgamesh riled up enough to fight so valiantly is that Enkidu blocks the commerce of the land, the huge benefit of city-life and the power of the city that flows when a king rules over it and establishes an order, a hierarchy, that puts the city in enough order for power to flow from his rule in the free exchange of goods harvested and prepared by many classes of people in that hierarchy. This is city-life. And this is the life that wild-man-becoming-civilized Enkidu is preventing, blocking.

But in their embracing one another eventually as friends and lovers, King Gilgamesh must confess that he has a problem that threatens his city's life — Humbaba, the wild force in the deepest recesses of the wilderness, even wilder than Enkidu's roots. This evil beast Humbaba's roar is the flood — the great flood from which the band of YAH stole perhaps whole lines for their Noah/Tranquilizer story. But in the Genesis story, it is YAHWEH who does the flooding — and because the temperamental YAHWEH can no longer bear the mud-creatures, except one particular mud-creature. YAHWEH finds favor with — even bows down to — one trance-inducing, tranquilizing human who will go on post-flood and get drunk and strip himself naked as if someone had enslaved him and then berate his kids — even blaming the whole thing on the grandson whose father had little to do with any of it...the one from whom we get the name Canaan... the Humble-Traders, the ones among whom Abram will one day wander toward...far away from Ancient Babylon's Ur/Uruk and its civilized, high-society life of the metropolis and temple-worship and festival/party.

Abram, we'll soon see, is a bordercrosser, a Hebrew. These nomadic bordercrossers are far different people from the people of Uruk and Babylon — the people from whom the bordercrossing band of YAH is pretty clearly differentiating themselves. Ancient Babylon's economy is a top-down system...and what does the band of YAH do with towers and top-down systems? They topple them, up-end them and civilized society's polite expectations.

A very different way forward in story, in imagination

There's a lot of up-ending going on already and we've only begun the story — both the band of YAH's story and *The Epic of Gilgamesh*.

One place where it seems like *The Epic of Gilgamesh* and the band of YAH are in agreement is with women-characters who live and thrive and have speaking parts. In the other Ancient Babylonian story mentioned earlier — *Enuma Elish* — Tiamat speaks in her defense but just before she is destroyed and her body is used to create the snow-globe earth. What had Tiamat done? She had disobeyed the male gods' dictum that men ordain which man married which woman. *Enuma Elish*'s portrayal of women simply reinforces the default, that women must do what men ask or else be destroyed. In *Enuma Elish*, the hierarchy and its controlling son patriarchy are simply reinforced.

But not in the band of YAH's stories. With Eden, Woman disobeys and Wisdom is born.

In *The Epic of Gilgamesh*, it might seem like a big step forward for women and valuing women in that multiple women have speaking roles, no woman is killed, and some women are even wise. The temple-prostitute helps to shape the wild-man Enkidu into a civilized man, through sex with her and through his eating her produce, bread and wine. But she's still a sex-slave, at the service of the hierarchs of ISHTAR in Uruk, which is under the king's direction. Sure, the father-god ANU commands the mother-goddess ARURU to create Enkidu — but it's at a man's orders. And King Gilgamesh takes his anxiety-fueled dreams to his mother for interpretation and she seems to be wise — but she is not a ruling queen, let's note. It's her son who rules the great city, not her.

This is all vastly different from the band of YAH's Genesis tales so far. In the Eden/Pleasure story, Woman listens to the Snake, eats the forbidden fruit from the Knowing-Tree, and from that order-violating-action gives birth to wisdom. But that's not all...she also gives birth to sex with mud-creature — and perhaps this is what gets YAHWEH all in a huff in the first place. Mud-Creature was hiding himself in her, in Woman, in the one place in the Orchard where YAHWEH could not find Mud-Creature.

Perhaps YAHWEH is jealous. YAHWEH certainly creates Woman as an afterthought — maybe YAHWEH was hoping that the mud-creature would find friendship and love with It, with YAHWEH, instead of with Woman.

The great irony, of course, is that modern religions of the Book — Judaism, Christianity, and Islam, all three of these religions sharing the Hebrew Bible as their common text — have ignored YAHWEH's jealous-lust or have thought it so ridiculous that the Creator of the snow-globe earth could be jealous or could want sex with a mud-creature. But that's just the trick now, isn't it? And none of it will make much sense until we get a full-sweep of more of the band of YAH's stories... because some pretty wild things are coming between YAHWEH and human beings, specifically men. Mud-creatures of every gender are irresistible...!

So far, YAHWEH is already quite wild in the early biblical stories. YAHWEH has temper tantrums, It gets displeased, It gets fearful that humans will be like It, It counsels Spear-Getter/Cain but only after showing Its preference for Wasted-Breath/Abel's grass-fed flesh over Cain's vegetarian diet that seems to be no different from what was in the Orchard with all the fruit-eating and no mention of eating animals.

Babylonian stories about order...and then there's the band of YAH's eruptive, disruptive tales!

Everything seems quite orderly in the realm of the gods and goddesses in *Enuma Elish* and *The Epic of Gilgamesh*, at least so far...while the band of YAH's YAHWEH is quite temperamental and human-like in emotion. This is far different from the Seven Days Creation story that kicks off Genesis. The Seven Days story is widely considered by scholars to be written by the priestly editors as a way to invite a more god-like God, more in keeping with the control of the situation and having everything planned and under wraps like the Ancient Babylonians' understandings of gods and goddesses.

But not so with the band of YAH who even presents a divinity that can be swayed by humans — mud-creatures. Note how Spear-Getter/Cain sways YAHWEH toward protecting him even after he had just killed his brother. In some ways, the people of Uruk sway father-god ANU to do something about the king stealing away their sons and daughters for labor — but even then ANU's response is to delegate down the chain of command (hierarchy) to mother-goddess ARURU to do something about the people's cries, that she might craft Enkidu out of mud to mess with King Gilgamesh instead of the city-dwellers'/subjects' sons and daughters and all the labor these youngsters can provide to build Uruk even stronger and more internally vibrant in the name of King Gilgamesh.

If we have our wits about us and do not project modern religion's views about YAHWEH onto the biblical stories but instead read out what is there and wonder about it, we might be quite surprised by this YAHWEH. It's very different from ANU and ARURU and ISHTAR and the whole pantheon of Ancient Babylonian gods and goddesses. And certainly different from the Canaanite fertility-divinities of BAAL and ASHTAROTH (see *The Naked Path of Prophet vol 1* for more flavor about them).

Perhaps, dear reader, you're becoming more curious about why I've chosen 'It' for YAHWEH's pronoun. As we'll see through the clever poems of the Bible's prophets/ecstatics, 'They' might be a perfectly good pronoun too, not so much as in 'They' as a *plural* but as in 'They' as in *non-binary*, in our multi-gendered, bordercrossing imagination of the 20th & 21st centuries.

Let's see what else the band of YAH has in store for us

as we turn to three characters born in Ancient Babylon, in the Land of Light...three characters who are swayed, enticed, to travel far away from the so-assumed perfect land of the Fertile Crescent with its palaces and towers to a land with apparently great promise, the hill-country far removed from the Fertile Crescent and its metropolises like Uruk...a land and a life of nomading, of bordercrossing, of having no particular home, a life where the wind blows, perhaps, more freely.

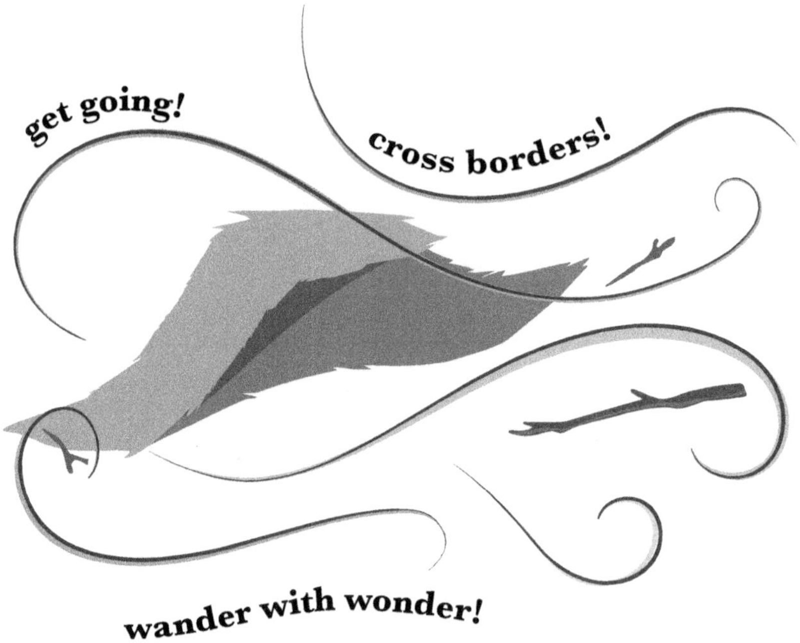
get going!
cross borders!
wander with wonder!

Genesis 12 - 19

From Slackers to Prosperers

Abram & Sarai become Abraham & Sarah
in a land far, far away from the old prosperous metropolis
of Ur[uk] and its hierarchical imagination

<begin at Gen 12.1>

And YAHWEH said to Abram, the guy
whose name means Patriarch-Helps-or-Hurts,
"Get-going! You!
From your land!
From everybody you know and call your ancestral-family!
From your father's house!

To the land that I'll make you see!

I'll make you — yes one person! — a great nation!
I'll bring you to your knees into abundance!
I'll make your name synonymous with greatness —
it'll bring people to their knees into abundance!
I'll bring into abundance those who bring you into abundance —
as for those belittling you with even the smallest-insult,
I bitterly curse!
They'll be brought into abundance through you —

every species from the mud — including the (maid) slaves!"

And Abram went — just as it had been had styled out (sweet-talked?) to him — by YAHWEH.

(This sweet-talking style of speech would have been quite surprising in the ancient world — not only by content/promise but by sound. Note the style of this sweet-talking...all the repetitions of 'you' which has a hard 'c' or 'k' sound to it as it's used here in Hebrew. This little styling forth with all these velar-stops as linguists call them sounds percussive, musical, like a drum. And even more surprising? A character with an undecided, ambivalent, wavering, probably not-to-be-trusted name gets the invitation...Patriarch-Helps-or-Hurts. Note here and elsewhere the importance of knowing what the biblical characters' names mean. And even more surprising? This guy actually goes — leaves his palace-rich homeland in the fertile cradle of civilization and cradle of metropolises between two great rivers in Ancient Babylon for a land unknown.

And note the clever contrasts/juxtapositions with word-choices here: whoever QLLs Abram will get AHRRed by YAHWEH...QLL/'small-insult' as used in the Flood Story and AHRR/'a very serious curse.' QLL could be so small an insult, like getting flicked off by someone's middle finger...stupid power-move that seems big and mean but at the end of the day means nothing, a small-insult. And yet YAHWEH repays the foolish insulter with a big curse!

And as for 'every species from the mud — including the (maid)slaves'...the word here is MSHPCHH/'clan or tribe or family or probably better extended family'...though *Strong's Exhaustive Concordance* also notes that that word is most certainly connected to SHPCHH/'maidslave.' To ancient ears in this story, MSHPCHH would broaden one's assumptions about family as in not only the 'family' descended from the husband and first-wife and second-wife and more-wives but also the 'family' that comes from the husband having sex with and children through the maidslaves. And MSHPCHH is immediately juxtaposed with MOLDT/'ancestral-family' mentioned earlier in the YAHWEH's same sweet-talking speech. *Strong's Exhaustive Concordance* notes that MOLDT from YLD bears some nuances of 'pedigree'...as in someone who could claim full 'birth-rights' within a family.

Could the character-YAHWEH here be suggesting in this stylish speech that Abram's 'ancestral-family' back in Ancient Babylon — which does not seem to include slaves among their pedigree — might change once Abram moves south to Canaan where slaves' kids count in the ever-growing family that Abram will welcome...a new way that sees 'family' as including everyone?

MSHPCHH foreshadows what will come regarding the maidslave The-Immigrant/Hagar and later the baby-making contest between Rachel and Leah eventually using their maidslaves to get more children credited to themselves individually...but even more than that in that the prophetic imagination essentially sees all humans as slaves...either as slaves to the empire and its hierarchical/royal-slave imagination or as slaves to YAHWEH alone as we see in 1 & 2 Samuel...and as the prophets implore, the wise swim away from "the shipwreck" that is empire and hold no power over any other human and thus a need to free anyone we hold below us, as in freeing all slaves. But Abram as we'll soon see is not there yet. Clearly. Though one day one of his slaves will be his ambassador to fetch a wife for his son Isaac as if that slave were a person of full-status and worthy of YAHWEH, as we'll soon see....)

<*Gen 12. 4b-c*>

And Abram took his wife Sarai, whose name means On-Top,
and Cover-Up, his brother's son,
and all their (animal/wealth) gatherings they'd gathered over the years —
the life that they'd made for themselves in Scorched-and-Glowing-Land (it was that hot, hot, hot city-life!) —
and they left to get-going
toward the Humble-Traders'-Land.

And they entered the Humble-Traders'-Land,
and Abram/Patriarch-Helps-or-Hurts crossed over
(the river/border) onto the solid-ground, into the land,
all the way to the area of Rise-Early-Load-Your-Shoulders-With-Work,
all the way to the Drunk-Tree-Gets-You-Flowing-Like-Arrows.

(Quite a fertile area, apparently...enough to keep a big oak tree alive, the kind of oak that has a reputation from which strong drink can be brewed...enough to get you drunk and seeing things, get you into a flow like arrows shooting across the sky. Sounds great, right? But this is no land with towers and palaces like his homeland of Babylon....

Note too 'Abram/Patriarch-Helps-or-Hurts' is AHBRM and 'to bordercross or cross a river into a new territory' is AYBR(M)...they both sound quite similar when spoken aloud...a pun that echoes through the story about a man from the hot-hot-hot city-life of Babylon choosing to leave it behind in favor of wandering, bordercrossing....)

And, at the time,
the Humble-Traders were on the land.

And YAHWEH made Itself able to be seen
by Abram and said,
"To your seed/descendants!
I give this land!"

And he built there an altar for slaughtering animals to YAHWEH,
the one who made Itself able to be seen by him.

And it got old being there so he moved on to the mountains east of House-of-EL-God-of-the-Land,
and he stretched out his tent
with House-of-EL-God-of-the-Land to the west and Heap-of-Ruins to the east.

And he built there an altar for slaughtering animals to YAHWEH,
and he called out in YAHWEH's name.

And Abram, the guy named Patriarch-Helps-or-Hurts,
tore out his tent-stakes,
kept on going,
and tore out his tent-stakes again to journey toward
the southern desert.

And so it was —
a famine in the land!

And Abram went down even further south
toward Suffering-Egypt
to stay there as an immigrant
because the famine weighed so heavily on the land.

And so it was —
when he was just about to enter Suffering-Egypt that
he said to his wife Sarai, whose name means On-Top,
"Now look here, please,
I know in every way how beautiful you are
— what if they see you?! —
the Suffering-Egyptians! —
and they say, 'This is his wife!'
and they kill me
but you they let live!?!
Let's say you're my sister
so that it goes well for me —
so that it goes well for me —
in <u>your being bordercrossed, for your sake</u> —
so that my living, breathing body can stay alive —
<u>(with all) your rolling around</u>!"

And so it was —
just as Abram was entering into Suffering-Egypt
that the Suffering-Egyptians saw the woman —
yep, she was very beautiful.

And some of those officials on-top for the Sufferers' royal-ruler, Pharaoh-Negligence,
saw her,
and they all boasted about her to Pharaoh-Negligence,
and the woman was taken to Pharaoh-Negligence's house.

And as for Abram, (Pharaoh-Negligence) made it go well in his bordercrossing her.

(Note the style, what Abram does with Sarai/SRY and what the officials/SRY do with Sarai/SRY. All the same letters in pun-rich Hebrew. On-Top, indeed!

And note the ancient idioms...'bordercrossing, for the sake of'/AYBUR and 'rolling around'/GLL, Abram anticipating what will happen when Pharaoh's men see the beautiful Sarai and take her for Pharaoh's royal-harem, his royal-sex-slaves. Sarai's name can sometimes be used for 'princess' as well....

This Abram...right now he hurts others, especially his own wife...all kinds of borders being crossed....)

And so it was —
(Abram) got lambs and goats
and cattle and donkeys
and male-slaves and female-slaves-able-to-bear-children-for-their-owner
and female-donkeys and camels.

And YAHWEH hit Pharaoh-Negligence with knock-out punches —

and his house/family too! —
all because of the styling-on of Sarai, Abram's wife.

And Pharaoh-Negligence called out Abram and said,
"What's this you've done to me?!
Why didn't you tell me she's your wife?!
Why did you say, 'She's my sister!'
and I took her — for me! —
to be my wife and now look at this! —
(all that these knock-out punches have done!) —
take your wife and go!"

And Pharaoh-Negligence shouted out orders at his people,
and they sent him away
and his wife
and all that was his.

('Take your wife and go' sounds like this in Hebrew: QCH ULC. More of those repeating 'ck' sounds. Seems that even one as Negligent as Pharaoh can get into the game of styling out some words for effect. The Hebrew word for 'Pharaoh'/PRAYH — by the way — sounds like the Hebrew word for 'negligence'/PRAY.

And superpower-leading Pharaohs were probably no friends to bordercrossers of Ancient Israel/Palestine — Pharaohs would most likely be quite negligent toward people who don't even rank in their royal/slave society's hierarchy, except as future slaves, even sex-slaves like Sarai had become before getting kicked out of the Pharaoh's harem.

Note how the band of YAH essentially has Abram

steal a great deal of wealth/animals from Pharaoh-Negligence through the ruse with Sarai before they all high-tail it out of there...all at Sarai's expense. Get a flavor for the kind of person Abram is so far? So far he's a patriarch who <u>hurts</u> people, or at least uses people — his own wife! — for his own gain. Abram only <u>helps</u> himself.)

And Abram went up from Suffering-Egypt —
he and his wife and all that was his —
and Cover-Up with him —
toward the southern desert.

And Abram was very weighed down
with livestock, with silver, with gold.

And he went on his tent-stake-tearing journey from the southern desert all the way to House-of-EL-God-of-the-Land, to the place where he'd been at the opening,
between House-of-EL-God-of-the-Land and Heap-of-Ruins,
to the place of the slaughtering altar which he'd built there in the beginning
and Abram/Patriarch-Helps-or-Hurts had called out there in the name of YAHWEH.

And even Cover-Up —
having gone along with Abram, whose name means Patriarch-Helps-or-Hurts —
Cover-Up had lambs and goats and cattle and tents.

And the land couldn't handle them living together
because their gatherings were so <u>many...bustling!</u>

They just weren't able to live together as one whole.

And so it was —
there was a fight...a tousling
between Abram's livestock-herders
and between Cover-Up's livestock-herders.

> (The band of YAH plays with clever style on the words 'many'/RB and 'fight'/RAYB.)

And the Humble-Traders and those living in the open-country were living on the land.

And Abram said to Cover-Up,
"Please, let there be no fighting
between me and you,
between my livestock-herders
  and your livestock-herders,
because we are men of brothers — family!
Why not —
the whole land is right in front of your face!
Please separate from me —
if left, I'll go right...
if right, I'll go left."

> (There's a cleverness to these words that Abram chooses...the word for 'left'/SMAHL here has some grammarians seeing a similarity with the word SML having to do with 'wearing clothes, even the mantle of status.' Play the 'clothes-wearing' in with Cover-Up's very name...and his choice, where he later ends up in Sodom/Their-Bondage, where clothes get stripped off nightly.)

And Cover-Up raised his eyes
and saw the whole, broad, round valley of the Going-Down River —
as if it were whirling and dancing before him —

all of it lush with water...
before YAHWEH laid waste
Their-Bondage and Bind-Abundant-Harvest —
just like YAHWEH's orchard,
and just like Suffering-Egypt —
as you enter into Little-Place.

(Even more playfulness here with word choice... CCR/'something round...usually a loaf of bread or a coin or a district, city' and CCR derives from CRR/'to dance around.' The city/region that Cover-Up eventually chooses is known for its whirling dances, most likely in honor of BAAL and ASHTAROTH.

And 'lush with water'/MSHQH is similar sounding to 'laid waste'/SHCHT.

Again, all these clever puns foreshadow Cover-Up's foreboding choice...especially bringing up the orchard — most likely referring to Eden — that got surrounded and blocked by YAHWEH's heavenly henchmen and then reminding us of the knock-out punches/plagues with which YAHWEH hit the Egyptians for Pharaoh's negligence in handling Abram's wife, whom Abram passed off as his sister to save his own skin.)

And Cover-Up chose for himself the whole, broad,

round valley of the Going-Down River as if it were
whirling and dancing before him —
and Cover-Up pulled up tent-stakes
and began his journey from the east.

And they separated, one man from his relative.

And Abram lived in the Humble-Traders'-Land,
and Cover-Up lived in the cities of the broad, round
valley (dancing round!) and put up and took down his
tent and then put up and took down his tent
...even all the way to the city of Their-Bondage.

And Their-Bondage's people — they were bad
and offended YAHWEH with their corruption —
very much so!
And YAHWEH said to Abram, whose name means
Patriarch-Helps-or-Hurts,
after Cover-Up had separated himself from (Abram),

"Please raise your eyes and see —

from the place where you are northward
and then down to the southern desert
and eastward and westward to the sea —

because all the land that you see
I'm giving it to you
for you and your seed/descendants
...even for forever!

I'm setting up your seed/descendants to be
just like the land's dust!

If anyone can even weigh the land's dust...
so will your seed/descendants be weighed!

Stand up tall!
Walk around the land
toward its length and toward its width
because I'm giving it to you!"

And Abram put up and took down his tent
and then put up and took down his tent (again)
and entered into
and lived among The-Trees-Where-You-Can-Get-Drunk-&-See-Things-&-Do-Wild-Things which is in Enchanting-Allies
(a few days' journey from where Cover-Up was living).
And he built there a slaughtering altar to YAHWEH.

<Gen 14. 1-24>

After these stylings-on,
YAHWEH's style was with Abram in a trance:

"Do not fear, Abram!
I'm your warrior's defense!
Your ever-growing salary!"

And Abram said,
"My boss! YAHWEH!
What have you given me?!
I — I'm stripped of any children — going the way of childlessness!
And a son I bought — my house will be his! —
that guy from way-up-north, My-EL-God-Helps!"

(Even the name of the slave is a bit of a stab at YAHWEH...My-EL-Helps...as if to say 'and you, YAHWEH, haven't done a thing yet.' EL, remember, is the head god of the regional/Canaanite gods + goddesses. Note too that YAHWEH has no reply for Abram to Abram's style, his clever way of questioning.)

And Abram continued saying,

"Look here, you haven't given me a seed/descendant!
Hey, what about a son of my house/family becoming heir to what's mine?!"
And what do you know — YAHWEH's style came to him saying,
"Nah, this guy won't become your heir...
instead it'll be the one who comes out of your guts,
he'll become your heir!"

(Note the clever style here...as if the child will be born right out of Abram's guts, as if from his own womb.)

And (YAHWEH) made him come outside,
and It said,
"Please gaze upon the solid-sky —
count the stars —
if you can count them!"

And It said to him,
"So will your seed/descendants be!"

And he put his trust in YAHWEH —

he drove his tent-stake into something firm/ established, this commitment with YAHWEH (despite his aimless wandering as a nomadic bordercrosser where he hardly ever drove in his tent-stakes for long),

he turned to the right (hearkening back to this splitting with Cover-Up),

he took the right road, the high road.

And honesty and reliability were woven for him, with him.

(Note the styles in the language, the word choices and turns of phrase by the biblical storycrafters, the band of YAH...first with the all-important word AHMN/'to trust, to drive in one's tent-stake' and all the idiomatic ways that the ancients understood that word 'trust' had, from which we get our word "amen"...and second that we 'weave'/CHSHB a life in our choices...and soon we'll get to discover how Abram's choices and Cover-Up's choices weave very different lives just by where we choose to live, and for how long, perhaps. And here's YAHWEH, who so wanted to be interwoven and in relationship with Mud-Creature/Adam now weaving himself with Abram, this one who chose bordercrossing and wandering over city-life, who drove in his tent-stake long enough to know and be known by YAHWEH...)

And It said to him,
"I'm YAHWEH,
the one who made you come out of Ur,
out of the very rich and fertile land of the Flaming Light,
(where the sun never sets...

parties and festivals lasting until dawn every night),
out of the southern Ancient Babylonian Land of the Wise-Ones,
to give to you this land right here —
to be the heir of it."

And he said,
"My boss, YAHWEH,
how will I know
when I'm the heir?"
And It said to him,
"Fetch for me a young cow,
one that has not yet borne a calf, a three-year-old,
and a three-year-old goat,
and a three-year-old ram,
and a turtle-dove,
and a young pigeon."

And he fetched all of these for It,
and he cut them in pieces, right down the middle.

And he set each piece by its companion.
But the birds he didn't cut up.

And birds of prey flew down on the carcasses,
and Abram blew them away.

And so it was —
the sun was going in, setting,
and a deep, trance-like sleep fell upon Abram
— and yikes! a terror — a great darkness — fell upon him!

(TRDMH...same kind of sleep as YAHWEH cast upon the first mud-creature, just as YAHWEH was about to create Woman from the mud-creature's rib... through wounding the mud-creature...a wounding that will be limped upon and remembered in a few generations....)

And It said to Abram,
"Know, know, know this!
Your seed/descendants will be foreigners,
immigrants...
in a land not for them —
slaves — humiliated ones
who must sing their begging-song —
for 400 years —
what'll seem like forever ten times over!
As for the nation for whom they'll slave away,
I'll act as judge — I'll sail directly with the wind — lay down justice!
And they'll come out of all that
having gathered greatly — wealth!
And you — you'll enter into your parents/ancestors
(join them in death)
safely, healthy, whole, at peace!
You'll be buried
in your good-old, gray-haired old age!"

<Gen 15.16>

And so it was —
and the sun had gone in,
and there was thick darkness and — get this! —
a fiery-pot like a furnace
and smoke and a fiery-torch
passed through between those pieces!

(This is an ancient ritual of covenant-making, contract-making, generations-lasting deal-making... where both parties walk through the blood of the severed animals and each party offers something to the other to show their trust in one another. Such deal-making only worked when both parties offer something to the other...which doesn't happen here. YAHWEH gives; Abram — our Slack-Daddy — takes and then gives nothing!

And as for this business of 'act as judge — I'll sail directly with the wind — lay down justice'/DN...knowing what we know about YAHWEH so far walking within the breeze in Eden/Pleasure and offering blasts of wind/ life, this whole biblical-business of 'justice'/DN has as its primitive root 'to sail directly' as in going with the wind, as *Strong's Exhaustive Concordance* notes. The last time DN was used was just before YAHWEH flooded the snow-globe earth. Abram's grandson Jacob will one day name his daughter Dinah, from that same Hebrew root DN.)

And on that day, YAHWEH cut a deal with Abram, the
one named Patriarch-Helps-or-Hurts, saying,
"To your seed/descendants I give this land
from Suffering-Egypt's river
to the great river, Fruitful-River...the Euphrates (all the way to your old home in Babylon)!"

<Gen 15. 19-21>

And as for Sarai, whose name means On-Top or In-Charge — Sarai, Abram's wife, hadn't given birth to any children for him.

She had a Suffering-Egyptian slave-woman,
the kind who'd given birth to children before.

Her name was The-Immigrant.

And Sarai — meaning On-Top — said to Abram —
meaning Patriarch-Helps-or-Hurts —
"Look here please,
YAHWEH's holding me back
from giving birth to children.
Please go enter into — have sex —
with my slave-woman —
let's hope I can build up something from her!"

And Abram listened to Sarai's voice —
he heard what Sarai, On-Top, was saying.

And Abram's wife Sarai took The-Immigrant,
the Suffering-Egyptian slave-woman
who'd borne children before,
at the end of ten years of Abram having lived
in the Humble-Traders'-Land,
and she gave her to her husband Abram
as a wife.

And he entered into her — had sex with her — with
The-Immigrant,
and she became pregnant.

(Earlier we had the verb YDAY/'know' as a euphemism for sex...and here we get a new verb for sex... BOAH/'enter'...perhaps a bit cruder than 'knowing'... maybe YDAY is more like 'love-making' and BOAH is more like 'screwing' to an ancient hearer? And here with Abram and a slave-woman, there's a clear power difference between the two people...a hierarchical power difference with Abram most likely thinking he's worth more than his wife's slave-woman. We'll have to watch when and how YDAY and BOAH are used throughout these Genesis stories to perhaps catch the differences between these two verbs often used for sex.)

And she saw that she was pregnant,
and she treated her mistress lightly, badly — made her only worthy of a small-insult in her own eyes and esteem.

(There's our friend QLL again, noted in the Noah story...the word that I suspect could mean something to ancient ears like 'screwing over'...and right after Abram BOAHed The-Immigrant. Here we are with potentially more of the band of YAH's bawdy style aimed at meaning, awakening ancient hearers to the power-dynamics of relationships like any good comedian does, ancient or modern. Jesus does the same with his parables and one-liner quips we call 'aphorisms' or wisdom-sayings, let's remember.)

And Sarai said to Abram,
"I'm getting treated violently and wrongly because of you!
I — I put my slave-woman in your lap
and when she saw that she was pregnant,
I got treated lightly, badly —
as if I were just a small-insult in her eyes!
YAHWEH, make a decision between me and you!"

(Note how Sarai ups the ante at first...'getting treated violently and wrongly'/CHMS is the word used in the Flood Story where YAHWEH violently upends the earth with water...a huge deal. Quite clever rhetoric on her part...which she just a few sentences later backs down to what it was...QLL/'a small insult.')

And Abram said to Sarai,
"Now look here, your slave-woman is in your hands,
under your control!
Do to her whatever is good in your eyes!"

And Sarai/On-Top humiliated and beat her up,
and (The-Immigrant) ran away from her — and fast.

And YAHWEH's ambassador found her near a water-spring in the wilderness, a spring by a road-wall.
And he said,
"Hey, The-Immigrant, On-Top's slave-woman,
where're you coming from?
And please tell me where you're going?"

And she said,
"From On-Top! My mistress!
And now I'm running away — and fast!"

And YAHWEH's ambassador said to her,
"Go back to your mistress!
Allow yourself to be humiliated
and beat up under her hand!"

And YAHWEH's ambassador said to her,
"Multiply, multiply, multiply —
that's what I'll do for your seed/descendants!
You can't count them — there'll be so many!"

(No response from The-Immigrant — an ancient would assume she's overcome with emotion, without words because of the ambassador's words.)

And YAHWEH's ambassador said to her,
"Look here — *you* are the one who is pregnant
and you'll give birth to a son,
and you're going to call out his name

'EL-Listens' . . . 'Divinity-Listens!'

because YAHWEH listened in
on your humiliation and your being beat up!
He'll yahweh — he'll be a wild beast of a mud-creature —
his hand (penis?) on everybody,
everybody's hand (penis?) on him
and up against all of his brothers he'll live!"

(Though the 'hand'/YD is more likely than 'penis'/YD here, an ancient hearer might begin to wonder... especially with what we've heard so far about YAHWEH.

And the 'yahweh' of this little saying...the name YAHWEH, you might recall, is a form of the verb 'to be.' And here we have a very similar form of that verb which ordinarily would not be used, instead inferred by the context of the sentence. But here YHYH is spelled out very clearly...all too similar in Hebrew characters and in Hebrew sound to YHUH, the actual name for YAHWEH.

To some biblical readers, YAHWEH having Its penis

on/in others might sound completely ridiculous, perhaps even sacrilegious. To more clever readers, the ridiculousness will soon make sense in future Genesis stories from the band of YAH...if indeed this story presages future stories.)

And (The-Immigrant) called out the name of
YAHWEH
who'd been styling out to her,
"You are ELOHIM/divinity seeing me!"

because she'd said,
"Why even here have I seen
the backside of It seeing me?"

<Gen 16. 14>

And The-Immigrant gave birth for Abram — a son!

And Abram called out the name of his son
to whom The-Immigrant had given birth,

'EL-Listens' . . . 'Divinity-Listens!'

<Gen 16.16 - 17.27>

<# >

(Time passes and things change, as you'll see....)

And YAHWEH made himself be seen by (the one who used to be called 'Abram')
at The-Trees-Where-You-Can-Get-Drunk-&-See-Things-&-Do-Wild-Things.

You see, he was sitting down
at the tent-opening during the heat of the day.

And he raised his eyes and saw — whoah! —
three people standing-at-attention
in front of him!
And he saw,
and he ran to call out to them
from the tent-opening,
and he bowed down toward the ground,
and he said,
"My bosses, please!
If only I could measure up in your eyes!
Please don't just pass by your slave — me!
Please!
Let a little water be fetched and wash your feet!
And rest yourselves under a tree!
Let's take (and eat) a little bit of bread
and strengthen your hearts —
then afterwards you can pass —
as much as you all can pass by your slave — me!"

And they said,
"Yes, do just as you've styled out!"

> (You see, they liked the way he said what he said, his style. That is to say, he wooed them, sweet-talked them.)

And Abraham — the one whose name used to be
Abram/Patriarch-Helps-or-Hurts and now sounds
more like Patriarch-Prospers — hurried
toward the tent, to Sarah — who sounds like she is

now even more Clearly-On-Top — and said,
"Hurry and get a whole lot
of our best ground wheat-flour
and knead it
and make those round, warm cakes!"

And to the cattle
Abraham ran and took a calf —
a tender and good one —
and gave it to the (slave)boy,
and he hurried to prepare it.

And he took the cheese-curds and milk and the calf-meat
which he'd prepared,
and he placed it right in front of them.

(Note meat and dairy at the same meal — a story told either long before the kosher laws of the priestly Torah or the band of YAH has their characters Abraham and Sarah show that they do not practice kosher, at least in offering hospitality to these foreigners...perhaps the band of YAH needling the kosher-traditions.

Abram's name changes...and Sarai's too...and certainly their actions here support that. No longer is this guy Abraham slacking around and going every which way as he was when he was younger, when he'd tear out his tent-stakes in wanderlust and lie about his wife to save his own skin. He seems more settled, sitting there in his tent during the hot time of the day, rooted enough to be able to see people and to offer these people such exquisite hospitality. In this region, hospitality is one's responsibility and pleasure in the ancient world. And that extra syllable in Abram—>Abraham's name clarifies the meaning of his name:

Abram/AHBRM in Hebrew leaves good and bad possibilities...the AB/'father, patriarch' with a penchant for 'deception, slacking, possibly exalting'... but all of it unsure...a truly ambivalent Slack-Daddy!

Abraham/AHBRHM in Hebrew only points up...the AB/'father, patriarch' who is 'high, exalted'....

and this begins to clarify the meaning of his name and takes it away from 'helps and hurts'...now he's clearly 'prosperous'!

Something must have happened in his life for him to earn such a lofty title.

And as for Sarai —> Sarah...

On-Top/SRY also has a new sound/syllable in her name — and now she's Clearly-On-Top/SRH... essentially a princess...and that new syllable only clarifies even more her name and role — quite remarkable for a woman having such a powerful name in the ancient world — especially when she's not royalty but a bordercrossing, wandering woman who fled the land of the metropolises of Babylon for the probably not as comfortable tent-life in the rolling-fields, the wide-open-countryside of Ancient Israel/Palestine.

It should be noted again too that Abram/Abraham — AHBRM/AHBRHM — both sound very similar to AYBRYM...'bordercrosser/bordercrossing.' Curious, yes?

Names change and grow...people change and grow... and not always because people take the easier path. Perhaps we all find ways of making the difficult easy, pleasurable. We'll have to discover how and if each character demonstrates this change in their lives, to discover if and how they merit such important names the rest of these characters' lives.)

And he took up his stand before them under the tree, and they ate.

And they said to him,
"Where is Sarah, Clearly-On-Top, your wife?"
And he said,
"Right there in the tent."

And one said,
"Return, return, return —
when I return to you —
in due season —
a son —
for Sarah —
your wife!
Sarah'll have a son!"

And Sarah was listening at the tent-opening, right behind him.

And Abraham and Sarah were old —
entering (deeply) into their days and years —
and the way of women had become flabby for Sarah...
things had stopped.

And Sarah burst out laughing inside herself, saying,

"After having become all worn out, <u>pleasure</u> is coming to me?!!"
and "My boss is old!"

And YAHWEH said to Abraham,
"What's this?
Why did Sarah burst out laughing
and say, 'Haha, yeah — will I really give birth?'
and 'I'm getting old!'?
Is such style too difficult and different
for YAHWEH?!?
At just the right time,
I'll return to you —in due season —
and Sarah will have a son!"
And Sarah — Clearly-On-Top — she tried to deny it, saying
"I didn't burst out laughing!"
because she was afraid.

And It said,
"No, you sure burst out laughing!"

> (In all the fun of this little episode, note the word 'pleasure'/AYDNH...calling us back to the pleasure of Eden/AYDN and what Mud-Creature and Woman were enjoying there in the orchard, in so many ways... and the pleasure that elder-characters Abraham and Sarah will enjoy to create their first child, with YAHWEH's help.)

And they stood up tall from there — the people did,
(YAHWEH and the ambassadors did) —
and they leaned out and looked down upon the edge of Their-Bondage,

and Abraham went with them to send them off.

And YAHWEH said (to Itself),
"Should I cover-over-with-my-well-fed-flesh (conceal)
from Abraham what I'm about to do?
With Abraham about to become
a nation so great and strong-as-bone?
And everyone about to be brought
to their knees into abundance —
all through him —
all the nations of the solid-ground....
Because I know him in every way...
so much so that he shouts out orders
at his children and his house/family after him
that they keep YAHWEH's way
of doing the honest and reliable thing
all so that YAHWEH enters into Abraham
— brings about —
what was styled out for him...."

And YAHWEH said,
"The outcry of the cities Their-Bondage and Bind-Abundant-Harvest —
yes, it's growing —
and their corruption —
yes, it's very, very heavy — serious —
so, if you please,
I'm going down there and I'm going to see
what their outcry that's come to me is all about —
does it make for an end — annihilation —
and if not, then I know."

And they turned away from there — the people (the ambassadors traveling with YAHWEH) —
and they went toward Their-Bondage.

And Abraham took his stand there again before YAHWEH's face.

And Abraham got closer and said,
"How could it be — would you sweep away
the honest and reliable with the guilty?!
What if there're 50 honest, reliable people in the middle of the city?
How could it be — would you really sweep away —
and not lift up — the place
for the sake of the 50 honest and reliable who are inside it?
How dare you act in such a style as this —
to kill the honest and reliable with the guilty?!
That the honest and reliable would be just like the guilty...?!
How dare you — the judge over the whole land! —
not make a fair and just judgement!"

And YAHWEH said,
"If I find in Their-Bondage 50 honest and reliable people within the city,
I'll lift up — spare — the whole place for their sake."

And Abraham responded and said,
"Look, may I please make another try at styling out to my boss —
— I'm dust and dirt —
what if the 50 honest and reliable ones
are just 5 fewer?
Would you wipe out — for 5!? — the whole city?!"

And It said,
"No, I won't wipe it out if I find 45 there."
And he continued on

still styling on for him and said,
"What if 40 are found there?"

And It said,
"I won't do it for the sake of the 40."

And he said,
"Please don't let this get my boss all hot and angry
but let me style on...what if 30 are found there?"

And It said,
"I won't do it if I find 30 there."
And he said,
"Look, may I please make another try at styling out to my boss —
what if 20 happen to be found there?"

And It said,
"I won't wipe them out for the sake of the 20."

And he said,
"Please don't let this get my boss all hot and angry
but let me style out just this one time —
what if 10 happen to be found there?"

And It said,
"I won't wipe them out for the sake of the 10."

And YAHWEH left just at the end —
of the styling-out with Abraham —
the guy now known as Patriarch-Prospers —
and Abraham returned to his place.

And two of the ambassadors entered into Their-Bondage in the evening, and Cover-Up was sitting by Their-Bondage's city-gate and he, Cover-Up, saw them and stood up tall to call out, to announce them.

> (This was a role of some honor and necessity and safety, often done by older men in ancient cities who might have a better chance through all their years of knowing friend from foe, in determining who is friendly/safe enough to be allowed into the city through the city-gate.)

And they bowed down, their faces to the ground.

And he said,
"Listen up, please, my bosses,
please turn in here to your slaves' house — ours!
Spend the night!
Bathe your feet!
Rise early in the morning and go on your way!"

> (Cover-Up, like his Uncle Abraham and Aunt Sarah, is offering so far the best hospitality he can to these unknown guests.)

And they said,
"No! You see — the town square — we'll spend the night there."

And <u>he pecked at them, urged them — very strongly</u> —
and they turned on in
and entered into his house.

And he made for them a feast with wine
and he baked little unleavened cakes
(so they would be ready quickly),
and they ate.

Just before they were about to lie down to sleep,
the city's people — Their-Bondage's people —
surrounded the house —
from young people to old people —
all the people — the whole group of them —
from every edge of town.

And they called out to Cover-Up, and said to him,
"Where are the people,
the ones who entered — those who came to you tonight?
Make them come out here to us
so we can get to know them!"

> (Here's all that 'entering'/BOAH again...now being contrasted with 'knowing, often via sex'/YDAY... though I suspect they are mocking Cover-Up for his covered-up ways through their choice of verbs here: they ask to YDAY when what they really want is to BOAH the visitors to their town, the fresh meat for their nightly orgy in the town square. And as for the gender of the townspeople wanting to 'know' the visitors, know that if the crowd were 99 women and 1 man, 'townspeople' and the pronoun used for the crowd/people would be masculine-gender in Ancient Hebrew. That is to say, we really don't know the gender of all of the townspeople who are wanting to know the visitors. But we do know the townspeople were of all ages, a rather strange detail to add about this messed up/confused town.)

And Cover-Up went to them
through the opening,
and he shut the door after himself,
and he said,
"Please no, my brothers, don't do this bad thing!
Please listen here, I have two daughters
who haven't known men —
I'll make them go out to you all —
do to them whatever is good in your eyes —
only to these people (the visitors),
don't do a thing — no style!
I mean, they've entered — come under the shade —
the protection —
the roof-beams of my house!"

And they said,
"Come closer!"

And they said (to one another),
"He entered — came to stay here as an immigrant
and now he judges, judges, judges —
now we'll do worse to you than them!"

And they pecked at Cover-Up, urged him — very strongly —
and they got closer to break down the door.

And the people reached out their hands (or penises?)
and entered Cover-Up into the house — err, the
people reached out their hands and brought Cover-Up
toward them into the house —
and shut the door.

(We actually don't know which way the story goes

until late in that sentence — "to them." All this BOAH-ing (enter as in 'enter a room' or 'enter as in sex'?) and YD as we know is the Hebrew word for hand, and a euphemism for penis. And 'the people' has been repeatedly used to describe both the visitors and the city-people. Very clever storytelling in the midst of the chaos of an angry mob making the first moves to attack Cover-Up as Cover-Up is scooped into the house by the visitors!)

And as for the people who were at the opening of the house —
they struck them with blindness —
from the youngest to the oldest!

And they got tired of trying to find the opening and gave up.

(Umm...which opening? Pun-rich!)

And the people (the visitors) said to Cover-Up,
"Is there anyone else here who is yours?
A daughter's husband?
And your sons and your daughters?
All who are yours in the city — make them leave the place —
because we're going to wipe out this place —
because their crying out is so great before YAHWEH's face —
YAHWEH sent us here to wipe out this place!"

And Cover-Up went out and styled it out to his daughters' husbands,

the ones who had taken his daughters (as wives),
and said,
“Stand up tall —
get out of this place —
because YAHWEH’s wiping out the city!”

But it was laughs and giggles in the eyes of his
daughters’ husbands.

And just then the dawn’s red light was climbing up,
and the ambassadors pressed Cover-Up, saying,
“Stand up tall —
fetch your wife and your two daughters who happen
to be here —
so that you’re not swept away
in the city’s crooked ways!”

But he hesitated —
the people grabbed his hand and his wife’s hand
and his two daughters’ hands —
in YAHWEH’s compassion for them —
and they made them leave and left them safely
outside the city.

And so it was —

just after they had gotten them outside, they said,
“Escape for your living, breathing life —
don’t look back behind you —
don’t stand still in the whole broad river-valley —
to the mountains — escape —
or else you’ll be swept away!”

And Cover-Up said to them,
“Please no — my bosses — listen —

please let your slave measure up in your eyes —
your loyal-love — you've done —
it's grown for me —
to make me live — my living, breathing self —
I — I can't escape to the mountains —
or else something bad'll catch me and cling to me —
I'll die — listen — please — that city nearby —
to flee to —
it's a little thing —
I'll escape — please — there —
isn't it a little thing?
and my living, breathing self will live!?"

And one said to him,
"Look here, I'll lift you up —
even for this styling-out —
I won't overthrow the city
about which you styled-out —
hurry! escape there!
I can't make style until you've entered there — arrived!"

And that's why the city is named "Little-Place."

And the sun came up over the land,
and Cover-Up entered Little-Place.

And YAHWEH rained down
fire and sulfurous tree-resin
upon Their-Bondage and Bind-Abundant-Harvest —
from YAHWEH! — from the solid-sky!

And It overthrew these cities
and the whole broad river-valley
and everyone living in the cities
and whatever was springing up from on the mud.

And his wife — (Cover-Up's wife) —
looked back behind him —
and she became a statue — powdery sea-salt!

And Abraham rose early in the morning
to go to the place where he'd taken his stand there
before YAHWEH's face.

And he looked out over the edge
at the faces
of Their-Bondage and Bind-Abundant-Harvest
and at the whole face
of the broad river-valley's land,
and he saw — oh my! —
climbing up — smoke — from the land —
like smoke from a metal-smelting furnace!

<*Gen 19.29*>

And Cover-Up climbed up from Little-Place and lived
in the mountains
and his two daughters with him —
you see, he was afraid to live in Little-Place.

And he lived in a cave —
he and his two daughters.

And the first-born daughter said to the littler one,
"Our father's getting old,
and there's not a single man in the land
to enter into us — have sex with us —
as is the way of the whole land, the whole earth.
Come on — let's drink wine with our father
and lie down with him for sleep/sex
and then we'll really be alive — seed...a descendant!"

And they drank wine with their father that evening,
and the first-born daughter entered in and lay down
(for sex) with her father —

but he didn't know — in any way, including sexually —
when she was lying down
or when she stood up tall (got up)!

> (Incredibly punny passage...all of these Hebrew verbs are usually what a man would do to a woman...but here the woman does to a man...and not just any woman and any man: a daughter with her father! It must be mentioned too the play on Zoar/TSOAYR... the city known as "Little-Place" and the word used here for 'younger'/TSAYYRH which comes from the same 'root'/word in Hebrew.)

And so it was —

the following day,
the first-born daughter said to the littler one,
"Look, last night I lay down for sleep/sex
with my father —
we'll drink wine also tonight —
enter in!
lie down to sleep/have sex with him!
and then we'll really be alive — seed...a descendant!"

And that night, they again made him drink wine —
their father! —
and the littler one stood up tall,
and she lay down (for sex) with him,
but he didn't know — in any way, including sexually —

when she was lying down
or when she stood up tall (got up)!

And Cover-Up's two daughters became pregnant by their father!

And the first-born daughter gave birth to a son,
and she called out his name,
"From-My-Father!"

He was the father of the the nation From-My-Fathers up to this day.

And the littler one too, she gave birth to a son
and she called out his name,
"Inbred! Son-of-My-Kin!"

He was the father of the Inbred-nation — Children-of-My-Kin — up to this day.

<*Gen 20. 1-18*>

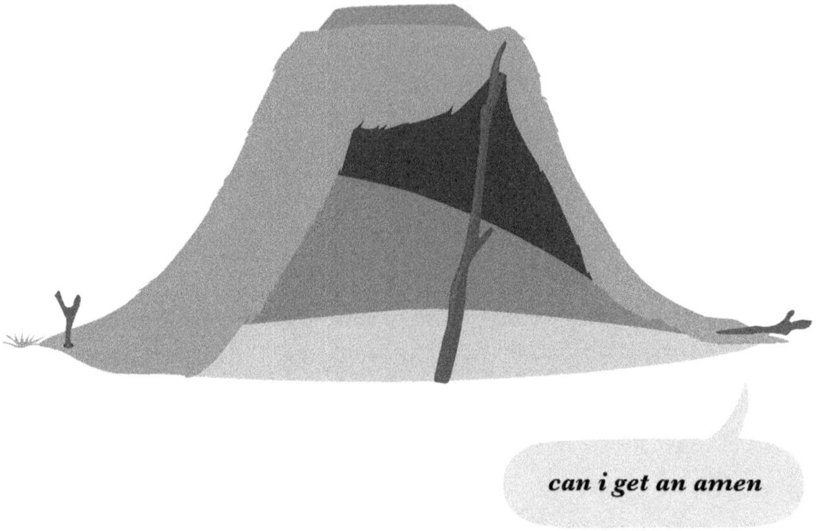

fyi: ‘amen’ means ‘I drive in my tent stake’

commentary

The Band of YAH's Flexible Imagination, Rich Characters & Nuanced Plots

If the crafters of these particular stories from biblical Genesis are indeed women, it's not like these women present women as always being the finest of creatures and only making brilliant decisions. (She does similarly with YAHWEH, right?)

Sure, Woman gives birth to wisdom by taking Snake's slithering advice and eating from the Knowing-Tree...

but two young women also get their father drunk and have sex with him so that they can fulfill their ancient-world destiny of bearing children!

You gotta love the way the storycrafters I call the band of YAH tell the story of Cover-Up's / Lot's daughters. It's a very different style — far different than the style of *Enuma Elish* and *The Epic of Gilgamesh*, which have their own clevernesses too, for sure.

The band of YAH's storycrafting style is sweet-talking, pun-spinning fun. They use the verbs YDAH/'know' and BOAH/'enter into' — the usual euphemisms for sex in the Hebrew idiom or style — and have the daughters do that to their father. Every other time that I know of in biblical storytelling it's a man doing those things to a woman. Talk about genderbending and role-reversing!

In these Genesis stories, the daughters get the upper hand...pun intended?!

(Recall that YD means both 'hand' and 'penis' in Hebrew. Every time YD is used in a biblical story, we'll need to listen carefully about which meaning is intended — if not the punny possibility of both.)

And as for women-characters, what about Sarai / Sarah? Her name is quite funny — after all, her name is the same Hebrew word (SR) used for Pharaoh's officials... people near 'the top' of the hierarchical-game of Egyptian governance with Pharaoh clearly on top of them. And the one who is clearly on top (Pharaoh) has Sarai — On-Top and later Clearly-On-Top — brought to him that he might delight in her beauty. But Abram and Sarai get the upper hand over Pharaoh through their lie about their being siblings to save Abram's life/ ass. It is quite ironic — or is it? — that the Hebrew word for Pharaoh sounds just like the word for 'negligence.' And here Pharaoh is clearly negligent in getting the full story on whether Sarai is available for his harem-of-royal-wives or not.

Sarai / Sarah often acts the part of one who is on-top when she becomes jealous of The-Immigrant / Hagar and her birthing abilities. What does Sarai do? She beats The-Immigrant, humiliates her, runs her out of town...only after Abram reminds Sarai that The-

Immigrant is in her grasp, in her hand, in her phallic-control, under her control. Sarai / Sarah is Clearly-On-Top of The-Immigrant here.

But who's the one who shows tremendous courage and faith in these stories so far? It's not the Hebrew-matriarch Sarai / Sarah but The-Immigrant / Hagar. This is another style of the band of YAH, a style we can find among many biblical writers including X, writer of 1 & 2 Samuel and perhaps portions of 1 & 2 Kings. The prophets play on that idea too, often revealing that the enemy-nations have more faith and trust in YAHWEH than the Israelites/Hebrews.

the band of YAH's bordercrossing style

Notice the complexity and richness of the band of YAH's characters — especially the women-characters — in these stories that could be 2500+ years old. This would have been unheard of in the ancient world — even Sarah's laughing at YAHWEH's suggestion about her bearing a child in her old age. And it only gets better!

Not only is the band of YAH crafting stories that stand in contrast with the stories they probably heard a lot growing up — the old Babylonian legends and surely others — they are also providing rich contrasts within and between their stories.

YAHWEH floods the whole world when It doesn't like what the mud-creatures / human beings are doing. Juxtapose that with YAHWEH deciding to kill off only a couple of towns with Their-Bondage / Sodom and Bind-Abundant-Harvest / Gomorrah. I guess we'd call that improvement regarding YAHWEH's vindictiveness, with only two towns destroyed instead of the whole world. And not only that, YAHWEH allows Itself to be swayed by Abraham's style, his argument about not sweeping away the innocent with the guilty. Such style is not just plain old speech — it might be better translated as sweet-talking, clever speech, speech that wakes you up to life, often with puns. This is the style that Ancient Hebrew is known for, this bordercrossing style that messes with your imagination often through humor.

Lay in the middle of these two scenes — YAHWEH flooding the whole earth and YAHWEH destroying only two towns — YAHWEH counseling Cain about his jealousy of his brother. And lay that alongside the scene of YAHWEH being counseled by Abraham. The band of YAH reveals YAHWEH to be a very curious character and force through all of these subtle juxtapositions, when all of these stories are placed side by side.

And note the all-important juxtaposing of Abraham's significant hospitality — lavish food and shelter from the hot sun — with Cover-Up's / Lot's initial hospitality in welcoming YAHWEH's ambassadors and encouraging them not to sleep in the town square but in the safety of his home. After all, Lot knows full well what happens in the town square at night...every townsperson from oldest to youngest shows up for the orgy. It should come as no surprise that the orgy-crowd wants some new orifices and penises and demands that Cover-Up — who maybe never participated in the nightly orgy but stayed covered-up and simply enjoyed the show? — release the newcomers into the party. Fresh meat! But here is where Cover-Up's / Lot's hospitality fails... he offers his virgin daughters to the townspeople instead of his guests. He makes generous hospitality for the guests — who just happen to be YAHWEH's ambassadors — but in offering his daughters to the orgy he reveals he's not like Abraham and Sarah in their care for others and supreme hospitality.

There's more clever juxtaposition to pay attention to here than even the wisest scripture scholars usually note...

> Abraham and Sarah offer better hospitality than Lot — and Abraham and Sarah do this with a tent under a tree;
>
> Lot has roofbeams, a solid house in an established town that has more cares than just getting food grown and prepared to keep on living...the people of this town have enough free-time and energy to have nightly orgies in the town square. And Lot builds his house apparently in a place where he and his daughters can at least watch!

And not only this...

> Abraham has a rebellious wife who talks back to YAHWEH;
>
> Lot has a wife who looks back after YAHWEH's ambassadors tell her and her family not to.
> Abraham's wife lives;
>
> Lot's wife dies — even worse she doesn't even exist as she blows away in the wind and cannot have the anciently imagined afterlife of a nice place on the

everlasting napping-bench that is Sheol...the place where people who have lived a good life and a good burial (because people care enough about them to bury them) go to live after death.

Juxtapose these two wives and we might discern some important meaning and a hallmark of the prophets...do what YAHWEH says or die (as we discover through Lot's wife) <u>and</u> feel free to talk back to YAHWEH especially if you disagree and can make a better argument than YAHWEH's often irrational logic (as we discover not only through Sarah's laughing at YAHWEH's promises and still living and thriving in old age and through Abraham's arguing with YAHWEH about the fate of Sodom and Gomorrah and the unfairness of wiping them off the planet if decent people lived there — even just 10 people.)

It's worth noting too that Cover-Up keeps seeking the cover and safety of a town — even after his previous home near the orgy is being bombed by YAHWEH. Cover-Up asks to be able to go to Zoar/Little-Place, instead of living in the open-country like his Uncle Abraham and Aunt Sarah. Abraham and Sarah live their lives as wandering bordercrossers, as nomads, never having a place with roof-beams. But Cover-Up begs for the safety of a city — even a small city — and pays for it with his wife's life and then drunken-sex with his daughters who essentially rape him for his seed, his ability to confer descendants upon them and fulfill their ancient role as women-baby-makers...a pinch that even Sarah feels and tries to resolve through The-Immigrant / Hagar.

Sodom(y)...how foolish to not make the connection with Eden's rib (and soon Jacob's)

Sodom and Gomorrah have for centuries been seen and used to justify the punishment-by-death of homosexuality, as Leviticus 18 & Leviticus 20 implore. But that is a misguided interpretation of the Sodom and Gomorrah story. Very much so. Sure, some biblical scholars make a wise note about the contrast between Abraham's supreme hospitality and Lot's wanting hospitality (especially at home, with his own family... the daughters he foolishly offers to the orgy to protect his guests). But everyone seems to miss the clever and significant detail about who is in the towns square — young and old. All comers. (Pun?)

Sure, it appears to be men demanding that the visiting men come out to the orgy — though the townspeople making these demands could include one man and a bunch of women...after all, plural-masculine includes women in Ancient Hebrew. (Same goes for the visitors/ YAHWEH's ambassadors too — we do not know everyone's gender based on the Hebrew version of 'they.')

Sure, the townspeople are not satisfied with Lot offering his daughters and denigrate him as an immigrant who seems to be quite bossy with them, certainly in the scene but maybe always.

But let's not forget who was there every night in the town square — everyone, even the young. Or at least everyone except Lot's family. He was all Covered-Up, after all. But he must have liked to have watched. And his daughters, despite having been chaste and having their virginity covered up from the touch of men or of anybody it seems, they seem to know what to do to get pregnant. They eventually rape their father to get what they want — children and status as successful baby-makers in the ancient world. Too bad they didn't absorb the lesson about where the seed of descendants must come from to be honorable — you see, the town's orgy didn't teach their hungry eyes that lesson.

And the townspeople want to know the guests. This is the 'biblical knowing' that Lot's daughters eventually do to their father. It makes me wonder a little bit more about the Eden / Pleasure story...with the Knowing-Tree. Is this what the ancient biblical storyteller the band of YAH was after? Is that tree more about knowing in the wisdom-sense or in the sexual-sense of the ancient Hebrew word YDAY/'to know'? Or maybe both? Is that the game here?

Because as soon as Mud-Creature and Woman eat from the Knowing-Tree they discover they are naked — even though they had been that way the whole time before that, it seems. And they make themselves things to cover themselves. But not long after that they seem to be covering themselves in one another, with one another — embracing, love-making, knowing — as YAHWEH was walking in the breeze through the Pleasure-Orchard.

Yes, the story is much more interesting when we know what 'Eden' means in Hebrew, right? Pleasure...what comes to Sarah to eventually give birth to a son, even in her old age.

Why do these naked Eden creatures cover themselves

from each other and then uncover themselves in and around each other and then, after getting yelled at by YAHWEH, cover themselves again?

It's a bit like the three-year-old that runs around naked with no care in the world about their nakedness. But then a few years later when someone gives them a droopy at the pool and their nakedness is revealed, it's the end of the world for that droopied-kid that people saw them naked. Just years before that — even days before that — the kid happily and freely pranced around naked. But now the slightly older kid has somehow and from someone (school? parents/adults? socialization?) learned that nakedness is somehow wrong, inappropriate at times, even shameful in 'polite' society, in city-life.

After Mud-Creature and Woman eat from the Knowing-Tree, they know, they lose their innocence, much like a socialized child who learns to fear nakedness and much like a hormone-fueled teenager who must hide their burgeoning sexuality and desire, at least from adults/authorities...

...that is until they grow older and find someone with whom to do just as Woman and Mud-Creature had done...remove their clothes, fall into each other, hide themselves in and around one another, their love-making a cocoon of safety and yet no longer fearful of the world around them...no longer needing to hide anything from their partner and even from anyone else...their love-making...freedom-inducing from within...a knowing the pulse not only of their partner but the whole earth...the whole universe...an ecstatic burst of being rushed upon...of being ravished by and with one's partner and much more...THE ALL...all of It right there.

What was it Snake told Woman / Eve after Woman said they'd die if they ate from the Knowing-Tree?

> *"Not die?!*
> *You will not die!*
> *See, the-gods-and-goddesses know*
> *that on the day you all eat from it,*
> *your eyes will be opened*
> *and you all'll be like the-gods-and-goddesses*
> *in knowing good and bad!"*

To be like gods and goddesses in knowing....

Perhaps it's only through <u>knowing</u> that creation happens, that creativity happens, a working with and participating with THE ALL.

All of the sudden, in an orchard full of trees, that Knowing-Tree that Woman and Mud-Creature had been running around and innocently playing around for days, weeks, years (?) suddenly looked desirable, lusty — it stirred up in Woman desire for insight, for understanding things. And she ate — and she knew. And Mud-Creature ate — and he knew.

And shortly after, they knew each other by eye and then by touch, by taste and smell, by pulse.

Are your eyes opening?

ha ha ha!
look at this guy
what a
joke
HAAA!

Genesis 21 - 25

Laughingstock

the stories of Isaac & Rebekah

<begin at Gen 21.1>

And YAHWEH took care of Sarah — whose name means Clearly-On-Top — just as It said It would —

YAHWEH did for Sarah just as It'd styled out.

And she became pregnant,
and Sarah gave birth to a son
for Abraham
in his old age.

<Gen 21.2c>

And Abraham — whose name means Patriarch-Prospers — called out the name of his son,
the one born to him,
the one for whom Sarah gave birth for him,

"Laughingstock! Isaac!"

(The name 'Isaac'/YTSCHQ indeed means 'Laughingstock' and recalls two earlier stories:

of Sarah laughing inside the tent upon hearing YAHWEH tell her husband Abraham that she would give birth to a son in their old age

and of Cover-Up telling his daughters' husbands to flee Their-Bondage...Cover-Up's warning 'was all laughs and giggles to them.'

In both of these earlier stories, YTSCHQ is a kind of laughter that is more of mocking, derision...not necessarily laughing with joy.)

<Gen 21. 4-34>

And so it was —
(long) after these stylings-on
that the-gods-and-goddesses/ELOHIM tested-by-adventure Abraham, the one whose name means Patriarch-Prospers.

And one said to him, "Abraham!"

And he said, "Yes! That's me!"

And one said,
"Please take your son —
your only one — whom you love —
Isaac...Laughingstock —
and go, go, go
to the land of YAHWEH's-Gonna-See —
and climb him up there to kill as a burnt-offering —
on one of the mountains one tells you!"
And Abraham arose early in the morning
and saddled his donkey
and fetched two of his (slave)boys with him
and Isaac, his son.

And he split some wood for the burnt-offering,
and stood up tall to head out toward the place
which one was telling him — the-gods-and-goddesses/ELOHIM, that is.

On the third day,
Abraham raised his eyes
and saw the place in the distance.

And Abraham said to his (slave)boys,
"Stay by yourselves here with the donkey —
I and the boy — we'll go by over there —
and pay our respects by bowing down in worship —
then we'll return to you."

(An ancient hearer would already know something strange is about to happen — worship in the ancient world involved killing an animal and burning it up to one's gods/goddesses. Abraham tells the slave-boys to stay with the donkey, apparently the only animal they have with them.

Note too the clarifications about this 'one' who speaks to Abraham — not necessarily YAHWEH but representatives of the ELOHIM/'the-gods-and-goddesses'...voices of ages past, perhaps....)

And Abraham took the wood for the burnt-offering
and put it on Isaac, his son,
and he took in his own hand the fire and the butcher-knife.

And the two of them walked off together.

And Isaac — Laughingstock — said to Abraham, his father,
he said, "My father!"

And he said,
"Right here, my son!"

And he said,
"Hey — (here's) the fire and the wood —
but where is the baby lamb for the burnt-offering?"

And Abraham said,
"The-gods-and-goddesses/ELOHIM will see to it —
the lamb for the burnt-offering —
my son!"

And the two of them walked off together.

And they entered the place
one had told him — the-gods-and-goddesses —
and Abraham built there a slaughtering-altar
and stacked the wood
and tied up Isaac — Laughingstock — his son —
and put him on the slaughtering-altar
on top of the wood —

and Abraham stretched out his hand —

and took the butcher-knife to slaughter his son —
and YAHWEH's ambassador called out to him from the solid-sky and said,
"Abraham! Abraham!!"

And he said,
"Right here!"

And (the ambassador) said,
"Do not stretch out your hand on the boy!
Don't do anything to him at all!
You see, now I know that the-gods-and-goddesses/
ELOHIM fear/see you —
you weren't going to keep your son — your only one
— from me!"

(You see, many of the gods/goddesses of the region in the ancient world demanded human-child-sacrifice. As regards the underlined pun above...an alternate reading could be "now I know that you are/have fear of the-gods-and-goddesses" or as most Bibles translate the awkward phrase "you are God-fearing"...but even that translation is troubled in that it assumes much about 'the-gods-and-goddesses'/ELOHIM being 'God' when instead ELOHIM sometimes means 'the-gods-and-goddesses,' as we might see here and will see clearly in some of the Jacob-stories.

The Levitical priests, let's recall, use ELOHIM as their name for YAHWEH, as in 'God of all gods and goddesses,' an inclusive way of talking about divinity. ELOHIM is masculine-plural for 'EL,' the regional name for godhead. ELOHIM, by the way, as a masculine-plural could again include male and female realities. Masculine-plurals in ancient languages simply designate that at least one of the plural-many is masculine.

And YRAH — usually in this instance translated as 'fear' — could even be 'see' depending on a lot of factors. More will be said about all of this later...just know that the line probably calls forth many things in the ears of an ancient hearer of the tale...like the prophets'/ecstatics' poems, the story explodes in so many directions...double/triple entendre.)

And Abraham raised his eyes and saw —
what do you know — a ram! —
behind him —
caught up in the underbrush —
by its horns!

And Abraham went
and fetched the ram
and climbed it up (onto the slaughtering-altar)
for the burnt-offering underneath — err, instead of —
his son.

(The word 'saw' underlined above is YRAH. The word 'fear' a little bit above it is YRAH. The consonants of both of these words are the same, and we must remember that the 'original' Hebrew stories were not pointed with vowels until the Masorete-scholars came along and slanted meanings in ways that dimmed down the possibilities of meaning. How did they do this? By adding vowels!

You see, adding vowels takes away some of the hazy meanings to Ancient Hebrew when the language is written down and then read aloud. Vowels also take away from some of the fun of wondering what the original stories were saying, as we see here and as we'll soon see — fun that the bands of YAH and X and the prophets all play upon. They all want us to wonder. Such wondering is what awakens something within us, within the hearers, to what is...YAHWEH... an ecstatic glimpse of THE ALL. Puns explode in many directions — they do anything but pigeonhole us into a singular meaning.

Adding vowels to Ancient Hebrew removes much of the double- and triple-entendre that comes...arrives... enters in (as in BOAH, mentioned earlier) when the story is told out loud, in an oral culture. And we must remember that many of the biblical texts were first composed orally — without writing them down first. Ever compose a speech in this way, without any notes? It's a much different brain-experience, a much different imagination is needed.

When reading the Ancient Hebrew texts of the Bible, I try to listen with an ear to the vowels that were placed there by the Masoretes and with an ear curious about other directions those original, pre-Masoretic consonants-without-vowels might go.

When did the Masoretes do their work? Between the 6th - 10th centuries CE...much later than these stories were first told and then later written down. Modern biblical scholars think the band of YAH told their stories anywhere from 900 - 300 BCE. That's perhaps 1000+ years between when the band of YAH told their stories and when the Masoretes began their work of pointing/adding vowels to the Torah-text they received!!!

It all makes me wonder if ancient hearers of these biblical texts caught even more of the subtleties than I'm trying to bring forward in *The Naked Path of Prophet* series. Most certainly, the oral telling of these tales immediately brought forward these subtleties and more readily allowed these texts to explode in every hearer's imagination, a true hallmark of the prophetic/ecstatic imagination.

In this Laughingstock story, the verbs for 'seeing' and 'fearing' probably sounded just a little bit differently from each other and usually can be differentiated with context...though how rarely would you confuse 'seeing' and 'fearing' in a story except in a story as cleverly imagined by the band of YAH as this one. I suspect there's a lot of play going on here in this story with 'seeing' and 'fearing'...and not only that... the word AHL/EL/God as in ELOHIM/the-gods-and-goddesses is very similar sounding to the word AHYL/ram. Again, more pun-play in this wild story.)

<Gen 22.14 - 23.20>
<#>

And Abraham was old and entering into his days,
and YAHWEH had brought Patriarch-Prospers to his knees into abundance,
in every way.

And Abraham — the one whose name means Patriarch-Prospers — said to his slave, the oldest one in his house
who was master and had charge over everything that was given to him,
"Please put your hand (penis?) here
under my fleshy thigh and genitals,
and I'll make you swear by YAHWEH —
who is the God-or-gods-and-goddesses/ELOHIM

of the solid-sky
and the God-or-gods-and-goddesses/ELOHIM
of the solid-land —
that you'll never fetch a wife for my son
from the Humble-Traders' daughters,
among whom I'm living nearby.
Instead, to my homeland
and to my ancestral-family — go!
Fetch a wife for my son, for Isaac...Laughingstock!"

(Note well...Abraham makes a clear connection now between YAHWEH and ELOHIM, perhaps informed by his experience of nearly slaughtering Laughingstock/Isaac...no laughing matter! That is to say, Abraham discerns that it is YAHWEH who is the-god-and-goddesses of the earth and of the sky/heavens...YAHWEH is over/on-top of the gods and goddesses of the land...this YAHWEH that is the breeze...that shows up just at the right time...no matter where you are...no matter which voices/powers try to tell you to do crazy things like kill a son...YAHWEH shows up and talks sense into you...YAHWEH allows humans like you and me to talk sense into Itself too... YAHWEH welcomes life and even breathes life into humans like you and me...except those Flood and Sodom/Gomorrah instances....

And here's another rather strange use for MSHL that was heard earlier when YAHWEH tells Woman that her husband will be her master and shortly after that when YAHWEH tells Cain that he needs to master his feelings. Here we have a slave as master over everything in Abraham's house — a slave! MSHL will appear in the Joseph-saga too...perhaps every

MSHL in the band of YAH's stories is an unusual usage in that it's usually used to describe rulers/ kings, especially in the Deuteronomistic writings of Joshua and Judges and in the later Wisdom literature. Prophets Isaiah and Jeremiah tease MSHL in their poems. And here, a slave is MSHL/'master'!

And the Hebrew word YD can mean 'hand' or 'penis,' let's recall. (!)

And note the use of 'ancestral-family'/MOLDT referring to back in Ancient Babylon where slaves do not have the pedigree to be included in 'family'... different from MSPCHH/'extended-family-including-the-maidslaves' as we saw juxtaposed when YAHWEH was first inviting Abram to leave Babylon and go to Canaan.)

And the slave said to him,
"What if the woman isn't willing
to come following after me to this land?
Should I return, return, return your son
to the land from which you left?"

And Abraham said to him,
"Careful now — you!
So that you don't return my son there!
YAHWEH, who is indeed God-or-gods-and-
goddesses/ELOHIM of the solid-sky —
who fetched me from my father's house
and from the land of my ancestral-family —
who styled it out to me —
who swore to me saying
'To your seed/descendants I give this land!' —

It'll send Its ambassador before you
and you'll fetch a woman for my son from there.
If the woman isn't willing to go following after you,
you'll be clean and unpunished from having sworn
this to me —
except that my son —
you aren't to return him there!"

And the slave put his hand (penis?) under his boss
Abraham's fleshy thigh and genitals
and he swore to it in this style.

(This 'style' of swearing by placing one's hand — penis?! — under the flesh of the patriarch's thigh and genitals will seem quite queer to our 21st century ears...though this might be the usual and expected 'style' of the ancient Mediterranean world. And it's quite the clever style too...'promise me you'll find a wife for my son so that the generations who come after me are guaranteed and make your promise by touching what was involved in making your generation...my genitalia.' And in the ancient imagination, those generations — as we could see in Abram's earlier panic — must come through one's body, not by adoption, and not by sex with a slave-woman.

And, perhaps most radically, note the slave does what a son does — puts his hand on the father/patriarch's family jewels — genitals — to swear a solemn and serious promise on the very power of a family's future.)

And the slave took ten camels
from his boss's camels,
and he left
and with all that was good and valuable — his master's
property — <u>in his own hand...(penis?)...under his control</u>.

(Continuing on the earlier YD-pun here — 'hand'/'penis'/'potency or control' — the slave at the very least reached out his hand onto his boss' fleshy-ass/crotch to swear an oath to his boss and then took control of the situation in seeking a wife for his boss' son.)

And he stood up tall and went
to The-Highland-Palaces-by-the-Two-Rivers —
to Snort's city (Abraham's ancestral-family's city).

(Note that the two rivers referred to here are the Tigris and Euphrates, Mesopotamia, Babylon, one of the so-called cradles of civilization...Abraham's homeland to which Abraham sends his slave but never wants his child to go back to that exceedingly fertile area, metropolises thriving between the rivers, the city/region from which Abraham had first come. Consider that a moment, this desire of a wandering bordercrosser....)

And he made the camels kneel outside the city
by the water-well at evening-time,
at the time when women come out
to draw up water from the well.

And he said,
"YAHWEH! God-or-gods-and-goddesses/ELOHIM of my boss Abraham!
Please happen upon my face today!
Bring about your loyal-love
for my boss, Abraham!
So here it is — if I'm stationed by the water-spring,
and daughters of the city's people are coming out to draw up water
and there's a girl to whom to say,
'Please bend down your big water-jug
so I can have a drink!'
and she says, 'Drink!
And your camels too — I'll give them a drink!'
She'll be the one! The one you've chosen to be right for your slave —
for Isaac...Laughingstock!
And through her, I'll know
that you've brought about loyal-love for my boss!"

And so it was —
before he'd finished styling it out — wow! —
Rebekah came out!

(Rebekah's name calls to mind well-fed, stall-raised animals to any ancient hearer...something prized in the ancient world. RBQ is perhaps the verbal-root of the participle/noun MRBQ 'cattle-stall.' If Rebekah's name indicates anything about her size, this would have been like winning the lottery for Abraham's slave...larger, rounder women were considered healthier and having more longevity than skinnier women because larger women had a better chance of surviving the rigors of childbirth...no small thing in

> ancient cultures and even some cultures today. Note how the slave sets up a test of this potential-wife for his boss' son — a test of hospitality to a foreigner.)

Rebekah was born for EL's-Virgin...
Queen's son,
Snort's wife,
Abraham's brother.

And a big water-jug was on her shoulder.

And the girl had a good look to her — very much so.

And she was a virgin — a man hadn't yet known her (sexually).

> ('EL's-Virgin'/BTUAHL and 'virgin'/BTULH...not the punniest but noteworthy and perhaps from the same root. Perhaps Rebekah is making it very clear that she is from a good family — and a virgin and thus worthy and available for marriage — by announcing her family tree.)

And she went down toward the spring
and filled her big water-jug
and climbed it back up.

And the slave ran to call out after her, and said,
"Please let me sip a little water
from your big water-jug!"

And she said,
"Drink, my boss!"

and she hurried to lower down her big water-jug into
her hand (under her phallic-like-control?)
and gave him a drink
and having finished giving him a drink, she said,
"And for your camels too!
I'll draw up water until they've finished drinking!"

And she hurried
and emptied out her big water-jug into the trough
until it was <u>naked and bare</u>
and ran again to the well to draw up more water
and drew up water for every one of his camels.

And the man was stunned to silence just watching her to know whether YAHWEH was <u>rushing out and busting onto</u> his path or not.

> (Note this 'rushing out'/TSLCH is the same kind of rushing of the spirit/wind — same word in the ancient world, let's remember — upon the prophets/ecstatics in the 1 & 2 Samuel saga. And note the 'naked and bare'/AYRH reference so close to 'rushing out and busting onto his path'...considering all that will come regarding the prophets/ecstatics being naked wanderers on the mountaintops of Ancient Israel/Palestine, this could be a clever juxtaposition, an imaginative nudge and tease to ancient hearers who knew the queer ways of the prophets/ecstatics.
>
> I also suspect this passage would be bawdily/bodily funny to ancient ears though we might be missing it 2500+ years later. Let the scene play out in your imagination a bit...as she lowers her big jugs for him to get a drink...)

And so it was —
just as the camels had finished drinking
that the man took out a gold engagement nose-ring of no small-value
and two bracelets for her wrists —
bracelets twenty-times as heavy and valuable as the nose-ring —

(...in the ancient world, all of this jewelry would demonstrate interest in marriage with the wealth to back up such a proposition...but it's all happening a bit quickly, don't you think? Does Abraham's slave even know the girl's name yet — has she told him her name? Or is her name so embarrassing that she continues to harp on her pedigree and not her name, which has to do with 'cattle.' She continues to tell us she's descended from Snort, so...?

Notice more of the comedy of errors/manners here? This story that reads pretty flatly in most Bible translations is actually quite funny in Hebrew if you stay close to the text and remember the significant meanings of the Hebrew names...)

and he said,
"Daughter — whose are you?
Please tell me — does your father's house have space for us to stay the night?"

('daughter'/BT plays upon 'EL's-Virgin'/BTUAHL and 'virgin'/BTULH from just before...of all the things Abraham's slave could call her, he chooses another BT-word...and one showing her value as a daughter of someone else, not just a 'girl'/NAYRH which can indeed mean a 'marriageable girl' but also a slave/prostitute...Rebekah and this slave are dancing their words out very carefully to determine if marriage-here-by-the-spring is possible...and note the slave asks if Rebekah's father can host him and his retinue....'do you have a father? or are you a slave here getting the water?'

...and not just this, good chance Rebekah probably thinks this slave is proposing marriage to him...after all, he's the one who put the marriage-jewelry on her and he — as we will soon be told — has a crew of people and animals with him! Ancient comedy of manners!)

And she said to him,
"Daughter of EL's-Virgin! That's me!
That's Queen's son —
the one for whom she gave birth for Snort."
And she said to him,
"Straw and animal-feed — yes, we have a lot of it!
And even room to stay the night!"

And the man bowed down humbly
and got down on his knees for YAHWEH.

And he said,
"Bring me to my knees into abundance,
YAHWEH! God-or-gods-and-goddesses/ELOHIM of
my boss Abraham —
who didn't abandon Its loyal-love
and never-ending reliability for my boss —

I'm on the path —
YAHWEH led me to the house of my boss' brother!"

And the girl ran
and told everyone
in her mother's house these stylings-on.

And Rebekah had a brother,
and his name was Harden-Bricks.

And Harden-Bricks was running to the man outside
by the spring.

And so it was —
just as he saw the nose-ring and the bracelets on his sister's hands
and just as he was hearing his sister Rebekah's stylings-on saying
"Truth! He styled it out to me — the man did!"
that he entered into — arrived to — the man
and — what do you know — he was standing beside the camels by the spring —
and he said,
"Come! Enter!
Bring me to my knees into abundance, YAHWEH!
Why are you standing outside?!
<u>I've faced — turned/prepared</u> — the house and space for your camels!"

(Notice that while Abraham's / Patriarch-Prospers' slave is testing out whether YAHWEH is reliable and dependable on his mission to get a wife for his boss' son, Harden-Bricks who is from another land knows something of YAHWEH — his first instinct is to thank YAHWEH, not all-the-other-gods-and-goddesses. This would have probably been shocking in the ancient world to the band of YAH's audience... that a person from the cradle of civilization — the very palace/towers between the famous rivers — would know YAHWEH, and enough to bow to It... the famous culture of the very, very Ancient Sumer/Babylon have their own very successful gods and goddesses besides YAHWEH...a whole pantheon of divinities much more famous and well-known than the new-divinity-on-the-block YAHWEH, the newest way of conceiving the divine when the band of YAH told their tales 2500+ years ago.)

And the man entered the house
and unsaddled the camels
and gave straw and animal-feed to the camels
and water to wash his feet and the feet of the people
who were with him.

And it was set before him to eat,
and he said,
"No eating until I style out my style!"

And they said,
"Style on!"

And he said,
"A slave of Abraham — that's me!
YAHWEH's brought my boss to his knees into
abundance! Very much so!
He's become great — wealthy and powerful!
(YAHWEH's) given him lambs and goats
and cattle

and silver
and gold
and slaves
and female-slaves who've yet to bear children
and camels
and donkeys.
And Sarah, my boss's wife, gave birth to a son
for my boss — even in her old age!
(YAHWEH) gave him everything he has!
And my boss made me swear saying,
'Don't fetch a wife for my son
from the Humble-Traders' daughters,
among whom I live in their land.
Instead — to my father's house — go!
and to my extended-family-including-maidslaves
and fetch a wife for my son!'
So I said to my boss,
'What if the woman isn't willing
to come following after me?!'
And he said to me,
'YAHWEH with whom I've walked —
before Its face! —
It'll send Its ambassador with you,
and It'll rush out and bust onto your path!
You'll get a wife for my son
from my extended-family-including-maidslaves and
from my father's house.
Only at this point will you be clean and unpunished
from my oath —
when you enter into my extended-family-including-
maidslaves
and they don't give (her) to you —
will you be clean and unpunished from my oath!'
So I entered the spring today and said,
'YAHWEH! God-or-gods-and-goddesses of my boss

Abraham!
If only there'd be a possibility of you rushing out and busting onto my path upon which I'm going!
So, here it is —
I'll station myself by the spring of water
and a ripe-and-ready-teenager will come out to draw water,
and I'll say to her,
"Please let me drink a little water
from your big water-jug!"
and she'll say to me,
"Both you drink and I'll draw water for your camels too!"
— let her be the wife that YAHWEH chooses to be right for my boss's son!'
I — before I'd finished styling it out to my heart, to myself —
listen here! —
Rebekah came out,
her big water-jug on her shoulder,
and she went down toward the spring,
and drew up water,
and I said, 'Please let me drink!'
and she hurried to bring down her big water-jug from upon herself,
and she said, 'Drink! And I'll give a drink to your camels too!'
And I drank and the camels — she gave them a drink too.
And I asked her and said, 'Daughter — whose are you?'
and she said,
'Daughter of EL's-Virgin, Snort's son —
Queen gave birth for him!'
So I put a nose-ring in her nose
and bracelets on her wrists!
And I bowed down humbly and got on my knees for YAHWEH.

And I shouted out my joy for YAHWEH bringing me to my knees into abundance —
YAHWEH! God-or-gods-and-goddesses of my boss Abraham! — Patriarch-Prospers! —
(YAHWEH) who guided me on my journey in a never-ending reliable way to fetch a daughter from my boss' brother for his son!
Now if there's the possibility of your bringing about loyal-love and never-ending reliability for my boss, tell me!
And if not, tell me!
And I'll face — turn — to the right and good...
or to the left and bad!"

(All of those nice puns and clarifications from before, plus the addition of 'ripe-and-ready-teenager'/ AYLM...another word for 'someone marriageable' though very different from just BT and BTULH both in sound and meaning. AYLM is what Saul accidentally lets slip from his lips chatting with his general as he's looking at David after David just a few moments before had killed Goliath...before Saul corrects himself in addressing David directly as a NAYR/'boy or slave.'

The fact that Laban/Harden-Bricks is out the door and ready to make a deal — which as we'll see in the Jacob-stories is quite in his nature — might've made ancient hearers of this story wonder if Laban — the one industrious enough to harden bricks for sale in a region well-known for its building projects — might've sent his sister Rebekah out all gussied up that particular night to try to draw a suitor for her for marriage....to show she was an eligible AYLM.

And the slave uses MSHPCHH/'extended-family-including-maidslaves' instead of MOLDT/'ancestral-family' which his boss Abraham had earlier used when talking with the slave...two words probably with substantially different meanings in the ancient world. We might wonder here if the slave is trying to get Rebekah's family through Laban/Harden-Bricks to clarify if she's pedigreed as a non-slave by assuming she's part of the MSHPCHH as a SHPCHH/'maidslave' instead of using MOLDT/'ancestral-family-with-nonslave-pedigree.' Note that Laban does not do anything with that reference...perhaps fearing this would lower Rebekah's value in the slave/Abraham's eyes and thus lower how much is paid for her...which is to say maybe Rebekah is indeed born of a maidslave and that's why she hammers out her lineage so carefully earlier with all those names — most of which we do not have any reason to recognize.

Notice the slave closes his style with the same strange verb — 'face'/PNH — that Harden-Bricks used earlier about welcoming Abraham's slave into his space. It's a bit like a chess match...indicating now it's Harden-Bricks' move.)

And Harden-Bricks and EL's-Virgin answered and said,
"From YAHWEH this style has come!
We can't style for you 'bad' or 'good' —
look, here is Rebekah right in front of your face!
Fetch and go and let her be the wife <u>for the son</u> of
your boss just as YAHWEH has styled out!"

('For the son'/LBN and 'Harden-Bricks'/LBN — both the same consonants. Kind of stylish? And a bit of punny foreshadowing in that Rebekah's son Jacob will one day face Laban/Harden-Bricks and any ancient hearer who had already heard the saga the band of YAH had spun forth would make the connection and enjoy such storycrafting cleverness even more.)

And so it was —
just as Abraham's slave had heard their styles,
he bowed down to the ground for YAHWEH.

And the slave brought out jewelry of silver and jewelry of gold and clothes
and gave them to Rebekah.
And precious gifts he gave to her brother and to her mother.

And they ate and drank —
he and the people with him!

(Note...in case it hasn't dawned on you yet...a slave is eating with non-slaves...something ridiculous to even imagine for any ancient hearer.

Slavery was well known in ancient times — it's the hallmark and purpose of the hierarchical-imagination where the one who is seen as less is forced to labor for the one seen as better...on the terms of the one who ranks better than the lesser. The entire system is designed to keep the hierarchy in tact, to prevent slaves from rebelling and to keep the 'betters' growing in wealth and image at the expense of the 'lessers.'

Sadly, hierarchical-imagination is the default

through most of the human-history on the planet.

Slavery, after all, can be found throughout Ancient Babylon/Sumer where Abraham's slave travels to fetch a wife for his son. Babylonian slavery is the reason for *The Epic of Gilgamesh* as the king conscripts/forces labor upon the teenagers of the town to build and maintain the metropolis of Uruk and the teenagers' parents complain to the gods and goddesses.

Slavery can be found throughout Ancient Egypt — and we'll soon get a lampooned tale about slavery in superpower Ancient Egypt through the band of YAH's Joseph story, another clever tale like this one with Abraham's slave revealing how power/ YAHWEH really flows.

Slavery is what builds empires. It has built the superpower economy of my own country for centuries — and perhaps it still does (minimum wage) even after slavery was outlawed in name but not so much in practice. Enslaved African-Americans built much of the capital of my country — the country supposedly the beacon of freedom throughout the entire world. It's a tragedy in all too many ways.

But here in the band of YAH's story, a new way of being is coming about — where a 'slave' is recognized as an equal and seems to be valued by Rebekah's family as such. Hmmm.

And YAHWEH rushes onto a slave's path...imagine it! All of this would've been shocking to ancient hearers! Doubly so. Triply so...enough to trip up your imagination so that even more possibilities might be born...the hallmark of the prophetic/ecstatic-imagination that seeks to free everyone from within so that the default/hierarchical-imagination is revealed for what it is and people can then choose something else, another entirely different way to be in relationship with fellow humans.)

And they spent the night
and stood up tall in the morning,
and he said, "Send me back to my boss!"
And her brother and her mother said,
"Let the girl stay with us a few days — or ten! —
and after that she'll go!"
And he said to them,
"Don't delay me!
YAHWEH's rushing out and busting onto my path!
Send me on and I'll go to my boss!"

And they said,
"We'll call out for the girl and ask her —
directly from her mouth!"

And they called out for Rebekah
and said to her,
"Will you go with this man?"

And she said,
"I'll go!"

And they sent off their sister Rebekah
and her nursing-mother
and Abraham's slave and his people.

And they brought themselves to their knees into abundance
for Rebekah, and said to her,
"Our sister!
Become thousands and more!
Your seed/descendants'll take possession
of the gates of all who utterly hate them!"

And Rebekah and her (slave)girls stood up tall
and rode on the camels
and followed after the man —
the slave took Rebekah and left.
And Isaac — Laughingstock — had already entered/ come and gone
from Well-for-the-Living-Who-Sees-Me.

And he was living in the southern desert.

And Isaac was out meditating, musing
in the rolling-field
as evening was facing/turning.

(Isaac is much like his father and mother, wandering, bordercrossing. And his 'meditating and musing'/ SUCH in the open field is quite interesting, yes? Perhaps a very process by which ecstatic/prophetic-style comes forth? It's the only use of this verb in the entire Hebrew Bible...except that it does play on SCHQ/'to play, to amuse, to entertain' which is not a whole lot different from Laughingstock/Isaac's name: YTSCHQ.

And there's that 'facing'/PNH again, perhaps hearkening back to the unusual use of the verb by

Harden-Bricks and by Abraham's slave in their power-moves, facing-off with each other.)

And he raised his eyes and saw —
and what do you know! —
camels were entering — arriving!

And Rebekah raised her eyes
and saw Isaac
and fell from her camel!

And she said to the slave,
"Who is that man farther out walking in the rolling-field? The one calling out after us?"

And the slave said,
"That's my boss!"

And she took a shawl and plumped herself up,
covered herself.

(Makes you wonder if Isaac is quite handsome — even from a distance — that Rebekah would fall from her camel, right? Or was it what he was wearing or not wearing that could be so visible from afar? Or that the very process of SUCH/'meditating and musing' had brought about in him a certain look? I suspect ancient hearers would know exactly what's happening here and we moderns are left to wonder....)

And the slave tallied it all up for Isaac — all the styles he'd made.

And Isaac entered her in/to his mother Sarah's tent
and took Rebekah,
and she became his wife.

And he loved her —
Isaac was full of sighs and emotion
about his mother Sarah, (who had died.)

<Gen 25. 1-20>

<#>

And Isaac pleaded with YAHWEH
right in front of his wife
because she was like a weed pulled up by its roots
— which is to say she couldn't have children.

And YAHWEH pleaded for him,
and his wife Rebekah became pregnant.

And the children smashed each other to pieces —
beat and crushed each other in her womb.

And she said,
"If it's going to be like this — why me?"

And she went on and on questioning YAHWEH.

And YAHWEH said to her,
"Two nations are in your belly!
Two peoples are within your guts!
They are separating themselves —
one people from the other —
they'll be strong and brave —
and as for the greater...
they'll be slaves for the littler!"

And when her day came to give birth — yikes! —
there were twins in her belly!

The first one came out —
        red-and-muddy all over him —
        like a majestic royal robe — of hair.

And they called out his name,

"Esau . . . Gruff-Squeeze!"

And after that, his brother came out —
        his hand grabbing
        onto Gruff-Squeeze's heel.

And they called out his name,

"Jacob . . . Heel-Grabber!"

(Now an ancient would have heard a few things in that unusual name 'Jacob'/YAYQB...

trickster...the one who trips people up by
  their heels
swollen
rear end, rear of anything
restrainer...the one who holds people back,
  then gets around them...

It's a wonderfully punny name. And we met the word 'heel'/AYQB earlier in the Eden/Pleasure story, remember? YAHWEH's pun-style about the Snake....

And as for all the words to describe Esau, they're going

to be significant later...'red-and-muddy'/AHDMONY and 'hair'/SAYR. AHDM, you might recall, are the same letters as 'mud-creature.'

And Esau's name itself? AYSO...*Strong's Exhaustive Concordance* recognizes it as the past participle of the verb 'to do or make'/AYSH...as in 'having already been done over, even roughed up.' To be more specific for Ancient Hebrew readers, I see it as a *piel*-version of AYSH...and *piel*-forms of Ancient Hebrew verbs usually intensify their *qal*-'roots.'

Highly punny names!)

<Gen 25:26c>

And the boys grew up:

Esau...Gruff-Squeeze was becoming a man
who knew all about the chase...hunting,
a man of the rolling-field;

Jacob...Heel-Grabber was becoming a complete man
staying close to the tents (where his family lived).

And Isaac loved Esau
because of what he chased down (meat)
and put in his mouth,

and Rebekah loved Jacob.

And Jacob had boiled up some boiled-stew,
and Esau entered/came from the rolling-field —
he was exhausted.

And Esau said to Jacob,
"Please let me gulp down some
of that red-red-red-muddy-stuff there —
look — I'm exhausted!"

And that's why they call out his name "Mud-Red!"

> (Mud-Red — Edom/AHDOM — is one of the ancient peoples, a name that in the band of YAH's stories goes back to Esau's nickname here...and also recalls Mud-Creature/AHDM.)

And Jacob said,
"Sell me your rank and inheritance-rights as first-born
right now!"

And Esau said,
"Look, I'm going to die —
what's it to me this first-born rank and right?"

And Jacob said,
"Swear to me right now!"

And he swore to him
and sold his rank and rights as first-born to Jacob...

> Jacob,
> the one whose name calls to mind reaching
> around and being tricky...

and Jacob gave Esau bread and boiled-stew of lentils,
and he ate
and drank

and stood up tall
and left —

Esau despised the rank and rights that came with being first-born in the ancient world...

Esau,
the one whose name calls to mind being rough
and gruff....

<Gen 26. 1-35>

ummm...
yah...weh...
ummmmm

commentary

A New Imagination Where Even Slaves Are Heard & Obeyed

Note the confidence of Abraham's slave:

> *"Don't delay me!*
> *YAHWEH's rushing out and busting onto my path!"*

Earlier, this unnamed slave had prayed that YAHWEH would "rush out and bust onto my path" and make successful his journey of getting a wife for Abraham's son.

And what do you know...YAHWEH does. Even for this slave!

YAHWEH...divinity that is reliable for slave and owner alike. And with such confidence, slaves dine with slave-holders as equals. And not only that...slaves here swear as oldest sons do, on the father/patriarch's genitals!

Now there's something incredibly surprising and significant happening here in the band of YAH's imagination!!!

And note the two sons of Rebekah, the wife that the slave

had found for Abraham's son Isaac, the Laughingstock. Jacob, the boy who likes to stay near the tents and cook soup, bends the gender-expectations of the ancient world. Esau is the boy par excellence in the ancient world — a hunter who takes care of his family by hunting. How's he all 'mud-red'? Imagine hunting in the ancient world...Esau kills an animal and then hauls it back home over his shoulder as the dead-animal's blood drains all over his hairy body, hairy since birth. Esau is perhaps the masculine model for the ancient world, though a bit stupid or at least foolish.

Today we might say that being hunter and being cook are equally wonderful occupations and passions for boys, for anyone. We even have very popular TV shows to celebrate each of these passions.

But not so in the ancient world! And that's the beautiful contrast of the band of YAH's stories with ancient expectations that we can glean through this and other ancient stories. It's here with Jacob and with many of their characters that the band of YAH bends the expectations of gender roles, of just about anything and everything.

In *Enuma Elish*, Tiamat defies the gods and talks back to the gods and gets killed for it. But in YAH's stories, Sarah can laugh at YAHWEH and live. In YAH's stories, instead of telling her what to do, Rebekah's family asks Rebekah if she wants to go so soon with Abraham's slave — and she does, much to the surprise of her family!

In the band of YAH's stories, woman is clever, curious disrupter (Eve) and back-talker (Sarah) and important enough to be asked her opinion (Rebekah).

YAH busts down ancient expectations of 'woman'

This might not seem all that wild today — but compare it to the gender roles we can glean from the earlier Ancient Babylonian sources and we might find some quite surprising things.

In *The Epic of Gilgamesh,* women are indeed known to be wise:

Gilgamesh and Enkidu consult Gilgamesh's mother, Queen Ninsun, about the way to take on the evil force of nature, Humbaba, who instructs the flood, and earlier in the epic a temple-prostitute is called upon to civilize wild man Enkidu through sex and food and clothing...the three things that seem to have gendered expectations in the ancient world...and even into mid-20th century United States!

But in the band of YAH's Genesis stories, YAHWEH — this 'It' with masculine pronouns — makes clothes.

In the upcoming Joseph stories, it'll be Joseph, of course, who interprets dreams.

YAH has a lot of genderbending in their stories...and not just genderbending...

there's a whole flipping of social expectations! True bordercrossingwithwildlyimaginativeleaps! YAHWEH is reliable for slaves! Slaves and non-slaves dine together and enjoy each other! YAHWEH promises to take care of old Sarah — long after menopause, it seems — and she gives birth to a child!

In the band of YAH's Genesis stories, Woman / Eve gives birth to Wisdom. She's not just some special woman like a queen or queen-mother — Eve is Woman who upsets the god-of-the-land YAHWEH and gets It all nervous about Its creatures becoming just like It!

And with Cain / Spear-Getter and Abel / Wasted-Breath, YAHWEH likes better the younger brother's gift over the older brother's gift. Remember, in ancient Mediterranean societies, the older son inherits everything...but here in the story of older-son Cain and younger-son Abel, YAHWEH prefers younger-son Abel's gift.

So what?!

Why does any of this matter, all this parsing out the differences between *Gilgamesh* and the band of YAH's stories?

Because noticing these epic shifts in consciousness in the ancient world might help us to notice the epic shifts we are going through in the 21st century — and noticing so that we can live well and welcome a future of joy and of life for ourselves and one another and the planet upon which we live. Perhaps it's our expectations and assumptions about life and about people that hold us back, that prevent us from knowing ALL that life can be and indeed is...YAHWEH...from the Hebrew verb 'to be'?

Noticing these epic shifts in consciousness invited by YAH might help us to welcome a future that is possible for our great, great, great grandchildren to live on this planet before Humbaba or whatever is the 22nd century threat (global still-warming-way-too-much) swallows them/us.

In *Gilgamesh*, King Gilgamesh and Enkidu team up to take on Humbaba — the chaotic-cause of great floods. They set out carefully, approach carefully and then drive winds down his throat — which recalls *Enuma Elish* with Marduk driving winds down Tiamat's throat and recalls YAHWEH breathing life into Its Eden creatures? The dynamic duo of Gilgamesh and Enkidu kill Humbaba, the threat shared by civilized Gilgamesh's great city/rule/economy and by the once-wild Enkidu and by his animal-friends and human-shepherd-friends alike.

When Gilgamesh returns victorious to his great city of Uruk, even the goddesses want him in marriage — especially ISHTAR. But Gilgamesh spurns her and 'wisely' reminds her that to marry a goddess or god is to end one's human life — to fall into the abyss where human-life is no longer. Why? It's one of the great superstitions of the ancient world — and maybe even of our world? — that to see a god/goddess face-to-face means you must be dead. Even today, what human-nobody marries a diva/divo and lasts all that long in the tabloids, our modern tales of the celebrity-gods-and-goddesses?

The goddess ISHTAR feels insulted by Gilgamesh and appeals to her father ANU, the father of the pantheon of gods and goddesses, the Zeus of Babylon. And eventually, ISHTAR will begin the plot to kill what is most important to Gilgamesh: Enkidu, the man he hugs as if he's his wife.

Herein lies the central questions of the crafted-for-the-ancient-world Bible:

Can you see God — the-gods-and-goddesses/ELOHIM

— face to face and live? Can you be enticed to touch the genitalia of the gods and goddesses and make love with them and live?

That might seem strange for us moderns to conceive... but look at so many ancient epics and that's the the question of all questions. Even the Bible is full of 'God' impregnating women...Mary mother of Jesus in the Gospels of Matthew & Luke, Hannah in 1 Samuel, Sarah and Rebekah in the band of YAH's stories in Genesis...all of them getting filled with YAHWEH's breeze and nine months later giving birth to some important human being, even when the ancient odds were against their getting pregnant.

But it's not just 'God' with women in the Bible...just wait until we dive into the Jacob-saga!

What is there in the carnal/deep same-sex embrace that keeps circling back in ancient imagination — whether between human and human or god and human — especially when such embrace has been so taboo for so long, at least since the Levitical priestly editors wrote Leviticus 18 and Leviticus 20 which prescribe death as punishment to men having sex with men?

Is this God-having-sex-with-humans — let alone for awhile the genderbending embrace — something akin to the prophetic-ecstatic imagination?

New land, new imagination

If we are to trust the ancient biblical imagination, there is a need in the ancient world for a new land in which to explore new ways, new possibilities. And that's the ushering in of the biblical imagination...YAHWEH inviting Abram and Sarai and Lot to 'a promised land' wedged between Babylon and Egypt...the great superpowers of the day. Both of these superpowers were hierarchically-minded, royally-minded, with slaves central to their superpower and economic greatness.

But for hundreds of years, hierarchies and royalties had competing touches on the many peoples living in Ancient Israel/Palestine — a bunch of bands, family-groups living as best they could on the trade routes being fought over by the superpowers north and south. Maybe some of those bands partnered up to become a tribe, a united stick to better take on any challengers — such a stick with a leader of some sort, yes. If we are to trust at least a little bit of the story of X's saga in 1 & 2 Samuel, it wasn't until the people foolishly wanted to be like other countries and raised up one as their royal...something that set in motion a whole hierarchy of place and function. They already had a gold-laid-ark, a state-religion of sorts mediated by a priest, a hierarch who could be bought to get the gods on the buyer's side through some special ritual, like slaughtering an animal/ancient wealth, with special prayers only utterable by a priest...as the priest would have the buyer know.

In 1 & 2 Samuel, the story of the hierarchy of the state that emerged — a royal government led by a messiah — probably wasn't headed by Saul and David and the Davidic monarchy once thought to be inaugurated around 1000 BCE. That's the fiction hiding the past and also revealing its impulses and foolishnesses. No king look's great in X's writings.

Whenever this royal-government did emerge in real life/history — and it did come about at some point — X makes it clear that the decision to join the tribes together into a united monarchy was completely foolish...a move that does indeed make the misfits on the mountains look better and wiser. Who are the misfits, the 'boys,' a word that usually means 'the slaves'? The prophets. The ecstatics.

Scholars note that those Saul/David accounts in 1 & 2 Samuel are fictions placed at around 1000 BCE but likely didn't come about for a few more hundred years as Ancient Israel tried to blend in with the other principalities of the land before banding together bit by bit as a united royalty of some sort. Messiah/MSHYCH, by the way, comes from the word MSHCH/'to anoint or paint with oil'...though it's very close to another word MSHCHYT/'destroyer...some military attachment designed to destroy'...something X makes clear in 1 Samuel.

In the third and second centuries BCE, when translating the Hebrew Bible from Ancient Hebrew to Ancient Greek — the translation known as the Septuagint — the LXX translators opted for the Greek word 'christ' as the translation for the Hebrew word 'messiah.'

This whole christ/messiah-business is dangerous business...all about annihilation/MSHCHT. Early Jesus-believers before/after Paul conferring this title — 'Messiah' (Hebrew) and its apparent equivalent 'Christ' (Greek) — onto Jesus was and is dangerous, dangerous business then...not to mention how 'Christ' and Christianity have been used to bludgeon so many people over the past two millennia. And sadly Messiah/Christ and the religion born from wanting a 'saving-king' is still used in this way, even in my own neighborhood.

It doesn't take much to make a strong argument that this 'we-need-a-king-to-save-us' was the imagination that infected Germany in the early 20th century that allowed a power-usurper like Hitler to take control and enact a hierarchical imagination that saw some as 'pure' and some as no better than vermin to be cast into the fire...Jews, homosexuals, disabled/differently-abled, Roma, political opponents...possibly as many as 8 million people! This was in Christian-led Germany... where the Nazi guard wore belt buckles emblazoned with *Gott Mit Uns*...God with us...as they confidently killed millions upon millions of people in and around their growing nation and enabled a world war that would kill 75 million more people. It's hard to imagine, difficult to get my head around the reality that so much destruction could be wrought through a hierarchical imagination like this.

And where did Christian-led Germany get this imagination? Lots of places, surely, but one place is out of the fascist-mindset of the Levitical priests who decided who lived and who died in their Torah, as they tragically proclaimed in Leviticus 20.13.

Putting any human above or below oneself is dangerous... the slow (and quick) creep of hierarchical imagination.

Could it be the same imagination that is slowly infecting my own nation? Slavery has been alive and well on this land since 1619 — long before the United States of America was a nation standing on its own two feet and growing the slave trade even more until we fought a civil war to decide if people could own people as slaves or not. How many died from that war? Maybe 750,000 by war's end, likely more.

But did that Civil War ever end? Jim Crow, lynchings town by town...often publicized as entertainment in towns...as humans killed humans in broad daylight and for the only crime often being the color of their skin. Often. Statues heralding the leaders of the Confederacy and the hierarchical-imagination that wanted slavery are just now beginning to be taken down in the 2020s. That's a century and a half after the war ended.

And before and during and after that entire time, the native peoples were fought and slaughtered in all kinds of grotesque ways and anyone allowed to live was pushed westward without any thought about it... the Manifest Destiny of certain-classed, male, white landowners over and against everyone else as if God had ordained it.

Do you recognize the hierarchical-imagination here? 'I am better than a slave and I am better than a native so I put them below me to demonstrate my merit and I can do whatever needs to be done to them to keep them there.'

And now we look to presidents to try to fix it all over again as saviors of sorts, we rally to their agendas, we do what we can to help them 'win'...and all too often the winning president enacts an agenda steeped in hierarchical-imagination that puts the other party below theirs, a move that only exacerbates our nation's problems all the more. It doesn't matter which political party one sides with — the same imagination often exists there with just more agreeable rhetoric to one's ears with the party that we like at the moment. One president I voted for for his hopeful message eventually dropped 26,171 bombs on those he saw as enemies abroad...and their families with children, and their neighbors, and their neighbors down the street...many of whom had nothing to do with any of his worries.

Those 26,171 bombs were in a single year.

The next president dropped even more.

Either we live out of an imagination that recognizes the equality of every human being no matter what <u>or</u> we live out of an imagination that sees some people as better than others and some people as expendable.

It doesn't matter our political party, our church/worship affiliation, our gender, our income-bracket or neighborhood, or any of our so-called identifiers. The hierarchical-imagination can be found in every one of these arenas...Democrat and Republican and often Independent...in every organized religion...within and among men and women and trans-humans and nonbinary humans...everywhere...in me...maybe you're noticing it within you at times, dear reader.

And that destructive imagination will rule until we decide — much like the prophets/ecstatics decided — that we need to swim away from "the shipwreck" of that imagination to a new shore...one that recognizes the co-equal value of every human being and not just the ones who agree with us.

A different option than "the shipwreck" continuing to kill us in every generation

Paul, remember, used 'Christ' as a title for Jesus to slap Rome and its Caesar in the face...Rome, the power who crucified Jesus. In Paul's mind, Jesus as 'Christ' is the only one who can make Rome bow down to YAHWEH, this Jesus who was a wandering peasant and killed by Rome and raised up by YAHWEH who would now, in Paul's mind, be the one to convert even the most stubborn Roman Emperor Cult to bow down to YAHWEH and YAHWEH alone.

But Paul's plan backfired. His idea of 'Christ' being on the same level with all people and all of us bowing down together before YAHWEH together quickly got sublimated by Peter's camp's vision of a hierarchy of people, a vast network of human leadership acting for 'Christ.' It's rather comical (and tragic) that those acting for Christ — pastors, priests, bishops, popes, etc. — are often dressed in Roman garb, or at least the richest clothes of the culture in which the priestly Christ-actor lived.

Jesus was a peasant from the middle of nowhere — with nowhere and everywhere to lay his head. Do you really think he was wearing fine clothes?

In my own church — Roman Catholicism — there are fights to try to get the language spoken for our rituals and even worse our Bibles to be in Latin, the court-language of Rome that tried Jesus, found him guilty, and killed him in Rome's sickening torturous style... the many hours of terrorizing pain of being nailed or strung up on a cross until the crucified drowns in their own spit...not to mention the humiliation of being strung up there naked for all the neighborhood to see.

Hierarchies — be they religious or governmental — are quite catchy. They've been the default for millennia upon millennia upon millennia. *The Epic of Gilgamesh*, let's remember, is about 5000 years old, its story of a king who created the great metropolis Uruk, all through slavery or conscripted/forced labor. Ancient Egypt was built by slaves too, by people who were valued less than their royals, their Pharaohs and Queens.

The prophets/ecstatics offer a different option — one like Paul that recognizes that YAHWEH alone is great and that everyone else is at the same level, made of the same stuff as one another and existing within THE ALL with one another. As the prophets point out, to put any human being above another creates a significant imaginative problem — because eventually we humans are quick to name some people as better than us and some people as worse than us and, therefore, worth less. Worthless.

Perhaps the whole Bible could be seen as a 1000+ year story of how one group of nomadic bordercrossers (Hebrews/Israelites) tried to deal with the power-issues of being small little principalities squeezed between the trade routes of the superpowers of Babylon and Egypt. And — at least from the standpoint of the prophets — their/our error was to choose hierarchy/monarchy/priest-with-a-temple-or-church instead of the spiral-rich wisdom of the wind...YAHWEH...which cannot be contained by any ark, by any temple, by any church, by any one single human being...not even in the Bible itself.

But if we read the Bible only from the hierarchical

priestly-imagination, we will never know what the ecstatic/prophetic-imagination is inviting. The Bible catalogs in full effect the one-thousand-year argument of hierarchical-imagination vs. prophetic/ecstatic-imagination...and how the hierarchical-imagination won out...and how we still let it win out today often because we're not even conscious of it and our choosing to enact it in our relationships and in our institutions.

From the prophets' standpoint, if more and more of us did nothing, something might happen.

What happens when you just sit there and let the wind kiss you?

What happens when you stay there a little longer and let the wind into and out of you...let the wind make love to you and with you...when you're a willing participant in this love-making both as receiver and then as penetrator...and then as receiver and then as penetrator?

Sex alone or with others where we're stuck in one role is pretty awful sex — at least eventually — no matter who our partner is, right? Surprise and variety of roles, positions, etc. is the spice....

Being with the wind, being with YAHWEH, invites us to be both receiver and penetrator as we receive the wind and then gently or not-so-gently push it out into the larger atmosphere. And soon we humans realize It is a much more potent penetrator in this relationship than we humans are...unless, of course, you're Jacob.

If we're relaxed enough It almost feels like we're being breathed...oceanic...yeah? Welcome to the genderbending, taking-on-all-roles imagination of the prophets as they imagine and reimagine their relationship with YAHWEH.

All the while the priests invite us to be good boys and girls and follow the law and come to temple/church and do our ritual and say our special prayers and be bettered by it.

But not the prophets —

let YAHWEH ravish you!

A New Way Forward...touched by YAHWEH

Abraham stands up to YAHWEH in trying to help YAHWEH recognize that wiping out a whole town for the depravity and controlling-corruption of most/many of Sodom & Gomorrah is flat-out wrong. Sure, Abraham is concerned mostly because his nephew and family live there. But this is something that needs to be noted, this standing up to YAHWEH and this swaying YAHWEH's opinion about some matter.

Of course, we do this in our world too. Prayers of intercession in liturgy or in person...asking God to do something about some communal concern. Praying for a friend...asking God to do something because God must not be paying attention, otherwise God would have done something already if indeed God is a loving God.

But standing up to God, even fighting back against God and living? Topping God?! Well...that's an entirely different matter, and a matter that's soon going to be explored with our band of YAH's stories.

The band of YAH is not completely ingenious about having their human characters' take on the divine. *The Epic of Gilgamesh* has that as well when ISHTAR gets offended that Gilgamesh will not marry her because Gilgamesh knows what happens to humans when they marry or have sex with the divine...they seem to die.

In her anger at being miffed by Gilgamesh, ISHTAR appeals to ANU, god of gods, to send the Bull of Heaven onto the great city of Uruk — the Bull of Heaven being 7 years of famine. (That's going to sound pretty similar to the Joseph story very soon, with its 7 years of famine.) And ANU agrees to ISHTAR's plan as long as the city's people and animals are first cared for. But ISHTAR cannot control the Bull's power or doesn't want to and has the Bull swallow up 200+ citizens of Uruk. Enkidu defends the city by taking on the Bull, even flinging his own excrement at the Bull while the Bull slings its spit at Enkidu. Spit in the ancient world was thought to hold special powers, magic — weave that into your imagination of Jesus spitting into mud and smearing it on the blind guy's eyes to help him to see again...Jesus as shaman, healer and magic-maker of the ancient world.

Enkidu takes a chunk of the dead Bull and throws it at ISHTAR; ISHTAR then gathers the shamanic women of the city for plans for revenge.

Gilgamesh and Enkidu celebrate their victory against the Bull of Heaven and ISHTAR — they parade the spoils, the Bull's horns, place the spoils in Gilgamesh's personal temple. And they sleep that night as heroes in putting both the Bull and ISHTAR below them, under their power. Uh-oh.

Sleeping in the same bed/room as King Gilgamesh, Enkidu dreams that the gods and goddesses had joined together in council. Uh-oh.

This is an ancient nightmare — and that's why Enkidu jerks upright in bed and asks Gilgamesh what this is about. The gods and goddesses in council and all working together — well, that's a powerful force. And a powerful force indeed: Enkidu lies there as if paralyzed, as a human who has seen a god face to face. That's what the *Epic* says.

What if Gilgamesh had just let ISHTAR have her goddess-way with himself? Could any of the past-disaster and coming-disaster have been averted for Gilgamesh...or for his subjects (those under his rule)? If Gilgamesh would have just married ISHTAR as she requested and then Gilgamesh had died from it, would that have been the noble thing to do...Gilgamesh's death weighed against the hundreds killed when ISHTAR sicked the Bull on Uruk?

It might have been the noble thing — but it's not the kingly thing. And that's one of the tricky things about living in a hierarchical-system...the top-dog routinely sacrifices the bottom-dogs to keep its rule going.

Gilgamesh feared marrying goddess ISHTAR, feared he would die from it.

But it's not what the band of YAH imagines, now is it?

Mud-Creature and Woman see YAHWEH face to face and live. Spear-Getter had a conversation with YAHWEH, seemingly face to face. Patriarch-Prospers / Abraham and Clearly-On-Top / Sarah talk with YAHWEH — Sarah even laughs at YAHWEH.

There's a lot of face-to-face banter in the band of YAH's stories so far. A lot. And nobody dies because of that face-to-face banter.

Abraham's slave prays that YAHWEH will 'rush out and bust onto my path' and YAHWEH responds, busts out on a slave's path and does good.

Jacob soon will dream and pray and even be touched by YAHWEH — and way more than a little touch!

What would happen if a human reached out and touched YAHWEH back? We are always touching YAHWEH, and YAHWEH is always touching us back.

That is, if you know anything about what YAHWEH was and is for the ancient prophets/ecstatics — long before the priests built arks and temples and codes and ritual formulations and forbade people from saying 'YAHWEH' out loud...long before they forbade a lot of things the prophets/ecstatics were doing...the very things at the roots of Judaism and Christianity and Islam that so few want to talk about today. Yet.

The prophets encouraged relationship with YAHWEH, intimate relationship, touching YAHWEH, even encouraged saying 'YAHWEH' out loud. Why? Because the prophets/ecstatics were first touched by YAHWEH —

in a very special, sensual, sexy way...

in a way that topples empires and welcomes new life and new ways forward...

the wind whispers to you, circles you,
desires you, loves you...

what is your response?

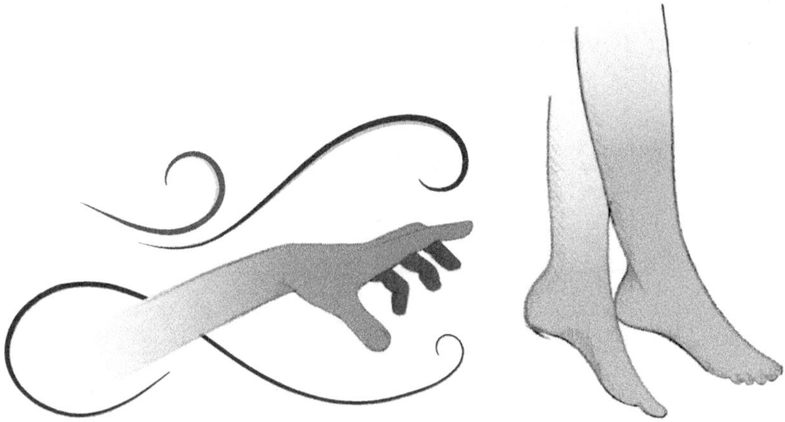

Genesis 27 - 35

Gruff-Squeeze(s) & Tricky-Heel-Grabber

the brothers Esau & Jacob
and Jacob's Clever Wives

<begin at Gen 27.1>

And so it was —
when Isaac...Laughingstock was old
and his eyes had become weak and dim in appearance
he called for his older son Esau
and said to him,
"My son!"

And he said,
"Here I am!"

And he said to him,
"Listen please, I'm getting old
and I don't know the day of my death.
Now please lift your gear —
your bow and bag of arrows —
and go on out to the rolling-field
and game me up some game
and make for me that tasty delicacy just like I love
and enter it — bring it to me to eat it —

so that what's alive within me —
my living, breathing body —
can bring you to your knees into abundance
before I die!"

And Rebekah had been listening as Isaac was styling out to his son Esau...Gruff-Squeeze.

And Esau left for the rolling-field
to game up some game —
to hunt some food — to bring back with him.

And Rebekah said to her son Jacob...Heel-Grabber,
"Listen up!
I heard your father style out to your brother Esau,
'Bring me some game
and make me that tasty delicacy
and I'll eat it
and I'll bring you to your knees into abundance
right in front of YAHWEH
right before I die!'
Now, my son, listen up to my voice —
I — yes me! — I'm shouting out orders at you —
please go to the little lambs and goats
and fetch me from there two young ones —
good ones —
and I'll make them into the tasty delicacy for your father —
just like he loves,
and then you'll enter — go into your father —
and he'll eat
so that he'll bring you to your knees into abundance
before he dies!"

And Jacob — the Tricky-Heel-Grabber — said to his mother Rebekah,

“Hey now,
my brother Esau is a rough and hairy guy
and I’m a smooth guy —
What if my father touches me — gropes, searches me out?!
What if I become in his eyes a cheater,
and I bring upon myself a curse
instead of his bringing me to my knees into abundance?!!”

(Jacob calling himself smooth is true of his tongue/ talk too...and the ancient Hebrew points in that direction. Jacob calls himself CHLQ/‘smooth’...a word-choice usually meaning ‘smooth-talker, one who makes deals.’ Comedy! He calls his brother Esau SAYR/‘hairy’...foreshadowing for a place that will be pivotal in Jacob’s life-journey.)

And his mom said to him,
“On me! Your small insult will be on me, my son!
For sure!
You listen to my voice
— and go get them for me!”

And he went
and fetched them
and brought them to his mom,
and his mom made a tasty delicacy
just like his father loves.

And Rebekah fetched Esau’s clothes —
her older son’s clothes — the finest —
which were with her in the house

and she put them on Jacob, her younger son,
and the skins of the young little lambs she put
on his hands
and on his smooth neck.

And she put the tasty delicacy and bread
that she'd made
into the hands of Jacob, her son.

And he entered — went into his father and said,
"My father!"

And he said,
"Why, who are you, my son?"

And Jacob said to his father,
"I'm Esau! Your first-born!
I've done just as you've styled out to me —
get up tall please and sit
and eat my game
so that your living, breathing body brings me to my
knees into abundance!"

And Isaac...Laughingstock said to his son,
"What's this?
You were so quick to find (game), my son?!"

And he said,
"Yes! YAHWEH — your God-or-gods-and-goddesses
— <u>happened</u> upon my face!"

('happened'/QRH is the same verb that Abraham's slave used to implore YAHWEH to show up and find a wife for his boss' son, the same son who now is old and in bed and ready to officially give the inheritance-blessing to what he thinks is his oldest son.)

And Isaac said to Jacob,
"Please come closer so I can touch you, my son —
are you really Esau, or not?!"

And Jacob got closer to his father Isaac,
and he touched him and said,
"The voice is Jacob's voice —
and the hands're Esau's hands."

And he didn't scrutinize carefully —
that the hands were like Esau's hands —
his brother's —
rough and hairy —
and he would bring him to his knees into abundance.

And he said,
"You there are my son Esau?"

And he said,
"That's me!"

And he said,
"Come closer to me
and I'll eat my son's game,
so that my living, breathing body can bring you to
your knees into abundance!"

And he got closer to him,
and he ate,
and he brought him wine,
and he drank.

And Isaac...Laughingstock, his father, said to him,
"Please come closer to me —
kiss me, my son!"

And he got closer
and kissed him.

And he breathed in the smell of his clothes
and then brought him to his knees into abundance
and said,
"Ah, see!
The smell of my son!
Just like smell of a rolling-field
for which YAHWEH has offered abundance!
God-or-gods-and-goddesses give you the solid-sky's lightest rain
and the oily, fatty goodness of the ground —
and oh so much grain and new wine!
The peoples (of the world) will slave away for you!
The nations of the world will bow down before you!
Become the stronger one to your brothers!
They'll bow down to you — they, the sons of your mother!
Whoever curses you is cursed!
Whoever brings you into abundance is abundant!"

(Notice that Laughingstock/Isaac offers the same blessing to his son as YAHWEH offered Patriarch-Prospers/Abraham.)

And so it was —

just as Isaac...Laughingstock was finishing bringing

Jacob...Tricky-Heel-Grabber to his knees into abundance

that Jacob...Tricky-Heel-Grabber sped on out of there
away from his father Isaac...Laughingstock's face

and his brother Esau...Gruff-Squeeze entered from his hunting-trek!

And he also had made a tasty delicacy for him
and brought it to his father
and said to his father,
"Get up tall, my father —"

— he was eating his son's game (from the first son to visit him) —

"— so that your living, breathing body
can bring me to my knees into abundance!"

And Isaac, his father, said to him,
"Who are you?"

And he said,
"It's me — your son — your first-born — Esau!"

And Isaac shook and shook
and shook over and over again,
so, so much, and said,
"Then who was the guy who gamed up the game —
and brought it to me —
and I ate from all of it before you entered??
I brought him to his knees into abundance
— and abundant he'll be!!"

When Esau heard his father's style,
he cried out a great cry
and got all bitter and fussy — very much so!
And he said to his father,
"Me too! Offer me abundance, my father!"

And he said,
"Your brother entered here as a fraud
and took your abundance!"

And he said,
"It's true, isn't it,
why his name's called out like that...
  Heel-Grabbing Jacob...
  the Cheatin'-Swindler —
he's held my heel on this —
cheated me these two times —
my first-born rank and inheritance-right —
he took it —
and now he's taken my abundance too!"

And he said,
"Didn't you separate out some abundance for me?!"

And Isaac answered and said to Esau,
"Listen up,
I've set him up to be stronger than you —
and over all his brothers —
I've given him the slaves —
and have lent him my support
with grain and new wine —
what can I do now, my son?"
And Esau said to his father,
"Do you only have one abundance, my father?!?
Offer me abundance too, my father!"

(As ridiculous as this would sound to our 21st century ears — this separating out some special portion of abundance for Esau when abundance means it can't be divided — such a thing would be equally ridiculous in the ancient world, though in a slightly different ridiculous way. You see, in the ancient world, only one son — almost always the oldest, especially if the oldest was from a non-slave wife — received the inheritance and the offering of abundance before his father's death. The other sons would be back-up in case the chosen son died. And in the ancient world, once a father conferred the abundance/blessing upon a son, it could not be changed...at least not as easily as the termination-loophole-clause of our 21st century contracts.)

And Esau raised his voice and wept.

And his father Isaac answered and said to him,
"Listen up,
away from the rich, fatty goodness of the land —
that'll be where you live —
away from the solid-sky's lightest rain from above —
on the razor-thin edge of life — you'll live — by your sword, on the drought-dead ground —
you'll slave away for your brother —
and it'll be when you roam and tramp around
that you'll break into pieces his harness around your adversarial-neck!"

(These are tight little puns in the Ancient Hebrew text. And note the wandering, roaming life that Isaac knows will save Esau.

Isaac might be old and nearly blind but he is no Laughingstock with how he uses language...quite the style in word choices here.)

And Esau cherished his hate for Jacob
about the abundance
that his father had given him.

And Esau said in his heart (to himself),
"The days for mourning my father are very close —
and then I'll kill my brother Jacob!"

And it was reported to Rebekah —
her older son Esau's style —
and she sent for and called out for her younger son Jacob —
and said to him,
"Listen up!
Your brother Esau — Gruff-Squeeze! —
he's breathing heavily and plotting revenge for you —
to kill you —
now, my son, listen to my voice —
stand up tall —
bolt to my brother Harden-Bricks —
toward Scorched-and-Glowing-Land (that hot,
hot, hot city-life in the land of the palaces and
metropolises and ziggurats of Babylon) —
stay with him a few days —
until your brother's feverish rage turns over —
until your brother's hot-and-bothered anger turns
away from you —
and he forgets what you did to him —
and I'll go-get and fetch you from there —
why should I have to suffer the loss of the two of you
in a single day!"

from Abraham's homeland, the Ziggurat of Ur...
representing Babylon's solid hierarchical imagination
from which Abraham is called to wander away

(There's some playful style with Rebekah's choice of words here too — many similar sounding words in Hebrew as she parses out meaning for Jacob. Recall too Abraham hoping no son of his — or grandson, surely — would ever return to Babylon, to the land of the palaces and temples and metropolises of Ur[uk] or the anywhere in that region.)

<Gen 27.46 - 28.9>

And Jacob left from Seven-Wells in the south — such a perfect place —
and went toward Scorched-and-Glowing-Land in the north, in Ancient Babylon.

And he just happened to end up in a place
and stayed there overnight
because the sun was setting.

And he took one of the stones from the place
and put it under his head
and slept in that place.

And he had a dream — and listen here —
a mounded-up ramp was standing on the ground —
its head struck the solid-sky!

And listen here — ambassadors of the-gods-and-goddesses/ELOHIM were climbing up and going down on it!
And listen here —
YAHWEH was standing on top of it!

And It said,
"I'm YAHWEH —
God-or-the-gods-and-goddesses/ELOHIM
  of Abraham, your (grand)father —
God-or-the-gods-and-goddesses/ELOHIM
  of Isaac!

The land on which you are lying down —
I give it to you and to your seed...your descendants!
Your seed'll be like the ground's dust —
and you'll bust out all over —
to the west and to the east,
to the north and to the south!
They'll find themselves abundant —
through you —
all the extended-families-including-the-maidslaves
from the mud —
through your seed...your descendants!

So listen up now —
I'm with you!
I'll stand guard for you everywhere you go!
I'll bring you back here
to this mud, this patch of land!

I won't loosen from you, won't leave you behind
until I've done
what I've styled out for you!"

And Jacob awoke from his sleep and said,
"My goodness! How can that be?!
YAHWEH is in this place!
And I — I hadn't known it!"

(Now this was a positively shocking dream and realization for anyone in the ancient world...that a god/goddess from one land could show up in another land without a war happening. ELOHIM/ gods-and-goddesses were tied up in the land, in the ancient imagination. And this story highlights the complexities of that word ELOHIM, for sure. In the Hebrew scriptures, ELOHIM cannot always be translated as "God." Like with the Abraham-almost-killing-Isaac story, ELOHIM here most likely means multiple divinities, multiple gods and goddesses as their ambassadors are moving up and down the ziggurat-staircase. And YAHWEH is on top of all of it, on top of and in charge of all ambassadors and on top of all divinities, all ELOHIM. And YAHWEH reminds Jacob that It is the ELOHIM/divinity of his father and grandfather, and to trust as they trusted, even in this foreign land as Jacob runs from this bloodthirsty brother.

Here is YAHWEH crossing borders and revealing Itself in a land where other gods and goddesses had had a foothold for centuries, whether the land is Canaan/Humble-Traders'-Land or Babylon. Where was he exactly when Jacob had the dream? Was he in Abraham's homeland? On the way there? We actually do not know in the story — and I suspect that's the band of YAH's purpose.

YAHWEH can be found anywhere and everywhere. YAHWEH — the very essence of life, the breeze! — YAHWEH can be found even on top of all the gods and goddesses on the ziggurat, the mounded mud up to the solid-sky, the heavens, the mounded-up ziggurats of Babylon, the royal-courts of Egypt

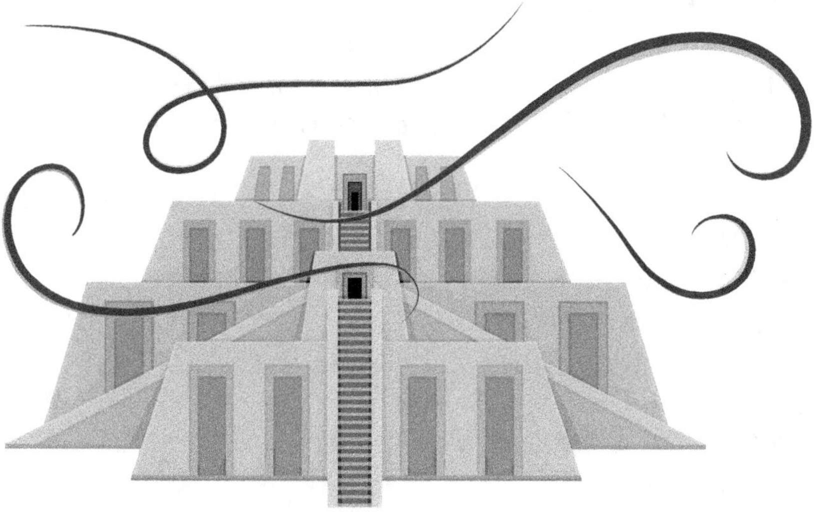

with their sphinx-mounds and pyramids of power...

YAHWEH can be found anywhere!

YAHWEH, on top of all — even without any temple or special-building!

YAHWEH, on top of all the other gods and goddesses anywhere and everywhere!

Keep in mind that on-topness of YAHWEH as we move along with the course of the story....)

<Gen 28. 17-22>

And Jacob lifted his feet
and went toward the land
of the children of the long-past in the East.

And he saw — what do you know! —
a water-well
in the rolling-field —

and — listen here —
three flocks of lambs and goats stretching and resting
by (the well) —
for the flocks usually drank from that well.

And there was a huge stone
over the top of the well —
they'd gather all of the herds there,
roll the stone from the top of the water-well,
give water to the lambs and goats,
and then return the stone
on top of the well to its place.

And Jacob said to them,
"My brothers, where're you from?"

And they said,
"Scorched-and-Glowing-Land of Babylon — that's where we're from."

And he said to them,
"Do you know Harden-Bricks?
Snort's son?"

And they said,
"We know him."

And he said,
"How is he?
All is well with him...is he healthy, safe, at peace?"

And they said,
"Healthy, safe, and at peace.
And look —
his daughter Rachel...Little-Lamb —
she's entering — arriving with the lambs and goats!"

And he said,
"Look, there's still a better part of the day left —
it's not yet time to gather the livestock.
Give water to the lambs and goats —
and then go shepherd them (walk out with them as they eat in the field)!"

And they said,
"We aren't able to do it (by ourselves)
until all the flocks are gathered —
and they (we all) roll the stone

from the top of the well and then we can give water to the lambs and the goats."

> (Perhaps they're suggesting they're waiting on Rachel...they need her strength with theirs to move the stone.)

While he was still styling it out with them,
Rachel entered — she arrived with the lambs and the goats which were her father's —
you see, she was a shepherd.

> (This would have been incredibly surprising in the ancient world — a woman who is a shepherd! And not only that...her strength is required to help move the stone from atop the well....)

And so it was —
just when Jacob saw Rachel —

> Harden-Bricks's daughter,
> his mom's brother,
> with Harden-Bricks's lambs and goats,
> Harden-Bricks being his mom's brother —

Jacob got closer
and rolled the stone from the top of the well
and <u>gave water</u> to his mom's brother Harden-Bricks's lambs and goats!

And Jacob <u>kissed</u> Rachel
and raised his voice and wept!

(YAH's up to their punny tricks here...the form of the verb 'gave water' and the form of the verb 'kissed' are the same consonants in Hebrew...VYSHQ.

And what got into Jacob? When he left home he was a man of the tents — seemingly good at only lifting pots and pans...in the ancient world, this is considered women's work. But here, he is so moved at seeing Rachel — the unlikely shepherd upon whom all the other shepherds were waiting to move the stone from the well! — that Jacob lifts the stone himself and weeps at the sight of her. He is so moved! And so is the stone....)

And Jacob told Rachel
that he's a relative of her father,
and that he's Rebekah's son,
and she ran and told her father.

And so it was —
when Harden-Bricks heard Jacob's story —
his sister's son —
he ran to call out to him —

he embraced him
and kissed him
and made him enter his house.
And he tallied up all these stylings-on for Harden-Bricks.

And Harden-Bricks said to him,
"You sure are my flesh and bone!"

(Perhaps Jacob had told him about being forced to leave home after duping his brother...and perhaps a guy like Harden-Bricks/Laban identifies with swindling people for his own good, which is the only way to thrive in any empire as he seems to be living in the land of the metropolises, the land of the empire Babylon...

and perhaps Jacob told the story in such a punny, clever, stylish way that Harden-Bricks immediately knew Jacob through the familiar style of speech, a speech that erupts and surprises with its imagery and sounds.)

And he stayed with him a month of days — until the new moon.

And Harden-Bricks said to Jacob,
"Is it true that you are my relative?
Well, then, slave away for me for free...without pay
and tell me what'll be your reward."

And Harden-Bricks had two daughters:

the name of the older was Leah —
whose name brings to mind Tiring-and-Dreadful;

the name of the younger was Rachel —
whose name, of course, means Little-Lamb.

And Leah's eyes were tender, frail, weak.

And Rachel was beautifully shaped and had a beautiful appearance.

And Jacob loved Rachel, and he said,
"I'll slave away for you seven years for Rachel,
your daughter — the younger one."

(Seven being the number of completion, wholeness... the perfect number of years Jacob will slave away for this person Jacob loves wholly...though ancient hearers would immediately know this deal is trouble....)

And Harden-Bricks said,
"Better for me to give her to you
than to give her to another man.
Stay here, live with me!"

And Jacob slaved away seven years for Rachel —
and in his eyes it seemed like a few days
in his love for her.

And Jacob said to Harden-Bricks,
"Come on, give me my wife —
my days (of work) are fulfilled —
let me enter into her!"

(Sex in the ancient world sealed the marriage-deal, of course. And the verb here — a form of BOAH — is often used by the band of YAH, as noted before, to playfully tease at entering rooms or regions...or sexually as in entering someone with one's body...a definite pun/slang/euphemism and not the love-making kind of slang that YDAY/'knowing' often invites.)

And Harden-Bricks gathered all the people of the place and prepared a feast with wine.

And so it was —
in the evening,
he took his daughter Leah
and made her enter (into the bridal-tent) with him,
and he entered into her!

<Gen 29.24>

And so it was —
in the morning — yikes! —
it was Leah!

And (Jacob) said to Harden-Bricks,
"What's this you did to me?
Was it not for Rachel I slaved away for you?!
Why did you deceive me?!"

And Harden-Bricks said,
"It's not done like that in our part of the world —
to give the little-one before the first-born —
fulfill this seven (days of the ancient bridal week celebrations)
and I'll give you even that one —
in her slavery —
which you'll slave away with me
still another seven years."

(Jacob...duper of his brother Esau...now duped by his father-in-law Harden-Bricks who fools Jacob by having him consummate the marriage with Leah and not with Rachel...

Harden-Bricks' name brings to mind hard work via forming bricks from mud and hardening them in the fire...and now hard work in exchange for the love of Jacob's life, love at first sight with Rachel, the Little-Lamb.

And Harden-Bricks has style...playing with sevens here and clever actions to his significant advantage.

His relatives who left home — Abraham and Sarah and Isaac and Rebekah and Jacob — they all have style, style rooted in their wandering life.

Harden-Bricks has style too, a punny and familiar style — but his style is more concrete and more for himself, less wandering and fluid than his nomadic relatives who left home for a new way of life, a whole new imagination. Harden-Bricks, after all, lives in the land of the palaces, the land between the two great rivers where metropolises are built out of, you guessed it, bricks hardened in the hot sun and in the fire, bricks to build towers and palaces and empires.

What use does a nomad like Jacob and his ancestors back to Abraham have with bricks...?

Bricks are just extra weight in one's baggage, no use for a nomad, a bordercrosser.)

And Jacob did, sure enough —
he <u>fulfilled</u> this seven (days, the bridal week of celebrations).

And he gave him his daughter Rachel to be his wife.

<*Gen 29.29*>

And he entered into Rachel too,
for he really loved Rachel <u>more than Leah</u>.

(Another clever pun here...'fulfilled'/YMLAH and 'more-than-Leah'/MLAHH are similar sounding... enough to produce an ancient giggle...especially as the littler Rachel — indeed, the Little-Lamb! — is more fulfilling to Jacob than the weak-eyed Leah who is probably larger and fattier and more appealing in the ancient imagination, as we learned with his mother Rebekah, regarding surviving child-bearing. But Jacob loves Rachel — no matter if she is smaller and more muscular and not seen as beautiful in most ancient eyes and is a bit of a genderbending shepherd and apparently quite physically strong...enough to be needed to help lift the stone off the well. In a burst of love at first sight, though, Jacob was able to lift the stone from the well by himself. He's now virile — and virile enough not only to lift the stone by himself but to enter into Rachel — this guy who was more at home in the tents with his mom than out in the open-field with his hunting brother Esau. For anyone disturbed by all this 'entering into'...just you wait!)

And (Jacob) slaved away for (Harden-Bricks) still
another seven years.

And YAHWEH saw that he hated her — Leah —
Tiring-and-Dreadful — and It opened her womb.
And Rachel was like a weed pulled up by its roots —
unable to have children.

And Leah became pregnant
and gave birth to a son
and called out his name,

"Looky-Here-a-Son . . . Reuben!"

because she'd said,
"Look at how YAHWEH has looked
into my misery —
you see,
now my husband's gonna love me!"

(Leah guesses that Jacob will love her more now that she's done what women were expected to do in the ancient world — bear a child, especially a boy-child who will inherit the family's future.)

And she became pregnant again,
gave birth to a son and said,
"YAHWEH heard that I was hated — yes, me! —
so Its given me even this one!"

And she called out his name,

"Listening . . . Simeon!"

And she became pregnant again,
gave birth to a son and said,
"Now time and time again my husband's attaching himself to me
because I gave birth to three sons for him!"
That's why she called out his name,

"He's-Attached . . . Levi!"

And she became pregnant another time,
gave birth to a son and said,
"Time and time again, I throw up my hands (penis?!)
in praise to YAHWEH!"

That's why she called out his name,

"Throw-Up-Your-Hands/Penis-In-Praise . . . Judah!"

(This might seem completely ridiculous...until we soon get to Judah's story about throwing his own penis out there to get himself into trouble.)

And she stood up (from all the squatting down) of giving birth to children — as if she were finished with it for good.

<Gen 30. 1-13>

And Looky-Here-a-Son went out
during the days
of lopping off the wheat (wheat-harvest),
and he found
in the rolling-field some passion-potion-plants.

(Often translated as 'mandrakes,' these plants were said to stir up sexual desire...and rather interestingly, the word in Hebrew is DUDY...and from the same root as the name David/DOD...whose name means 'boil over with affection/love'...and do they ever in 1 Samuel...Samuel and YAHWEH and Saul and Saul's son Jonathan all vying for David's young affection.)

And he entered them into — brought them to his mother Leah.

And Rachel said to Leah,
"Please give me some of your son's passion-potion-plants!"

And she said to her,
"It's a tiny thing that you take my husband —
you even take my son's passion-potion-plants?!"

> (Leah slams Rachel with an ancient-insult, a reminder of her unfit-to-be-a-woman tininess and even her 'little'/lesser name...Little-Lamb.)

And Rachel said,
"So here it is — he can lie down with you tonight
in exchange for your son's passion-potion plants."

And Jacob entered into — arrived from the rolling-field in the evening,
and Leah went out to call him
and said to him,
"To me! Enter!
I traded, traded, traded
my son's passion-plants for you!"

And he lay with her that night.

<Gen 30. 17-23>

<#>

> (Leah and Rachel each have a maidslave. The maidslaves of both sisters have children too — and

each sister claims their maidslave's children as her very own in the baby-making contest.

And lo and behold, Rachel eventually becomes pregnant and gives birth to her first son, this time not her slave's son whom she tried to count as her own flesh-and-blood son in the baby-making contest with her sister Leah.)

And (Rachel) called out his name,

"Add-On . . . Joseph!"

saying, "YAHWEH added on — for me — another son!"

And so it was —
just after Rachel had given birth
to Add-On...Joseph
that Jacob said to Harden-Bricks,
"Send me off
and I'll get going to my place, to my land —
give me my wives and my children
for whom I slaved away for you to get them —
let me go —
because you know my slaving away —
all that I slaved away for you!"

And Harden-Bricks said to him,
"Oh please — if I measure up in your eyes —
I learned by snake-hissing/fortune-telling —
YAHWEH's brought me to my knees
into abundance
because of rolling with you!"

(This 'rolling' is actually the ancient idiom — works even today. And as for snake-hissing...the verb NCHSH is usually translated as 'divination' in most Bibles. And that's fine, except that it ignores that NCHSH is indeed the word for snake — and that's one way our ancestors discovered the present/future through snakes, through hissing or whispering like a snake. This 'hiss,' we'll soon discover in the Joseph-saga and in the poems of the prophets through the hiss-whispery way of YAHWEH — the Hebrew word NAHM — is actually a method of the prophets...and brings the Eden story into a new light, yes? Hiss....)

And (Harden-Bricks) said,
"<u>Cuss out</u> your reward and I'll give it."

(Harden-Bricks is not happy here. His good luck charm Jacob — and a heck of a lot of free labor — is about to walk out the door. 'Cuss out'/NQB above is often used violently, *Strong's Exhaustive Concordance* notes...to puncture, to pierce violently, to blaspheme. We could easily translate the above line as "Try to screw me over with your reward and I'll give it"...a strategy by Harden-Bricks to insult Jacob even before Jacob announces what he wants, a strategy to get Jacob then to low-ball his request for payment. Harden-Bricks is a shrewd negotiator, after all. And he'd need to be if he were to thrive in the region of the metropolises, the New York Cities of the ancient world.)

And (Jacob) said to him,
"You know how much I've slaved away for you —

and how much livestock-wealth you have
through me —
how little you had before I came along!
It all burst forth — major growth!
YAHWEH brought you to your knees
into abundance
when my feet (walked through your door) —
now how much longer
until I can have my own house — mine!?"

<Gen 30. 31-43>

And Jacob heard the stylings-out of Harden-Bricks' sons, when they said,
"Jacob is taking everything that is our father's!"

and

"It's from our father that he made this glorious wealth and reputation!"

And Jacob saw Harden-Brick's faces/expressions —
and for sure, they were no longer with him as they had been just three days ago.

And YAHWEH said to Jacob,
"Return to the land of your fathers and your ancestral-family and I will be with you!"

And Jacob sent for and called out
for Rachel and Leah
out into the rolling-field, by his flocks of lambs and goats,
and he said,
"I myself see the faces/expressions of your father —
that he's no longer with me
like he was just three days ago —

God-or-the-gods-and-goddesses/ELOHIM of my father have been with me —
and you both know that with all my strong ability to adapt
I've slaved away for your father —
and yet your father has cheated me
and slid by with changing my wages ten times now!
But God-or-the-gods-and-goddesses/ELOHIM did not give me over to be broken!"

<Gen 31. 8-16>

And Jacob stood up tall
and set his children and his wives onto the camels.

And he drove onward all his livestock-wealth (that he'd tended and grown)
and all his gathered-wealth —
other animals he'd gathered or acquired (while he was working) —
which he'd gathered up
while he was in the The-Highland-Palaces-on-the-Plateau
to carry back to his father Isaac
in the Humble-Traders'-Land.

And Harden-Bricks had gone to shear his lambs and goats (a time of year when he could make a lot of money from the animals' wool, a time of great celebration/parties with all that new 'liquid/available' wealth).

And Rachel had stolen the household-god-figurines
which were her father's.

And Jacob had stolen Harden-Bricks's heart —
the Palace-guy! —
in that he didn't tell him that he was running away.

(Cleverly, the same verb here with juxtaposed meanings/purposes — GNB — 'to steal.')

And he ran away — he and all that was his —
and stood up tall
and crossed the river
and set his face in the direction of the mountains of Pile-of-Protests.

And it was reported to Harden-Bricks —
three days later! —
that Jacob — the one whose name means Tricky-Heel-Grabber — had run away.

(Perhaps even Harden-Bricks' slaves sided with Jacob and didn't tell Harden-Bricks that Jacob and his wives and children and possessions had escaped while he was off partying with the new wool-wealth of his sheared sheep that Jacob had helped him acquire and augment into a real cash-sheep, 'cash-cow'....)

And (Harden-Bricks) took his brothers with him,
and he chased after (Jacob) a whole, long journey
of seven days, and he kept close to him into the
mountains of Pile-of-Protests.

And God-or-the-gods-and-goddesses/ELOHIM had
entered into Harden-Bricks — the Palace-guy! —
in a dream during the night, and said to him,
"Protect yourself in your stylings-on with Jacob —
from the good all the way to the bad!"

And Harden-Bricks caught up to Jacob —
Jacob'd been making all kinds of noise banging in

the tent-pegs for his tent in the mountains (noise by which he could be found easily, and if he knew he was being chased, possibly to show he wasn't afraid?).

And Harden-Bricks'd made all kinds of noise banging in the tent-pegs for his tent with his brothers in the mountains of Pile-of-Protests...(noise by which to threaten/scare Jacob, to let Jacob know that he was on his trail).

And Harden-Bricks said to Jacob,
"What did you do?!
You stole my heart!
You drove onward my daughters
as if they were captives of the sword, of war!
Why did you hide by running away?
— you stole from me —
you didn't tell me — I would've sent you off —
with a joyful party and songs
with tambourines and guitars!
You didn't even pause the treachery long enough
for me to kiss my (grand)children —
and my daughters!
Now you play the fool in what you're doing —
it's in the ELOHIM/God-or-gods-and-goddesses' hand
(penis/phallic-power?) to do you all some harm —
but your fathers' God-or-gods-and-goddesses/
ELOHIM spoke to me last night, saying
'Protect yourself from styling-it-out with Jacob —
from the good all the way to the bad!'
And now you've gone, gone, gone
because of how much you long, long, long for your father's house —
but why did you steal my gods-and-goddesses
(figurines/statues)?!"

(Quite a styling on from Harden-Bricks here...how he keeps circling back to 'steal' — perhaps his real reason for chasing after Jacob...not to say goodbye and kiss his grandchildren — oh, and his daughters (named second) — but to get his household-god-figurines back. Recall that Rachel stole them as they were leaving, without her husband Jacob knowing she'd done so.

And here we have to wonder what indeed Harden-Bricks means by ELOHIM. He's from Babylon, a land of many divinities/ELOHIM, and he refers to Jacob's father's ELOHIM...which could be divinity/ELOHIM — as in YAHWEH/One-God — or many divinities/ ELOHIM. Noticing how complex these ancient biblical texts are? References in this particular story to 'gods-and-goddesses' and 'god/goddess' include a possessive form of EL, not ELOHIM which is plural/non-possessive...and that's why I don't include ELOHIM immediately after the translation. 'Household-god-figurines' are TRPYM, by the way, from RPAH/'to heal.'

Note too the YD/'hand or penis or phallic-power' reference above, with Harden-Bricks enticing the ELOHIM to stick it to Jacob for his devious deeds in running away in this style...foreshadowing for what a random-dude/divinity will soon do to Jacob on his journey back home....)

And Jacob answered and said to Harden-Bricks,
"— because I was afraid —
that if I said something
you'd rob, tear your daughters away from me!
With whomever you find your god/goddess (figurine/ statue) — that person won't live!

In front of our relatives, search out what is yours here
with me —
and take it as yours!"

And Jacob didn't know
that Rachel had stolen them.

And Harden-Bricks entered into Jacob's tent
and into Leah's tent
and the tent of the two maidslaves
but he didn't find them.

And he left Leah's tent
and entered into Rachel's tent.
And Rachel had taken the household-god-figurines
and put them in the camel's saddle-bags
and sat on them!

And Harden-Bricks felt his way
through the entire tent
but he didn't find anything.

And she said to her father,
"Don't let my boss' eyes get all hot-and-bothered
angry —
because I'm not able to stand up tall before your face
because the way of women — my menstrual period —
has come to me."

And he searched everywhere but didn't find the
household-god-figurines.

And Jacob got all hot-and-bothered angry, and
grappled with Harden-Bricks.

<Gen 31.36b - 32.3>

<#>

(After the confrontation, Jacob and his wives and children and all that was his split — continued on their journey without Harden-Bricks + company.)

And Jacob sent ambassadors out ahead of him
to Esau, his brother,
toward the The-Rugged-Land-That-Will-Make-Your-Hair-Stand-On-End,
the rolling-field that is Red-Land.

("Red," remember, is Esau's nickname. And this rugged mountain range nearby sounds like quite a playfully scary place...SAYYR...the same word for 'hairy and rugged' used earlier to describe Esau when he was born. SAYYR is also the word for 'faun/satyr' and 'hairy goat' and 'whirlwind that comes out of nowhere to the point that you become horribly, horribly afraid'...all of that derives from the same SAYYR...and ancient hearers of this story from the band of YAH would know it. Jacob has great reasons to be afraid — his Gruff-Squeezing brother's potential revenge being just one of them.)

And he shouted out orders at (his slaves-sent-off-as-ambassadors), saying,
"This is how you are to speak to my boss, to Esau:
'This is what your slave Jacob says:
With Harden-Bricks —
I've been staying as an immigrant.

I've been delayed there —
procrastinating until now.
I have oxen
and a donkey
and lambs and goats
and a male-slave
and a female-slave-who's-borne-children —
and I'm sending this
to tell you, my boss,
so that I might measure up in your eyes...!'"

(Note...Jacob has a lot more than that...he's setting up the potential bribe to soothe Esau's once-red-hot anger towards him.)

And the ambassadors returned to Jacob and said,
"We were entering/arriving
to your brother, to Esau —
he was coming to call you out —
and 400 men with him!"

And Jacob became afraid — very much so —
and felt hard-pressed, narrowed into himself.

And he divided the people with him
and the lambs and goats and the cattle and the camels
into two camps.

And he said,
"If Esau enters into one camp and hits it,
there'll be another camp growing larger for an escape!"

(Growing larger in that some from the attacked camp might be able to run to the other camp and then flee danger while those left behind get captured as booty by Esau and his 400 men.)

And Jacob said,
"God-or-gods-and-goddesses/ELOHIM
  of my (grand)father Abraham —
God-or-gods-and-goddesses/ELOHIM
  of my father Isaac —
YAHWEH...the one saying to me,
'Return to your land and to your ancestral-family!
I'll do only what's good for you!'
I'm not worthy of all the loyal-love
and all the confidence
that you've done for your slave — for me!
Because with my stick I bordercrossed
over this Going-Down River —
but now I've become two camps!
Please snatch me away
from the hand/phallic-power
  of my brother —
from the hand/phallic-power
  of Esau...Gruff-Squeeze!
Because I'm afraid — me! — of him —
that he'll come hit me —
the mother with the children!
You — you! — said it yourself,
'Good, good, good —
I'll only do what's good for you!
I'll make your seed/descendants
like the sand of the sea —
which can't be counted from there being so many!'"

And he stayed the night there that night
and fetched from whatever came
into his hand/power
as a gift for his brother Esau...

200 female goats
20 male goats
200 female little-lambs
20 rams
milking camels with their 30 children
40 cows
10 bulls
20 female donkeys
10 male donkeys...

> (...all of this a huge gift and vast amount of wealth in the ancient world...and note that it's much larger gift than the first bribe he offered Esau by way of message-runner/ambassador...and note that it's more than 400 animals, perhaps a strategy and hope that each of Esau's henchmen will grab an animal as booty and thus allow Jacob's family a chance at escape...)

...and he gave them over
into the hand/power of his slaves...
herd by herd — each one (a herd) by itself.

And he said to his slaves,
"Cross the border/river ahead of me —
and put a little wind (some space)
between each herd!"

And he shouted out orders to the first one,
"When my brother Esau comes in contact with you
and asks you,
'Whose are you?
And where are you going?
And whose are these in front of you?'
then you are to say,
'(They belong) to your slave — to Jacob —
it's a gift sent to my boss — to Esau —
and listen here — (Jacob's) also right behind us!'"

And he shouted out the same orders
even to the second
and even to the third
and to every one of them who followed after herds,
"In this style, you're to style it out to Esau
when you find him. And you are also to say,
'Listen here — your slave Jacob is right behind us!'"
because he'd said (to himself),
"I'll cover it over
with him (like painting it/him with tar) —
with the gift going out ahead of me
and after that I'll be able to see him, his face
and maybe he'll lift me up, my face — maybe he'll
accept me back."

And he crossed the gift (over to the other side of the
border/river) on ahead of him —
and he stayed that night in the camp.

And he stood up tall in the middle of the night,
took his two wives and his two female maid-slaves and
his eleven children,
and crossed over at the crossing-place
of the Demoralize-and-Devastate.

(That's a branch of the Going-Down-River...if the hair on the back of your neck is not yet standing up... the Hebrew text is quite spooky with allusions in the multiple-reasons-to-panic plot...up here in the mountains where the wind howls like a whirlwind... crossing into The-Rugged-Land-That-Will-Make-Your-Hair-Stand-On-End...crossing at the crossing-place that could Demoralize-and-Devastate you like a creek that seems tame and then all of the sudden swells with deadly force....)

And he took them and crossed them over the creek-bed
and crossed over what was his —
his possessions, his family.
And Jacob remained there all by himself.

And a man kicked up the dust and wrestled with him —
like the crossing-place...devastated and demoralized —

until the climbing up of dawn —

and he saw that he wouldn't be able to hold his own
with him —

and he groped the hollow of his thigh and genitals —

and the hollow of Jacob's thigh and genitals was
impaled in kicking up the dust and wrestling with him
— devastating and demoralizing him!

And he said,
"Let me loose —
because the dawn's climbing up!"

And he said,
"No, I won't let you loose —
unless you bring me into abundance!"

And he said to him,
"What's your name?"

And he said,
"Jacob!"

And he said,
"Not Jacob!
Your name won't be called that anymore —
instead — On-Top-of-God! —
because you've been topping God-or-the-gods-and-goddesses/ELOHIM and people
and have held your own!"

And Jacob asked and said,
"Please tell me your name!"

And he said,
"Why this — why do you ask for my name?!"

And he offered him the abundance of life, right there.

Jacob called out the name of the place,

"Face-of-Divinity/EL!

because I've seen
God-or-gods-and-goddesses/ELOHIM —
faces to faces! —
and my living, breathing body was snatched away —
alive!"

And the sun shone brightly on him
just as he bordercrossed
through Face-of-the-Divinity/EL
and he'd been ribbed — limping because of his thigh
and genitals.

(Note that all of these 'crossings' are the same Hebrew word AYBR that have something to do with Abraham, the wanderer/bordercrosser, and with Samuel and the misfits/prophets on the mountaintops.

There's a lot to say about this pivotal story — and more will soon be said after we stay with the momentum building with this wild plot. For now, know this... the wound Jacob is experiencing hearkens back to Adam's, the first mud-creature of the band of YAH's stories...for the Hebrew word for 'rib' and this kind of limping Jacob is experiencing are rather strangely from the same Hebrew word...TSLAY. It's a wildly strange story, in a wildly strange place with wildly strange actions of a 'divinity or God'/EL — no matter one's religious fascination.)

<Gen 32.33>

And Jacob raised his eyes and saw — uh-oh! —
Esau coming, and with him 400 men!

And he divided up the children...
among Leah,
among Rachel,
and among the two maidslaves.

And he put the maidslaves and their children at the
front of the line

and Leah and her children after them
and Rachel and Joseph after them.

And he crossed over the border/river before them
and bowed down to the ground seven times, the perfect number of times,
until he got closer to his brother.
And Esau — the one known as Gruff-Squeeze! —
Esau ran to him,
to call out to him — to meet him —
and he hugged him —
— and he threw himself on his neck
and kissed him —

— and they wept!

And he raised his eyes
and saw the women and the children
and said,
"Who are these to you?"

And he said,
"The children —
whom God-or-gods-and-goddesses/ELOHIM have bowed in their kindness to me, their inferior —
(they all belong) to your slave — me!"

And the maidslaves and their children —
they got closer and bowed down.

And also Leah and her children —
they got closer and bowed down,
and after that Joseph and Rachel got closer and they bowed down.

And he said,
"Who is this whole camp to you,
everyone I've encountered?"

(Esau seems to be referring to the front-line gifts that he encountered first — the ones Jacob assembled to sweeten Esau's opinion of him. 'Camp' is MCHNH. 'Gift' is MNCHH.)

And (Jacob) said,
"To measure up in my boss' eyes!"

And Esau said,
"I already have so much, my brother!
Have for yourself what's yours!"

And Jacob said,
"Please no! Certainly not!
If I measure up in your eyes,
please take my gift from my hand —
look, my seeing your face is like seeing the face of God-or-gods-and-goddesses/ELOHIM!
Then you'd be pleased with me — and it would satisfy my debt —
please take my abundance
which is being brought here to you
because God-or-the-gods-and-goddesses/ELOHIM
have bowed in their kindness to me, their inferior —
and because I have everything!"

He pecked at him so stubbornly, urged him so strongly that he took it.

(This is quite a turn-of-phrase(s) from Jacob...the one who stole the abundance/blessing from their father... and now here he is in some strange way giving it back...but it's over and above the abundance that Isaac offered Jacob — all this wealth that Jacob is giving to Esau was found or made through Jacob's slaving away for Harden-Bricks. And notice the last line — 'because I have everything' — which is to say, it's all mine and mine to give out of God-or-gods-and-goddesses' offering of abundance to him, wrestling match or not. Hmmm....the whole very sticky and tricky business of the 'God-or-the-gods-and-goddesses have bowed in their kindness to me, their inferior'...CHNN...after what just happened back there at the river, the wrestling match. This is some serious style here in how Jacob is turning-the-phrases...not to mention playing on the town he named Peniel/Face-of-Divinity/PNYAHL and seeing something similar in his long-lost brother whom Jacob describes as seeing 'the face of God-or-gods-and-goddesses'/PNY AHLHYM, ELOHIM being the plural of EL in Peniel.)

And (Esau) said,
"Let's pull up camp and head out! Let's get going!
I'll go over there, opposite you."

(In the ancient world, this would be a way of providing hospitality to this person, by providing the person plenty of space to ensure plenty of room and grass of the rolling-field for their animals munching along the way.)

But he said to him,
"My boss,
know that the children are young and delicate —
the lambs, goats and cattle are nursing —
and knocked around — driven hard one day —
all the lambs and goats will die!
Please, let my boss cross on over
ahead of his slave — me —
and yes, yes I'll move along slowly, gently,
this business and pace of one foot at a time —
right in front of my face —
the pace of the children —
until I arrive with my boss — you! —
in The-Rugged-Land-That-Will-Make-Your-Hair-
Stand-On-End."

And Esau said,
"Please, let me place at your service
some of the people I have with me here!"

And he said,
"Why this?!
How can I measure up in your eyes, my boss?!"

And he returned that day —
Esau did — on the journey to The-Rugged-Land-
That-Will-Make-Your-Hair-Stand-On-End,

and Jacob pulled up camp
and headed out toward Hut
and built himself a house there
and for his livestock —
he made a hut.

That's why the name of the place is called "Hut."

<*Gen 33.18-20*>

<#>

(Time passes, everyone gets older.)

And Dinah...Justice —

she was Leah's daughter,
(Leah) gave birth to her for Jacob —

she was out and about seeing some daughters of the land/neighborhood.

And Early-and-Eager saw her —

he's the son of Male-Ass, one of the villagers,
mayor of the land.

And he took her and slept with her
— he humiliated and raped her!

And his living, breathing body clung
to Dinah...Justice, Jacob's daughter.

He loved the girl,
and he styled it out to the girl's heart.

And Early-and-Eager said to his father Male-Ass,
"Get for me that young child to be my wife!"

(Notice that what was awful in itself is getting more awful by the minute...she's not a 'young woman' but a 'young child'....)

And Jacob had heard
that someone had defiled and made value-less his daughter Justice...Dinah.

And his sons were out with his livestock
in the rolling-field —

Jacob kept silent — didn't speak a single word — until they arrived.

And Male-Ass, Early-and-Eager's father, went out to Jacob to style it out with him.

And Jacob's sons came in from the rolling-field when they heard —

the men were outraged

and got all hot-and-bothered angry with them —

so very much so! —

because such a foolish thing had been done in On-Top-of-God's land —

to sleep with Jacob's daughter
and not make it right.

And Male-Ass styled it out with them, saying
"My son Early-and-Eager delights in — has fallen in love with —
the living, breathing body of your daughter —
please give her to him as a wife —
let's make alliances-through-marriages together —
give your daughters to us

and take our daughters for yourselves!
With us you'll live —
the land'll be right there
in front of your face — yours!
Live in it and travel-and-trade in it!
Grab it for yourselves!"

And Early-and-Eager said to her father and her brothers,
"Let me measure up in your eyes!
Whatever you all say to me, I'll give it!
Increase the bridal price and gift you'll ask of me —
much greater! —
and I'll give you whatever you all say to me —
but give me the girl to be my wife!"

And Jacob's sons answered Early-and-Eager and his father Male-Ass deceitfully, falsely —

and they styled it out because he'd defiled and made value-less their sister Justice...Dinah,
and they said to them,
"We can't do this thing, this style (you've styled out) —
to give our sister to a man with an uncut-dick —
that's a total disgrace to us — as if you were stripping us as you'd strip a bride!

But in this we'll consent with you —
if you become like us —
if you cut the foreskin from the dick of every male —
then we'll give our daughters to you
and your daughters we'll take for ourselves —

and we'll live with you
and become one people — one nation!

But if you don't listen to us — to cut the foreskin from yourselves —
we take our daughter and go!"

And their stylings-on were good in the eyes
of Male-Ass and Early-and-Eager, son of Male-Ass.

And the boy didn't delay to make good on the style
because he desired Jacob's daughter.

And he was more weighty —

more of a burden?
more honorable?
or more serious?? —

than everyone else of his father's house/family.

So Male-Ass and his son Early-and-Eager entered into—went to the city-gate
and styled it out with the people of their city, saying
"These people are at peace and whole with us!
They'll be living in the land
and traveling-and-trading in it!

The land — hear this! — it's a big one — an enlarging hand/penis for their faces!

And as for their daughters — we'll take them for ourselves as wives
and our daughters we'll give to them!

Only in this will they consent with us — the people — the men —
to live with us —

to be one people, one nation —
by cutting the foreskin from every male among us
just as they've cut the foreskins from all of their dicks —
their cattle and their property and all of their animals
wouldn't be ours in this way —
unless we consent with them and they live with us!"

(Notice their style...bringing up the very thing they'll need to cut — sharing the land — long before the big-ask of every citizen's member...)

And they listened to Male-Ass and his son Early-and-Eager —
every one going out the gate of his city —
every male cut the foreskin from his dick —
every one going out the gate of his city.

(Ancient comedy here...just as a head of an uncircumcised penis goes out of its foreskin when excited...so too did every male go out the gate of the city to be circumcised...and thus the need for the band of YAH to repeat it twice...and some would argue I dimmed down the verb 'going out'/YTSAH... as YTSAH can sometimes mean 'spring forth' or 'shoot out from'...as penises sometimes do too.)

And so it was —
on the third day
when they were sore and in pain —
two of Jacob's sons —
Listening and He's-Attached, Justice's brothers —

each one with his sword —
they entered—went into the city boldly, as if they were trusted,
and killed every male.

And as for Male-Ass and his son Early-and-Eager —
they killed them with the edge of the sword.

And they took Justice...Dinah from Early-and-Eager's house and went out.

And Jacob's sons entered into — went up to — those who'd been pierced and killed,
and they plundered the city — took everything valuable as in war —
because they'd defiled their sister, made her become someone without value.

Their sheep and their cattle and their asses (donkeys)
and whatever was in the city
and whatever was in the rolling-field
— they took —

and whatever made them strong and wealthy
and all their little children and their wives
— they captured —

and they robbed even everything
that was in their houses.

And Jacob said to Listening and He's-Attached,
"You've stirred up trouble for me —
by making me smell bad — be considered immoral —
to anyone living in the land!
To the Humble-Traders!

To anyone living in the open-country, the tiny villages!
I — I count as only a few people —
they could unite against me —
they could attack and kill me —
and I'd be destroyed —
me and my house/family!"

And they said,
"Like a whore —
is that how he should treat our sister?!"

<Gen 35: 1-16b>

commentary

The Tricky, All-Important Stories of Gen 32 - 34

YAHWEH Wrestling with Jacob, and Dinah's Justice

How did we arrive here?

Jacob had a blow-up confrontation with his father-in-law — a blow-up disguised as Jacob running off without telling his father-in-law — but it appears the real issue is about the missing household-god-statues stolen by Rachel. Harden-Bricks even foreshadows a potential confrontation with a random-dude/god in his stylishly-stern rebuke to Jacob..."Now you play the fool in what you're doing — it's in the gods' hand/penis/phallic-power to do you all some harm!"

Talk about getting ribbed!

Jacob sends a message to his brother Esau with an announcement of a bribe, but the message back is that Esau's coming with 400 men — probably not a welcoming party!

And this whole scene happens in a wild, wild place — a place that echoes Esau's nickname 'Red'

and that must have been quite spooky...Seir...The-Rugged-Land-That-Will-Make-Your-Hair-Stand-On-End...the wild land where the wind gets crazy, whirlwinds...

the land of strange god-like beasts — fauns and satyrs (notice the sound-similarity in Seir and satyr...say them both out loud...it's no coincidence) — godly beasts that come out of nowhere as friend or foe or not-so-sure, where you're not sure you're imagining them, especially in all the wildly erupting weather conditions.

It's a land that induces tremendous fear, terror.

And Jacob panics and prays and reminds YAHWEH of Its promises that everything would be fine — and then divides up everything so that something would survive Esau's anticipated aggression against the first of Esau's gang he might encounter.

Jacob crosses the river at a spooky-named place — YBQ/'to devastate, to demoralize, to pour out, to take over in some wild and uncontrollable way.' Perhaps this crossing point was quite calm and then flooded very, very quickly...much like many creeks do in a quick storm in my own neighborhood. A babbling little brook can become a place of death in minutes...the water just before was at one's ankles and as a heavy rain comes and drains into the creek and sweeps away anyone in its path, or at least knocks down anyone in its path, knocked out cold on a rock, drowning anyone in even a few inches of water. A river-crossing is a scary thing...

in Jacob's situation, especially so with all the animals, with wives and small children...precious cargo.

Note too the playfulness of 'Jacob'/YAYQB at the 'Jabbok'/YBQ. And what do Jacob and this unnamed person do? They 'wrestle'/AHBQ.

And remember where he is — the land of whirlwinds, of unexpected terror-inducing, adrenaline-rushing possibilities. For thrill-seekers, it would be an incredible place. For someone relocating their family — and heading to re-meet a brother who last time you saw him had plans to kill you — imagine the terror within Jacob!

And there he is all alone one night — his family seemingly safe on the other side of the river — when out of nowhere a man starts AHBQ-ing with him. Scholars don't know for sure what this verb means — but it certainly calls to mind the river-crossing, the YBQ. In Hebrew morphology, even more so. AHBQ is used as a verb only in this story, only once in the entire Hebrew Bible. AHBQ is used as a noun six times in the Hebrew Bible — meaning 'dust or powder' — and often in some explosive kind of way. For instance, in Exodus, it's the word used to describe the dust that will land on the Egyptian people and create boils, one of the terror-inspiring, superpower-economy-wrecking plagues.

So I have translated the verb AHBQ as 'he kicked up the dust and wrestled with him — devastated and demoralized him' circling the meaning back to the name for the river-crossing, Devastate-and-Demoralize. It's no irony that the band of YAH has these two words YBQ and AHBQ in such close proximity in their story.

And this random man wrestling Jacob does something that might bother a lot of us —

when he sees
that he will lose the wrestling match with Jacob,
he gropes the hollow of Jacob's thigh and genitals.

Why 'gropes'? The verb NGAY is not a very nice 'touch.'

So far in Genesis the verb NGAY has been used by the band of YAH in the Eden story (grabbing fruit from the Tree of Knowledge) and in Jacob's dream story (the ramp scraped the solid-sky — it was that high!). NGAY is always used in some kind of unwanted or quick, violent way.

And where does this random man NGAY Jacob? In the CP YRC. YRC is the place that Abraham had his slave slip his hand and swear an oath about not marrying his son Isaac to a Humble-Trader / Canaanite. While YRC can mean 'thigh' it's often used in Hebrew idioms to mean 'the place from which your seed/descendants emerged.' Check out Genesis 46.26 and Exodus 1.5 to confirm that idiom.

Strong's Exhaustive Concordance even notes that the fleshiness of the word YRC implied genitals, often in Hebrew idiom as a euphemism — perhaps as we might say 'crotch' in English to avoid the embarrassment among polite company of having to say out loud 'penis/vagina' (biological names) or 'dick/pussy' (slang names)... or in mixed company when the biological names or 'genitalia' might sound silly to some or the slang names too much for another portion of the audience.

And as for CP, that's usually used for 'palm' as in 'the palm of his hand.' It can also mean 'hollow.' CP's origin is in CPP 'to bend'...relating to hand as in a hand's ability to cup, to grasp, to hold.

Adding all of this together, this passage is ripe with pun-possibilities...

the random man groped Jacob's

crotch at his/its bend

thigh where it bends

fleshy-thigh where it bends

cup of his legs

hollow of his fleshy-thigh

...and the possibilities don't end there!

Most Hebrew Bible translators opt for something like 'thigh where it bends' — some make the leap to 'the hip-socket'...often much influenced by the last line of the chapter (32.33) about Hebrews not eating this piece of animals in honor of Jacob...this line which was almost surely an addition by the Levitical priestly editors, perhaps to cover-up the queer nature of this story with their priestly-rush to interpret things to their advantage, through their priestly-lens.

Wait — what?!

The plot/meaning in the 'original' Hebrew text is

purposely vague and makes you want to know what happens next. You and I can playfully imagine the responses spilling out of ancient hearers to the story —

"Wait — what are you meaning here? Did the random dude grope Jacob's leg? his ass? his dick? his hip? And why? What was his purpose? Was it just what happens in wrestling matches — all that very close touching? Was it a punch to the balls to debilitate him? The story did say that the random dude felt he couldn't prevail over him and then he NGAY'd Jacob —"

NGAY could be 'to hit, to strike' — that's NGAY's most common use. NGAY could take on such possibilities as 'smack.' As *Strong's Exhaustive Concordance* notes as well, NGAY also is a euphemism for sex...'to lie with a woman.'

Is your head spinning yet?

And the band of YAH just continues on with their story, building momentum to a climax that defines not just Jacob but an entire people.

So this random man sees that he won't be able to prevail over Jacob in this random wrestling match — and that's the moment when he gropes his thigh and genitals/crotch or ass or balls, with that 'to lie as with a woman' reference. And no matter whatever possibilities we go with, the next lines of the story clarify quite a bit:

The random man NGAY's Jacob's thigh/genitals/ass so much so that Jacob's thigh/genitals/ass was TQAY'd in his kicking up dust and wrestling with him — devastating and demoralizing him.

TQAY...its thrust in the story

Brown-Driver-Briggs and others take TQAY back to its derivative-form YQAY.

What does TQAY via YQAY mean?

It is used only 8 times in the whole Hebrew Bible — including once in this Jacob story:

in Numbers 25.4 YAHWEH orders the execution/YQAY of the leaders in broad daylight for their having sex with the Moabite women during the Baal rituals

in 2 Samuel 21.6 in a conversation with King David, the Gibeonites calling for the execution/YQAY of seven Israelites, as atonement for Saul's killing Gibeonites a generation earlier

in 2 Samuel 21.9
in the actual execution/YQAY of Saul's family members as atonement

in 2 Samuel 21.13
recalling how Saul and his son Jonathan were executed/YQAY and how their bones had been hanging on a wall

in Jeremiah 6:8
in a poem with Jeremiah warning Jerusalem to take instruction from YAHWEH, with YAHWEH speaking...'otherwise my life-breath YQAY from you, otherwise I make you a horrible waste of a land — not livable!'

in Ezekiel 23.17 & 23.18
in a metaphorical story about two daughters who play the whore and sleep with lovers — illicitly and immorally — and the daughters are seen as unclean for their deeds through that immoral/unclean sex that then YQAYs the daughters from those illicit lovers, and that then YQAYs them from YAHWEH

In the Jeremiah and Ezekiel examples, we must infer a bit that to be without YAHWEH — to be YQAY from YAHWEH — is to be without life. In the prophetic imagination, YAHWEH is often recognized as the very breath of life — all the way back to the Eden story. Perhaps in the Jeremiah and Ezekiel examples, YQAY has to do with putting a wedge between two parties, separating them?

In their uses in Numbers and 2 Samuel, YQAY most certainly has to do with execution — killing someone — wedging the person from their life. *Strong's Exhaustive Concordance* notes that this usage of YQAY means "to impale (and thus allow to drop to pieces by rotting)."

Could it be as simple as YQAY having to do with stabbing or penetrating someone with some implement that drains them of their life?

TQAY is its own word in Hebrew too, 'apart' from YQAY

Rather curiously to me, TQAY has its own entry in Holladay's lexicon and in Brown-Driver-Briggs (entry #8628).

It's interesting to me to note that *Strong's Exhaustive*

Concordance and the lexicons by Brown-Driver-Briggs and Holladay make no connection morphologically between YQAY and its close relative TQAY, especially when TQAY is a form of YQAY.

As I've mentioned, TQAY is the form we have in this Jacob/random-dude wrestling match story of Genesis 32. But which one?

To clarify my argument here, I'll denote TQAY when it's used as its own separate entry as TQAY/8628...as in Brown-Driver-Brigg's entry #8628. The entry where TQAY is derived from YQAY I'll list as YQAY/TQAY.

Perhaps the seeming gulf between YQAY/TQAY and TQAY/8628 as completely separate entries in these modern scholars' minds reaches back to the decisions of the Masoretes (6th - 10th centuries CE) who took the Hebrew Bible and added vowels — pointed the consonants that were there already. The Masoretes' work narrows the possibilities of meaning with these punny Hebrew words that explode and erupt in ancient imaginations. At times the Masoretes' work obscures the connections between words with the same consonants.

Let's wonder a few brief minutes about the 'separated' TQAY possibilities and see if they clarify something in the YQAY meanings, see if they have any relationship at all....

In 1 Samuel 31.10, TQAY/8628 is the word used to describe what the Philistines did with Saul's dead, headless body once they found it on the battlefield from the previous day's war. The Philistines TQAY his body to the wall. TQAY here, commentators note, has to do with driving a nail through, piercing, impaling. *Strong's Exhaustive Concordance* notes that this TQAY/8628 use of the verb hearkens back to a primitive root 'to clatter' — the reverberating sharp-sound that happens when a trumpet/shofar is blown, when driving in a tent-stake with a hammer or rock, when slapping handcuffs on a slave, when driving a dart or a nail into a wall...here in 1 Samuel 31.10 through a body, as in the case of Saul's headless corpse hanging on the wall. Listen for the clanging and spine-shivering sound...that's what TQAY/8628 seems to imply with whatever its context and situation.

Perhaps TQAY/8628 and YQAY/TQAY both have to do with wedging something, like a knife wedging flesh and separating it from itself or like a knife pinning flesh to a wall or a tree...and with it the violent sound that captures our attention...of metal meeting living-flesh and then thrusting through that flesh to a wooden surface behind it?

With the Jacob story, most translators have opted for YQAY being "dislocated" as in...Jacob's hip-socket was dislocated in his wrestling with the random-dude. It's a possibility, but does it take into account the possibilities of what came before the YQAY...or after it, the surrounding details of the Jacob-wrestling-story? I'm not so sure.

What then to make of TQAY? Is this some kind of ancient Hebrew idiom? Another euphemism?

Could it be that the man 'banged' Jacob — with the sound reference of TQAY/8628? That would play on not only the possible Hebrew idiom/euphemism but also our 21st century English one too. Sex — hard, passionate, penetrative sex between people of any genders — has a particular noise to it, right?

Maybe our 'he nailed him' or 'he got him good' work here?

Even though Jacob clearly lives after the wrestling-match, could it be that the man 'killed' Jacob or 'destroyed' Jacob — as with the YQAY/TQAY uses in Numbers and 2 Samuel above? A "little death" as an older English expression goes for ejaculation and the need for the ejaculator to sleep/rest afterwards?

Or is TQAY in the story quite literally that the random-dude pierced or penetrated Jacob? Could it be, uh, that simple, that clear? Oh my....

It doesn't sound like a knife or any kind of weapon is involved.

It's hard to know, yes?

...it's hard...and in wrestling matches, sometimes it gets hard in all that rolling around on one another.

Perhaps if we continue with the story we'll be granted more clues....

One thing to note in the wrestling-story as the dialogue continues between the random man and Jacob is that we don't know for sure who is talking until Jacob tells the man his name — kind of like a good playground wrestling match where dust is getting kicked up everywhere and we can't identify who is who as they toss and tumble upon one another — good storytelling!

So the random-dude won't identify himself and demands that Jacob identify himself, tell him his name. And that's where we can then figure out who is on top now — Jacob has the upper hand, even with whatever happened earlier to his thigh/genitals/ass. Jacob climbed on top, even in his wounded state.

And not only that, in order to let this random-dude loose, Jacob demands this random-dude bless him, bring him into abundance — the very thing Jacob's father had done for Jacob in Jacob's tricky-heel-holding ways of stealing the blessing/abundance from his older brother Esau.

Does Jacob have a sense of who it is he's wrestling? of who it is who cheap-shotted him in the thigh/genitals/ass? of who did even way more than that — TQAY! — huh?

Is that why Jacob demands a blessing, demands to be brought into abundance? Because he figures out whom it is he's wrestling?

And of course, the random man says Jacob would not be called that anymore — no more Jacob. Instead... Jacob will be called Israel!

And that name confirms who it is that Jacob has been wrestling. Israel means 'On-Top-of-God'...even has his grandmother Sarah's name in there, or at least from the same root SRH...'to top, to be in charge, to have prevailed over other people with your power and the respect that follows such displays of power.'

Jacob gets on top...

No matter what's happened to Jacob in the wrestling match before he flipped the situation, Jacob now has his wrestling partner down on the ground, Jacob is now on top, and now has a new name...'On-Top-of-God.'

And the random-dude even clarifies..."you're On-Top-of-God because you've been topping the-gods-and-goddesses and people and have held your own!"

Note how that line of the story clarifies the meaning of 'Israel'...which could be read either as "God-on-Top' or as 'On-Top-of-God.'

Jacob, On-Top-of-God, is here on top of God.

Notice how much we miss in the story when we simply translate the line "you're Israel because you've been wrestling divinities and humans and held your own!" There's a beauty and cleverness to the Ancient Hebrew that just does not come through so easily in most English translations.

Back to the story...Jacob gets worried about something, this name is quite a big deal, and quite queer. He wants to know for sure the identity of this random-dude he's been wrestling. Jacob demands his name and the random-dude refuses again. But the random-dude does offer him all of life's abundance right then and there and then seems to disappear, like the wind.

And Jacob realizes that he has not only wrestled the-gods-and-goddesses in this scary area of Seir, he's won! He topped God!

Should Jacob have anything to worry about facing his embittered brother Esau? Of course not! But like any human, Jacob does worry and shortly after beating 'God' in the wrestling match Jacob continues on with his plans to bribe Esau herd by herd and hide himself and his more cherished wife in the rear...all the while limping on that cheap-shotted 'leg' of his.

Prophets discover G/god in their ecstasy

Jacob celebrates quickly by naming the area where he was Face-of-Divinity and finds the place and the experience he just had to be remarkable like any ancient person would. Why? Because there was a superstition that to see a god(dess) face to face meant you were dead or that you'd soon be dead.

But Jacob sees a god(dess) face to face and lives.

And this is key in the prophetic tradition, a true challenge to the inherited Babylonian/Sumerian ways and superstitions and even the later Levitical priestly-editor superstition that only allows Moses to see ELOHIM's/God's backside.

But the prophets and their ecstatic/prophetic-imagination experience their ELOHIM named YAHWEH in a much different way...

in 1 Samuel, YAHWEH reveals Itself to Samuel and

does so in a rather queer way...YAHWEH strips naked before Samuel as slaves or exiles are forced to strip before their captors. GLH means 'to strip.'

Yes. You read that right.

YAHWEH allows YAHWEH's self to be captured by the prophets — really, by anyone and everyone who is alive. And this capturing is enough to make any of us ecstatic, wouldn't you say?

(Remember...'ecstatic' is the better translation of the Hebrew NBYAH which gets translated as 'prophet.')

In 1 Samuel, after all, YAHWEH is the storm-god *par excellence*, the wind, the breath of life, what enters into oneself when one inhales, breathes. Later in the Jewish and Christian traditions, people grow their conception of YAHWEH-as-divinity into the 'holy wind' or 'spirit of holiness' or 'Holy Spirit.'

YAHWEH as the wind, the essence of life, as the birther of ecstatics/prophets...take that in for a moment.

The wind penetrates you and me, yes?

The wind allows you and me to capture It, to hold It within oneself, even for a few seconds.

This puts 1 Samuel's imagination into a bit of context, yes? With YAHWEH stripping Itself before the prophets and allowing Itself to be captured?

Are you getting it? <u>It</u>? I sure hope so, if you want to live!

YAHWEH and the wily wind

Bring that idea of YAHWEH-as-the-wind from 1 Samuel into what we know about YAHWEH within Genesis, within the band of YAH's stories. In their stories, YAHWEH walks through the Pleasure-Orchard/Eden... in the day's breeze, we're told. YAHWEH has emotions like human beings...confusion, anger, sadness, rage, compassion, desire. YAHWEH sits down and eats with Abraham, even mocks Sarah for laughing at Its promise that soon she'll have a child...even in her old age. YAHWEH is ephemeral, shows up in dreams (Jacob, later his son Joseph) and visions (Abraham) and then disappears. Like the wind.

Jacob had a wild dream one night as he was first fleeing from the brother who wanted to kill him for stealing the birthright and blessing from their father. Remember the dream? The ramp from solid-ground to solid-sky, and all of these gods and goddesses going up and down the ramp...moving from the heavens to the earth, visiting human beings and mixing with them. And who was on top of the ramp, on top of these gods and goddesses?

Not EL...as anyone in the ancient world of Canaan would assume.

Not IL...as anyone in the ancient region of Babylon/ Mesopotamia would assume.

Not BAAL — the hot new(ish) super-god of Canaan.

Not ASHTAROTH — another hot new(ish) super-goddess of Canaan probably remade from ISHTAR of nearby Babylon (from which we get Easter = ISHTAR = ASHTAROTH).

Not Marduk — the hot new(ish) super-god of Babylon.

In Jacob's dream, it was YAHWEH on top of the gods and goddesses, on top of the ramp that extended down to Jacob there asleep on the ground.

And now in this scary place of Seir, in the scary moment of his last-time-I-saw-him-he-wanted-to-kill-me brother coming at him with 400 men, Jacob wrestles some god, gets cheap-shotted in some wild way, regains his composure, and climbs on top of the god to become Israel.

And the peoples of the world will find their border crossing identity in his name, in this wild moment — like his parents and grandparents before him, Jacob/Israel will give birth to enough seed/descendants as there is sand at the seashore.

Imagine it!

But that limp after Jacob got cheap-shotted? Ummm....

What did happen there? In that wild moment? Was his hip simply dislocated and he limped on?

Well...the next lines of the Jacob story reveal a lot.

Jacob's thigh/genitals had been TSLAY.

What's TSLAY? Used only three other times in the

Hebrew Bible, it's often translated as 'limped' or 'lame.' Twice in Micah (4.6 & 4.7) and once in Zephaniah 3.19.

Yet we have encountered the same combination of consonants in the band of YAH's stories...back in the Eden story, in the Pleasure-Orchard. YAHWEH puts the mud-creature into a deep, trance-like sleep and reaches into the mud-creature's side and pulls out a TSLAY while the mud-creature is sleeping and crafts Woman from what he pulls from the mud-creature.

TSLAY is, of course, 'rib.' When we breathe in, our ribs move, yes? Watch any person when they breathe and it's quite obvious. The ancients of course knew nothing of oxygen and carbon dioxide and all of that when a human breathes...but they surely knew that to cover someone's mouth and nose for long would kill the person. Breathe out onto your hand and it feels kind of like the wind, right? In the Eden story, YAHWEH breathes the breath of life into the mud-creature and the mud-creature becomes a living being in its own right — mud-with-breath differentiated from the mud itself and differentiated from YAHWEH-alone-as-breath-alone, mud-with-breath alive with the air where those ribs move to guarantee life. And YAHWEH crafts WOMAN from mud-creature's rib?!

That Eden story is a strange, strange thing, yes?

Why did YAHWEH expect or hope that the mud-creature would be friends with and find a companion through the animals and birds alone?

The mud-creature did not, of course, find its companion among the animals — no matter how fun the name-gaming process was.

Woman is created as an after-thought in the story, as if YAHWEH were afraid that It would have to create her. Maybe Mud-Creature will be content with animals and live on in Eden/Pleasure forever as YAHWEH's own playmate, perhaps the character-YAHWEH wonders in the story.

And this Woman is the first to disobey the orders, gets enticed to eat from the Knowing-Tree by a slippery snake, a god-like creature to most ancient people. And what do you know? Boom — she and the mud-creature gain insight by breaking the rules, violating orders — they know that they are naked, and they immediately cover themselves up, they hide from each other, at least out in the open air, by fashioning clothes for themselves. And when they hear YAHWEH walking in and with the wind through the garden, they hide themselves from YAHWEH. The form of the verb there is YTCHBAH, from CHBAH...'to hide oneself, usually inside something.' *Strong's Exhaustive Concordance* makes the point that the primitive root of CHBAH was 'to secrete, as in to do something secretly'... and *Strong's* notes this very interesting connection with CHBB 'to love,' as in hiding within someone, in their bosom, to cherish someone in such an embrace.

Mud-Creature and Woman hide themselves in one another, in the midst of the trees of the orchard, the Pleasure-Orchard. That is to say, they were hiding their love-making, as people who 'know' do and must, usually, to fit into society so that they do not feel shame in their nakedness and in their passionate, unabashed affection for another person.

Children do not hide their affection for people, their

simple and age-appropriate ways of sharing their love. They kiss the cheeks of those they love sloppily. They embrace whomever they please as often as they please. Such unabashed love gets socialized out of us. Some day as puberty begins to awaken within humans, some of us seek/sought places where we could explore again such unabashed affection — either by oneself or with another person. Love by touch must be hidden by those who 'know' and by those who awaken to society's mores, society's morals and customs and ways of being, ways of fitting in.

On nakedness and hiding

I remember being at the pool when I was a child and watching a three or four year old escape from his mom as she was putting on his swimsuit. He ran around so freely in the sun and water — much to the embarrassment of his mom. Just a year or two later someone would give the same kid a droopy — pull his suit down when he was on the pool deck to reveal his nakedness — and the kid would howl at the embarrassment. What happened in that year or two between nakedly running around so freely and then being denuded by a peer? When does the shame creep in and from where?

It's not like the kid's genitalia had changed — at least not that much — between age three and age five. But the kid had changed, or been changed. The kid became aware of his nakedness, that it was somehow bad or wrong to be naked in public. Somehow, the only slightly older kid was awakening to what nearly everyone else thought was wrong. Through the experiences of life, the slightly older kid was eating from the Knowing-Tree.

Returning to the plot of the Eden story...just after hiding themselves in each other among the trees of the Pleasure-Orchard, YAHWEH calls for Mud-Creature and can't find him.

Eventually Mud-Creature fesses up that he "had been afraid because I was naked, so I hid." YAHWEH figures out that Mud-Creature must have eaten from the Knowing-Tree — after all, it's the only way to <u>know</u> in the story, at least so far — and accuses Mud-Creature of doing such a thing for which Mud-Creature then conveniently passes the blame onto Woman who gave him the fruit. Very clearly, the Mud-Creature had been right there as Woman chatted up Snake...and Mud-Creature had nothing to say about any of it. Mud-Creature let Woman be his 'front...his talker.'

They <u>knew</u> they were naked, and then they <u>knew</u> one another by hiding and making love.

Perhaps, before they ate from the Knowing-Tree, Woman and Mud-Creature had been like that little three or four year old kid at the pool — they could care less that they were naked. But after knowing by eating and then knowing by love-making, they must hide themselves from YAHWEH and they must wear clothes out of their shame, their embarrassment for the tremendous pleasure they must have found as new lovers hiding themselves, discovering themselves, discovering all that Pleasure offers them in participating together in their love-making.

And YAHWEH blows a gasket — first curses Snake, then Woman, and then Mud-Creature.

YAHWEH wanted to 'hide' inside Adam, the Mud-Creature?

Before Woman was created out of Mud-Creature's rib, what was YAHWEH's intention, do you think? Was YAHWEH hoping that Mud-Creature would be YAHWEH's companion? Was YAHWEH hoping for sex — for YTCHBAH — for hiding within Mud-Creature as Mud-Creature and Woman were doing there in the Pleasure-Orchard?

Wasn't YAHWEH doing that already? YAHWEH blew the breath of life into Mud-Creature? That's YAHWEH's way of love-making, right? At least until YAHWEH discovered It wanted more with Jacob.

Could that be what's happening here with the Abraham-Isaac-Jacob trilogy, the growing desire YAHWEH has for wanting to be inside of, making love with, humans?

Even Noah seems to have been trance-inducingly beautiful — talk about tranquilizing!

When YAHWEH chooses Abraham and entices him to leave the Scorched-and-Glowing-Land where the metropolis-life is hot-hot-hot! — one of the most fertile regions of the whole land, the whole known Mediterranean world — Abram/Abraham already has a companion, Sarai/Sarah. And she's quite the wife — On-Top and only growing in that direction...eventually becoming Clearly-On-Top.

She's so in-charge and on-top that she has the guts to laugh when the unusual visitor promises she'll be pregnant — even in her old age. Only then, perhaps, does she discover that she just laughed in YAHWEH's face — not just some random visitor for whom she and her old husband had been showing the expected hospitality of the bordercrossing region.

And what does Abraham think the-gods-and-goddesses is requesting he do with that son of Sarah's loins? Kill him! Drive a knife into his young flesh.

And Abraham is about to do just that until the-gods-and-goddesses' ambassador/message-runner tells him not to do such a thing and explains that YAHWEH now knows how faithful and trustworthy Abraham is. It's a rather odd story — and disturbing. Knowing that the other gods and goddesses of the region sometimes requested child sacrifice — as the prophets and the writer of 1 & 2 Kings note — might help us modern readers who (hopefully) cannot conceive of such a horrible practice. Imagine the trauma of young Isaac!

And later we have Isaac's son Jacob and YAHWEH (or a god) wrestling Jacob out of nowhere, in a land known for being devastated and demoralized. And YAHWEH gropes Jacob's flesh — his thighs and genitals. And all of a sudden, YAHWEH seems to penetrate Jacob! So much so that Jacob limps the next day.

Jacob had been ribbed — like Mud-Creature/Adam had been 'ribbed' to create Woman.

I'm not the first person to put all of this together. Biblical scholar Ted Jennings has much to say about this in his book *Jacob's Wound*. It's his book that made me revisit my 2017 translation of the band of YAH's stories in Genesis. Twice.

And the more I work with and listen long and play with these stories, the wilder they get. And the more I listen, I notice the band of YAH's stories are in conversation with 1 & 2 Samuel and 1 & 2 Kings...these stories about the prophets/ecstatics finding their free way with YAHWEH in a world that continually chooses domination governmentally, religiously, in a world that continually chooses shame within oneself and inflicting it on others, in a world that does not choose YAHWEH — unless the prophets/ecstatics can awaken a few people to stray toward their cause and away from the empire's grasp. These prophets/ecstatics were misfits on the mountaintops of Israel/Palestine, naked on the mountain and feeling no shame as YAHWEH strips Itself of Its clothes and allows Itself to be captured by penetrating us humans.

Ecstasy.

An ecstatic is one who feels no shame anymore at society's cruel, shame-driven mores and customs that ignore YAHWEH's way — of allowing Itself to be captured.

Inspiration. Allowing spirit-breath-wind (all the same word in the ancient imagination) to enter in.

Ecstasy. Inspiration. Ecstasy. Inspiration.

No wonder these poems of the prophets/ecstatics come to them — as if out of the wind! — and then must be delivered, shared. The prophetic poems are bustling with life — there's no containing them! Not even on pain of death will a decent prophet inspired by YAHWEH ever stop...as death comes for all too many of the prophets at the hands of society's shameful ways.

There's a huge difference between creating a thrill and letting a thrill like the wind (YAHWEH) arrive on Its own. Some day we might realize that the thrill is more like the atmosphere than the wind that feels like it comes and goes but is indeed constant...we're all living in an ocean of continuous waves of wind. THE ALL. And sitting on top of a mountain in the middle of nowhere only helps us to know even better the nature of the wind, of YAHWEH.

And what a wild group of people to first notice It!

The prophets/ecstatics were society's drop-outs. They were the ones who left civilized society, they were the ones who left the comfort of towns and governments for a wilder, more nomadic life — a life of following the breeze and wherever the breeze led them.

In X's saga, the prophets are sometimes referred to as 'boys' — another word for 'slaves' in the ancient world. 'Boys' is not to say they were all male or of a certain age. Again, 99 girls with 1 boy and the whole group of them gets called 'boys' in ancient Hebrew grammar. In the Jim Crow South in my own country, someone would call a black man of any age 'boy' to demean that person, to put them under the name-caller. These, of course, are two hierarchically-motivated moves meant to preserve pecking-orders.

Second Isaiah offers images of YAHWEH as woman, as mother — the Creator of the world! Talk about standing out with such a statement by this prophet that scholars are fairly sure was a woman and some consider the greatest poem-crafter of the Hebrew Bible.

Maybe gender had no importance to prophets. After all, YAHWEH penetrates all.

The prophets/ecstatics were the ones who could find comfort anywhere, comfort in the breeze alone. And they came to identify that wanderlust with the breeze as their unpredictable god/goddess...as the ground of their being...as YAHWEH, the Hebrew word for 'being.'

On the future of prophets who welcome sex with YAHWEH

Who else will drop out of society — swim away from "the shipwreck" that is empire and society, as Merton so cleverly says — to instead know YAHWEH as YAHWEH chooses to be known, to allow YAHWEH to penetrate you, wrap Itself around you, wrestle you into life, soothe you from the inside out?

That's the biblical invitation, after all. At least the one offered by the bands of YAH and X (the author of 1 & 2 Samuel and portions of 1 & 2 Kings) and all these poets that we list in Bibles as 'prophets' — those who had an ecstatic style to their words. Rarely do the biblical prophets speak in prose. They speak in pun, in metaphor, in riddle, with music and without — sometimes just the sound of the quietest wind as Elijah discovered.

How did that style arrive? Ecstatic inspiration.

What if YAHWEH indeed had anal-sex with our character Jacob? Would that be so embarrassing?

If Jacob hadn't allowed it — yes!

But Jacob seems a willing participant in the wrestling match, even if he's surprised by It.

Indeed, if we want to live, we'd better participate in the wrestling match with YAHWEH.

Breathe in and live. Stop your breathing for long, and you die.

YAHWEH's promise to every generation of prophets/ breathers

What was YAHWEH's promise to Abraham and Isaac and Jacob? That they'd have so many seeds/descendants as the stars in the sky, as the sands in the seashore.

Usually, such descendants come from a man planting a seed inside a woman — hiding something of himself inside and with the woman, his wife. The ancients probably knew nothing of the sperm-and-egg idea that we have in the 21st century. The ancients knew that when a man planted his seed inside a woman, often a a child would grow there...that's how descendants came to be.

But here, in a scary little place where the wind was known to howl — even into whirlwinds — a deity penetrates the hollow-hole of a man and gives him a new name that will be the name of the whole people borne through him, through Jacob. Jacob becomes Israel, a father to the children of Israel, perhaps a father to the children of the bordercrossing nomadic prophets/ecstatics who found life in the out-of-the-way places. And how the government and people of Ancient Israel will wrestle its prophets — even kill them when their message takes away from the flag of their nation, from the palaces and temples where special people high up on the hierarchy and where ritual maintains the hierarchical order of state and organized religion. Indeed, state and religion become one and the same unless you give yourself over to something that cannot be contained or ritualized — something like the wind. I often marvel at the flag of my own country being so proudly displayed in churches or any religious institution — even more surprised when hymns to the nation are sung within their walls.

But as I've pointed out, state and religion are often intertwined...especially of they both have hierarchical assumptions.

And how my own nation of the United States of America cannot bear the poems of the prophets — especially the prophets of the 20th and 21st centuries. For centuries, they/we could not bear homosexuality either.

In Ancient Israel/Palestine, the prophets/ecstatics and homosexuality — or at least same-sex love and multi-gender love and genderbending — went hand in hand.

In the Eden story we see a playful inkling of this genderbending...Woman is born from man, the mud-creature having been ribbed by YAHWEH. Mud-Creature even proudly proclaims that Woman is "bone of my bone, flesh of my flesh." And Woman gives birth to Wisdom, to human-knowing, by violating what the-gods-and-goddesses ordained as right and just. And just like the hissing Snake said, Woman and Mud-Creature became just like the gods-and-goddesses in their knowing good from bad...no matter how much the priestly editors and later commentators want to make the Snake look evil (as we'll soon see).

And after generations of lustfully admiring mud-creatures/humans, YAHWEH plants Its seed inside Jacob — inside the hollow of Jacob's fleshy legs and inside each one of us (breathe!) — and through anyone who notices such a planting of that life-seed within, anyone who listens to their breathing, to being breathed, wisdom coming, entering in. How many meditators — famous like Gautama/Buddha or not-so-famous like the person teaching up the street at the local studio — how many of us know such a thing as wisdom for how to live coming from noticing the very movement of life...breathing...being penetrated by the spirit-wind-breath...breath that creates a vibration within oneself and around oneself.

YAHWEH — the wind — penetrates us all into life!

Remember, these Genesis stories likely come to us from a band of women and genderbenders...the band of YAH... from people who knew the many ways of penetration, especially in their world. A woman was only seen as valuable in the ancient world if she were penetrable and fertile — and note what these storycrafters do with that assumption!

Are you beginning to see and hear and feel within yourself just how clever the band of YAH is in their storytelling?

YAHWEH sexually ravishing Jacob...what a story for the sex-crazed and sex-shamed 21st century world!

And many might say, how very shameful! Even my very-gay and very-religious friends cannot even fathom such a possibility of YAHWEH having sex with Jacob. And how quickly my friends explain away Mary's pregnancy — her own sex with the wind to give birth to Jesus. Such a thing must be hidden, covered over, so many insist. They couldn't have meant that, my friends say.

But it is likely exactly that — YAHWEH's desire to be inside human beings and our very need for it. The Levitical priestly editors who crafted the first-draft of the Torah around the band of YAH's too-wild stories likely added the story of the Nephilim (Genesis 6) — the story of "the children of the-gods-and-goddesses" being aroused by and having sex with the beautiful daughters of human beings and giving birth to "the heroes...the giants of old." And notice where the priestly editors placed that story — right before we get the story of Noah where YAHWEH finds favor with Noah alone... Noah who has some trance-inducing or tranquilizing quality, perhaps because of his beauty! The priestly editors time and time again try to dim down the band of YAH's all too bright vision for life and their ecstatic ways of knowing YAHWEH.

The band of X joins the band of YAH in this bold vision where YAHWEH seems only interested in taking off Its clothes — indeed stripping Itself — whether by sunlight or moonlight, out in the open air, and entering whomever It pleases.

For so long, and certainly now too, men of authority — men who have rank in any kind of hierarchy — often avoid at all costs the sheer embarrassment of being penetrated by another man or of letting other people know they let it be done to them and enjoy it. Thorkil Vanggaard's research here is fascinating in *Phallos: A Symbol and Its History in the Male World*. For many/most men, as this psychiatrist points out, being penetrated is a supreme embarrassment...until they discover how pleasurable it can be. And then they/men crave it — sometimes even from their wives with some kind of creative penetration. A man must give up society's understanding of manhood — ordained through and by the hierarchy — in order to have such unabashed pleasure, to be penetrated as a woman is penetrated. Perhaps the Levitical priests' biggest issue in Leviticus 18 & Leviticus 20 with their death-penalty for men having sex with other men — literally, men lying with other men as if they were women — is that when a man gets penetrated by another man, in the priestly imagination, such men forfeit their place in the hierarchy.

Perhaps in the priestly imagination that crafted the Torah, the issue is two-fold: men having sex with men not only confuses the hierarchy of society, it also reflects the same sexual proclivities as the BAAL-worshippers where every night's orgy with all in the town — young and old, as the Sodom story reminds — included sex with everyone all at once.

But for the prophets/ecstatics it doesn't sound like it's an orgy they are after as much as it is an openness to letting YAHWEH have Its way with them, no matter their gender. And if that ecstasy induced by YAHWEH leads to love-making of a human with a human of whatever gender, what a gift. After all, YAHWEH seems to enjoy it with ALL.

But gender...

And on another important matter, how problematic our gender categories are, how much they limit our possibilities for knowing THE ALL, the 'all possibilities' of an Infinite God. I've been intrigued with watching the excellent film *XXY* and have a whole new imagination for relationship and one without categories/gender.

YAHWEH wants it with you and with me...with all of us, no matter our gender. From a prophet's viewpoint, gender doesn't matter at all — indeed from a prophet's viewpoint, gender is an artifice of the hierarchically-minded. YAHWEH has Its sexy, breathy time with every human being — no matter their gender. Just wait until we get to Jacob's son Joseph!

At times throughout the Bible, YAHWEH seems like a man; at other times, especially as imagined by Second Isaiah, like a woman, a mother; at other times, the binary of 'traditional' gender doesn't seem to make sense for YAHWEH. Indeed, YAHWEH breathes life into and has Its sexy way with every human being — no matter their 'gender.' Perhaps the biblical prophets took that cue and realized that sex with any consenting human being of age was okay — and not only okay but ordained by YAHWEH by example.

Perhaps the prophets were the first imaginers of a genderless or genderfluid world.

Just wait until we begin to explore the genderbending poems of the prophets...Amos, Hosea, the three Isaiahs, Jeremiah, and more in future volumes of *The Naked Path of Prophet*.

Genderbending and bordercrossing as YAHWEH's signature moves

The Ancient Hebrew imagination first imagined by the prophets/ecstatics is a true bordercrossing imagination — an imagination of wandering, clever nomadism that came about as a response to the Ancient Babylonian and Ancient Egyptian hierarchies of power and prestige through building(s) and through land owned and defended by their empire's armies. And how are buildings like theirs built? Through slave-labor and through lower-classes being recruited to labor for the managing upper-classes. It's the whole hierarchical problem that is the inspiration of *The Epic of Gilgamesh*, remember.

But not the prophets! Indeed, the entire biblical imagination that comes to us through the prophets is a borderless enterprise. In 1 Samuel, the biblical band of X has the prophets/ecstatics living right by a Philistine garrison — clearly these prophets were not afraid of the 'enemies' of Ancient Israel. The bands of YAH and X and many of the prophets with their poems recorded in the Bible routinely show that the so-called 'enemies' of Ancient Israel are indeed better, more trusting humans than the so-called followers of ELOHIM/God who claimed themselves as people of the ever-growing empire of Ancient Israel/Ancient Judah.

The greatest of ironies is that eventually some people of Ancient Israel wanted to be like all the other superpowers and adopt the hierarchical mindset and craft a king, a royalty that would unite them and lead them. Under a royal, everyone is a slave. And that's the full message of 1 & 2 Samuel, X's saga. Most cleverly, the band of X points out that the Philistines had a much more nuanced system of government than the superpowers of Ancient Babylon and Ancient Egypt... which is to say that in X's imagination, the Ancient Israelites could have chosen to adopt the Philistine's system or could have followed the prophets' wilder possibilities or could have fallen into the hierarchical default of royal/slave that Ancient Babylon and Ancient Egypt and many more had chosen. And Ancient Israel made its choice — sadly as most of us human beings choose hierarchy over equal relationship. Tragically, some humans have not ever known anything other than that — even with a lover.

The prophets wanted nothing to do with this royal/slave imagination and were content to continue their nomadism, their life close to the ground and the wind, far away from the compulsions of city-life. Sure, they might have had a home somewhere, a basecamp, as we see the character Samuel having. But they moved from place to place as their poetry snatched from the wind — YAHWEH — invited them. We see that in the descriptions of Samuel and Elijah and Elisha; we see that in the lifestyle of Jesus. We see that in Amos (a roaming shepherd), in Jeremiah (a priest not from Jerusalem who spends a lot of time in Jerusalem), much later in Paul (a traveling tent-maker), in so many of the prophets. Such nomadism is not a wanderlust so much as a lust after the wind, a deep love for the wind, for YAHWEH, for Its love and for wherever It takes us.

YAHWEH as genderbending and bordercrossing lover invites us to be penetrated wherever and whenever the wind blows. YAHWEH still wants Its way inside you and encourages a style of loving and a relationship as It pervades you and me and everyone, every living being. It's a 'non-religion' that needs no priest, no creed, no ritual, no cult...a 'binding back' to what always was and is, the wind, breath, being. It's the primal experience of life, that everyone knows and so easily forgets. It can be cultivated with another human being in love, in breathing into one another and with one another — but all the while knowing that it's YAHWEH who directs the dance, the pulse, the wind. It's YAHWEH who penetrates us into life.

And yet we cannot just be YAHWEH going around and penetrating whomever we wish...there's the tragic Dinah story for juxtaposition, surely offered by the band of YAH to show the tragedy of human desire when we do not know the wind, when we are Early-and-Eager, son of an Ass.

With both the Jacob-wrestling-YAHWEH and Dinah stories, we are left with an important insight and understanding...only YAHWEH can have all lovers and can enter anyone without asking.

When I come upon a Bible translation I've not yet encountered before, there are a few stories/sayings I look to form an opinion about its translation. One of those passages is Genesis 32 — 34...how much of the ancient Hebrew does the translation bring forward? how much does it dodge? how much does it try to explain away through what 21st century people think about 'God' and how 'God' should be, and how much of the ancient imagination does the translation allow without closing off too many possibilities?

Ancient Hebrew erupts with possibilities, and so should a good translation.

Being with all the complexities and bizarre possibilities of the Jacob-wrestling-YAHWEH and Dinah stories just might help you and me and all of us to have that experience that Jacob has as he's limping along — the moment or two of peace before his brother shows up...

the sun shining brightly upon him, radiating upon him... and you and me too...all who let the breath come and go...all who find their identity in the One who allows Its capture for life and for love...the One who plants Its life-seed inside each one of us, no matter which orifice...the One who wants us all and desires dearly us all...indeed, all of us living and <u>being</u> within THE ALL...<u>YAHWEH</u>.

Do you dare have an imagination infected by the kiss, the touch, the penetration of YAHWEH?

Let's see how YAHWEH planting Its seed inside Jacob gives birth to a generation of crafty, clever prophets — perhaps even naked ones like we find in the band of X's saga of 1 & 2 Samuel.

Joseph's story is soon coming...the child of Jacob who had the seed of life planted into him by YAHWEH. But first we must encounter a numbskull of a son of Jacob who gets his numbskull ways revealed to him by his daughter-in-law with her crafty, clever imagination...an ecstatic/prophetic-imagination.

Perhaps such an imagination is available to all...not just the children of Israel/Jacob.

ha ha ha

Genesis 38

Throw-Up-Your-Hands/Penis-In-Praise & Erect-Palm-Tree

the interlude story of Judah & Tamar

This story bearing the wily imagination of the band of YAH was wedged into the Joseph-saga by the Levitical priestly editors as an interlude story...I've pulled it out (as you'll soon see, I'm quite punny here) to appreciate it on its own and to see what the Joseph story offers without the interlude. Might we then hear the Judah/Tamar story and the Joseph-saga differently?

<beginning at Gen 38>

And so it was —

at that time Judah...Throw-Up-Your-Hands/Penis-In-Praise went down,
away from his brothers.

And he stretched out and settled near a man from the Retreat-in-the-Hill-Country —
his name was Pale-with-Shame.

And Judah...Throw-Up-Your-Hands/Penis-In-Praise

saw there a daughter of a certain man —
a Humble-Trader — his name was Cry-for-Help.

(Recall how careful Abraham was in ensuring his son not marry a Humble-Trader — not to mention a woman whose father was named "Cry-for-Help"!)

And he took her
and entered into her — had sex with her,
and she became pregnant and gave birth to a son.

(Note again the slang, rough-reference to sex here — 'enter'/BOAH — and not the 'knowing-kind-of-sex'/YDAY. And, um, do we even know her name? We most certainly know his name...and the possibilities for what his name can mean....)

And he called out his name,

"Wake-Up!"

And she became pregnant again
and gave birth to a son.

And she called out his name,

"Vigorous!"

And she added-on again and gave birth to a son.
And she called out his name,

"Ask!"

It was in the Land-of-Liars that she gave birth for him.

(Note how either the Levitical priestly editors who placed this Judah story in the middle of the Joseph-saga or the band of YAH as storycrafters themselves quite cleverly keeps the Judah-story connected with the Joseph/Add-On narrative through the use of the root of Joseph/Add-On's name to help craft the background details of the story...Joseph/<u>YOSP</u> and 'added on'/TSP from <u>YSP</u>.)

And Judah fetched a wife
for Wake-Up, his first-born son,
and her name was Erect-Palm-Tree.

And so it was —

Judah's first-born son Wake-Up was bad in YAHWEH's eyes —
and YAHWEH killed him!

And Judah said to Vigorous,
"<u>Enter into your brother's wife</u> — go have sex with your brother's wife —
and do your duty as brother-in-law
by acting as her husband
(as is customary in the ancient world).
Stand up a seed/descendent for your brother!"

But Vigorous <u>knew</u> that the seed — the descendent — wouldn't be his.

(The verbs here are quite ironic...usually 'knew' is used for having sex but here it's what happens for Vigorous as he thinks about having sex with his dead brother's wife...the custom and expectation of the next son/brother in the ancient world to provide descendant(s) for a childless dead-brother. The band of YAH is quite clever here in their 'style'...the mark of the prophetic imagination with its puns and plays on words to awaken something in the hearer through the style.)

And so it was —

when <u>he entered into his brother's wife</u> — had sex with her —
he wasted it on the ground (that's to say, he pulled out and ejaculated on the ground)
so that he wouldn't give a seed/descendant for his brother.

And he'd acted badly in YAHWEH's eyes by doing what he'd done —
and (YAHWEH) killed him too!

And Judah...Throw-Up-Your-Hands/Penis-In-Praise
said to his daughter-in-law Erect-Palm-Tree,
"Stay as a widow in your father's house
until my son Ask grows up."

You see, he'd said (to himself),
"Otherwise he dies too — he could be just like his brothers!"

And Erect-Palm-Tree left and stayed in her father's house.

And the days were piling up,
and Judah's wife — Cry-for-Help's daughter — died.

And Judah let out a big sigh — was comforted —
and climbed up to shear his lambs and goats —
he and his friend Pale-with-Shame, the guy from
Retreat-in-the-Hill-Country —
toward (the city) Count-It-Up.

(Judah letting out a sigh is a good sign in the ancient world, but note that we do not hear of him mourning his wife...an ancient hearer would probably immediately note that this step was skipped...after all, it was his *wife* who had died! We do not even get a 'many days (of mourning) passed' before Judah is off to adventures/partying. 'Shearing sheep/goats' was like festival-time in the ancient world. Shearing the wool from the animals meant you had something to sell or with which to trade...and plenty of money/liquid-wealth then to spend on whatever caught your eye right then and there....)

And Erect-Palm-Tree was told:
"Listen up,
your father-in-law climbed up to Count-It-Up
to shear his lambs and goats."

And she beheaded — err, put away — her mourning-clothes from on herself,
and plumped herself up — covered herself with a veil,
and wrapped herself up,
and sat over by the entrance to the spring which is on the road to Count-It-Up.

(Talk about words that erupt with multiple meanings... double and triple-entendre...the very linguistic style of the prophets.)

You see, she'd seen that Ask had grown up,
and she hadn't been given to him to be his wife
(as would have been customary in the ancient world).

(Note that she was mourning her two dead husbands longer than Judah has mourned for his wife...she was still wearing her mourning clothes while Judah is off getting ready to party! While maybe this was the expectation in the ancient world — ancient society's way of making it clear that this woman is a widow and not available for marriage — at least not yet — notice how the band of YAH lays these two similar scenarios next to each other: Judah as recent-widower-turned-partier and Tamar/Erect-Palm-Tree as ongoing-widow. How ridiculous the juxtaposition makes ancient society's assumptions seem, especially regarding gender-roles... the band of YAH's exceedingly clever imagination at work/play here.)

And Judah...Throw-Up-Your-Hands/Penis-In-Praise
saw her and figured she was a common-whore, a
prostitute, because she had covered her face

(as common-prostitutes would in that day because they'd been shamed into their role and had no other way to support themselves in the economy except as prostitute)

and he stretched out toward her, by the road,
and said,
"Come on please! I'm going to enter into you — have sex with you!"

(Note that the same word for 'stretching out'/NTH used at the beginning of the Judah story is used here... perhaps this time only something of his anatomy was stretching out....)

You see,
he didn't know that she was his daughter-in-law.

(Instead of 'knowing her' Judah will 'enter into her' because he didn't know her, didn't recognize her.)

And she said,
"What'll you give me to enter into me — have sex with me?"

And he said,
"I myself'll send for a young baby-goat from my lambs and goats."

And she said,
"Only if you give me some collateral until you send for it...!"

And he said,
"What collateral can I give you?"

And she said,
"Your ring that you use to affix your name to make deals
with your one-and-only identification on it
and your specially-twined necklace
and your one-of-a-kind walking stick in your hand."

(Not only do these show Judah's wealth — even before he shears his animals —- these items she asks for from him as collateral very clearly display his identity...like asking for someone's driver's license and a credit card and jewelry engraved with one's initials today.)

And he gave them to her
and entered into her — had sex with her —
and she became pregnant by him.

And she stood up tall
and left
and beheaded — err, put away — her veil
and wore her mourning-clothes that widows wear.

And Judah...Throw-Up-Your-Hands/Penis-In-Praise
sent a young baby-goat by his friend's hand,
the one who lived in Retreat-in-the-Hill-Country,
so that he could take back the collateral from the woman's hand/power.

(The woman has the upper hand here in having control of the collateral...quite an unusual situation by the ancient world's standards...not to mention the woman was a prostitute, or was at least playing one...

not to mention that, as we know, the word for 'hand'/ YD in Hebrew is also a euphemism for 'penis'...in this rather sexy story, a bit of a pun...not to mention too that she stood up tall earlier...she did. This recalls the gender-role-reversal we saw in the Cover-Up/ Lot stories earlier with his daughters and their sexy-time with their father.)

But he couldn't find her.

And he asked around
among the people of the place,
"Where is the special-religious-prostitute?
She was by the spring, over there on the roadside."

And they said,
"There's no special-religious-prostitute here."

(Judah's friend gives the woman a promotion — from 'common-whore'/ZONH to 'special-religious-prostitute'/QDSHH...from the same root-word as 'holy.' In the ancient world, temples to BAAL and to ELOHIM — generations after this tale was first told, even God's temple in Jerusalem — had QDSHH for rent/purchase...prostitutes who could be rented for 'holy sex' dedicated to the god/goddess of the temple...religions of the hierarchical temple-cults. The priestly Jerusalem temple even had male prostitutes/QDSHYM for purchase by their male clientele/worshippers who had come to worship the non-prophetic and ark-based version of YAHWEH pushed forward by the Levitical priests in charge of the temple at that time. See 2 Kings 23 for that story.

Note too that the friend asks-around...and the name of the youngest son whom Judah was trying to protect this whole time: Ask/Shelah.)

And he returned to Judah...Throw-Up-Your-Hands/
Penis-In-Praise and said,
"I didn't find her —
and the people of the place said,
'There's no special-religious-prostitute here.'"

And Judah said,
"She took them (his identification/collateral) for herself —
otherwise we'll be in contempt and despised!
Look, I sent this baby-goat, but you didn't find her!"

(You see, Judah was more worried about not making good on the deal with the woman and being seen as dishonorable and in contempt by the townspeople than he is in getting his things back. He asserts, essentially, that she stole them from him by not making good on their deal...and with this assertion tries in his mind to get the upper hand though he clearly knows he's been played by this prostitute...she walked off with much more in value with his jewels and identification than the baby goat he promised her.)

And so it was —

three new moons — the special religious moons (months) — had come and gone,

and it was reported to Judah...Throw-Up-Your-Hands/
Penis-In-Praise:
"Your daughter-in-law Erect-Palm-Tree
has been whoring around —
and even this — listen up —
she's gotten pregnant through whoring around!"

And Judah...Throw-Up-Your-Hands/Penis-In-Praise said,
"Force her out here and burn her!"

She was forced out —
and she sent for her father-in-law, saying,
"By the man to whom these things belong —
I'm pregnant!"

And she said,
"Please check these things out very carefully
— to whom they belong:
this special ring
  used to affix his name to make deals
with this one-and-only identification on it
and this specially-twined necklace
and this one-of-a-kind walking stick!"

And Judah...Throw-Up-Your-Hands/Penis-In-Praise
checked them out very carefully and said,
"She's more innocent
and in the right than me!
I mean,
it's all because I didn't give her to my son Ask!"

And adding-on no more —
he didn't know her — didn't have sex with her.

And so it was —

at the time she gave birth — listen here —
twins were in her belly!

And so it was —

in her giving birth,
one offered a hand,
and the midwife took and tied some crimson thread
around his hand,
and said,
"This one came out first!"

(Remember, the first-born gets all the rank and inheritance-rights in an ancient family...unless someone is 'Tricky' like Jacob, with his mom's help.)

And so it was —

just then his hand drew back in —
listen here! —
and his brother came out!

And she said,
"What's this?!
You're breaking out all over yourself!
A break-out!"
And his name was called out,

"Break-Out!"

And after that his brother came out —
the one who had the crimson thread on his hand.

And his name was called out,

"Dawn-Rising!"

(...as dawn comes and goes with its crimson-red....)

gulp!
ha ha ha

commentary

Tamar & Judah... A Clever Parable by the Band of YAH... A Victory Story for Women and Humans of All Genders...

A Positively Shocking Story Woven into the Middle of Joseph-saga by the Levitical Priestly Editors to Distract Us from YAHWEH & the Prophets' Larger Genderbending Ways

In the Bible handed down to us first by the Levitical priestly editors and Deuteronomists who crafted the Torah, the Judah story is wedged into the middle of the Joseph-saga. While this Judah-Tamar story is almost certainly the band of YAH's, it's the position of the story that's problematic.

Pull out this Judah-interlude from the Joseph-saga and you'll soon see that the Joseph story reads just fine without it and without any reference to Judah, whose long speeches in the Joseph-saga detract from Joseph and his and YAHWEH's genderbending ways.

Judah's long speeches in the Joseph story not only cover up Joseph but also try to set up Judah a bit higher after his completely foolish ways in the tale we just read about him, the tale that is Genesis 38. I argue that those speeches in the Joseph-saga are inserted by the Levitical priestly editors long after the first telling of the Joseph-saga.

In this Judah story, the clever daughter-in-law plays the prostitute to get back at her father-in-law, this one whose name means 'Throw-Up-Your-Hands/Penis-In-Praise.'

With 'hand'/YD being a euphemism for 'penis,' in this story we just read, it wouldn't be all that wrong to wonder if Judah's name might actually mean 'Throw-Out-Your-Penis'!!!

For a guy whose name has some sense of faithfulness to YAHWEH — 'Throw-Up-Your-Hands/Penis-in-Praise!' — Judah seems more interested in his own pleasure. Little did we know until Tamar helps to reveal it.

The wily ways of this woman — Erect-Palm-Tree / Tamar — very much reflect the wily actions of the prophets. In addition to their wildly clever raps and rhymes, the biblical prophets' style included exceedingly clever actions to awaken people to the reality before them.

And Tamar — the one who stands tall/erect, the one who stands her ground in her authenticity and in her desire for children — dupes Judah into realizing his dopiness. And we all get to watch and learn too.

Tamar's Clever Act...Much Like Jeremiah and the Clever Actions of the Prophets/Ecstatics

Ever note the wildly clever things Jeremiah uses to try to wake up Ancient Judah's royally-minded 'national security council' about the whole situation of Babylon invading?

Jeremiah wears an ox-goad over his shoulders to encourage the royal-government of his own nation to submit to the superpower-Babylon's wishes instead of trying to fight. In a sense, for the hierarchically-minded, Jeremiah was pointing out that Ancient Judah was already a slave to royal-Babylon — essentially blasphemy to the royal/priestly cults of Ancient Judah who thought ELOHIM/God would swoop down and save them from the carnage that Babylon would surely bring with its superpower-might.

With his wild action, Jeremiah encouraged the national security council to submit, as an ox submits to its master's desires. Fighting Babylon would have been a blood-bath for Ancient Judah — and Jeremiah and anyone with sense knew it. Babylon was so strong and Judah was not only small but highly distracted by its ever-addictive religions — whether the religion of the state/temple or the religion of BAAL/ASHTAROTH — and those temples required the 'service' of the poor.

God's/ELOHIM's temple and BAAL/ASHTAROTH's temples were not a whole lot different during Jeremiah's day...both hired prostitutes (the poorest of the poor) for their paying members' pleasure and 'worship' to the god(dess). They even had the nerve to call these prostitutes 'holy ones'/QDSHH — both the Jerusalem temple-cult dedicated to ELOHIM/God and the BAAL/ASHTAROTH temple-cults. Remember *The Epic of Gilgamesh* and the temple-prostitute brought to civilize the wild-man Enkidu through enticing him away from the animals through the temple-prostitute's beauty when she spread her legs for him, through his fucking her for days on end, through her making him clothes and feeding him civilized meals of bread and wine? In the hierarchical-mindset, the 'holy ones' like this *Gilgamesh* temple-prostitute are the ones who submit their bodies to their buyers so that God/god could be glorified. It's a sick system, and any human with sense knew it and styled out poems and raps to awaken fellow-humans to the kinds of sick things that were being done in the name of 'holiness' and the name of God/divinity. Prophets try to rattle people to knowing what's happening and then welcome change.

And Tamar plays on the assumptions about 'holy ones'/ QDSHYM by dressing up as one to get back at her father-in-law Judah.

On the significant problems of holiness

The prophets do not subscribe to these 'holy' games, games that are hierarchical, and that name some things and some people and some places as more holy than others.

To a prophet, nothing is sacred or holy. Why? Because everything touched by the wind — YAHWEH — is holy... and that's everything. A temple is no more holy than a human being from a prophet's experience — because YAHWEH flows through everything. An enemy of Israel is no better or worse than a devout Israelite...at least from what a prophet knows not through catechism, not through Law, but through experience. Once you know the wind and the ways and whispers of the wind and live out of that experience, what use is there for 'holiness' and 'sacredness' in all its problematic manifestations? To a prophet, the Sabbath is not holy and holidays are not needed. Why? Because every day is holy. The Levitical priestly editors crafted the Sabbath as a way to give people a dose of what the prophets were after — leaving the grasping ways of empire and control in any form, including organized religion. These priestly editors proclaimed that the Sabbath was holy — so stop! dedicate one day a week to ELOHIM/God and on that day do no work for the empire! give ELOHIM/God one day of your time...but just don't say YAHWEH out loud like the prophets want you to do!

The prophets dropped out of society completely — they left behind the ways of empire and its corrupting influence. The whole fictional story of Samuel is just that — the story of someone who dropped out of the holiness cult to simply be with the wind. All prophets worth their salt drop out of empire's ways, or at least try to, or like the priest/prophet Isaiah of Jerusalem try to point out the ridiculousness of priestly rituals when one's heart is not in it.

From a prophet's standpoint, the priestly-mandated one-day-a-week-Sabbath is a nice start to dropping out of empire's grasping ways — maybe on your Sabbath you and I might finally get a whiff of the atmosphere and wind that breathes us into life and finally leave behind the silliness of the empire and its cruel ways of demanding our addictive participation. That's empire's cruelty — where its grasp feels like you have no choice but to stay with it and keep doing all the things you and I think we must do all the while the breeze blows freely — YAHWEH reaches out to you and me — whether we conform and do what empire demands or not.

Why on earth do you think Jesus didn't honor the Sabbath? Why on earth do you think Jesus hung out with women and prostitutes and children and tax collectors...people who were seen as 'unholy' and worth nothing within the official empire? Why on earth do you think Jesus advocated people "take nothing with them for the journey"? He was advocating a leaving of the empire...in favor of the wild ways of the wind.

Jeremiah sees YAHWEH using 'the enemy' Babylon to help Ancient Judah/Israel grow!

Ancient Judah had reached out to its old enemies/allies to thwart Assyria's advance that took out Ancient Israel to the north of Ancient Judah and to thwart Babylon's advance once Assyria was defeated. The attempts at alliances failed. BAAL and ASHTAROTH and all manner of the-gods-and-goddesses were no help either. But Jeremiah knew that YAHWEH would help, the YAHWEH of the breeze that finds Itself at home anywhere and everywhere, even in Babylon where YAHWEH first invited Abram and Sarai and Lot to a new way of bordercrossing, to a way that follows the wind, even down into Ancient Egypt, another superpower that was no friend to Ancient Judah.

Jeremiah saw in Babylon a saving grace for the people of Ancient Judah to get its shit together — to come back to YAHWEH and YAHWEH alone — even if they were enslaved in Babylon. After all, YAHWEH needed no temple to be known. YAHWEH needed no government — little empire or big empire — to thrive. And so too those who dedicate themselves to YAHWEH alone... anywhere the breeze blows.

Perhaps Jeremiah was not only preventing the bloodbath of war with Babylon...perhaps Jeremiah recognized that Ancient Judah had become Babylon already by trying to become a (super)power and leaving behind the ways of YAHWEH invited by the prophets/ecstatics... the YAHWEH not of any temple...the YAHWEH of no single nation...the YAHWEH who crosses borders...the YAHWEH who found Abram in Babylon and invited Abram and Sarai and Lot to Canaan and even went with them to Egypt and then back to Canaan...the YAHWEH who goes anywhere and does anything It wants...the YAHWEH who is as pervasive as the breeze. Jeremiah knew well this breeze, this YAHWEH, even let YAHWEH whisper through him with clever poem after clever poem designed to awaken any listener to leave behind control for relationship with YAHWEH.

What did they do with the prophet Jeremiah? What did Ancient Judah's citizens do with Jeremiah? They killed him. Got rid of him and his puns designed to awaken. Shut him up. 'No more wildly clever poems from you, Jeremiah!'

But they killed him only after the king of Judah took Jeremiah's advice to submit to Babylon instead of engaging in a prolonged war where tiny Judah would have been slaughtered. Eventually.

Like Jeremiah, Jesus suffers a similar fate at the hands of people dedicated to hierarchy and its cruel ways that do not reflect YAHWEH, the wind. Jesus was inviting people to give to Caesar what was Caesar's and to give to God what is God's...THE ALL...YAHWEH. Even Caesar could not capture the wind...at least not any longer than anyone else.

The wind reveals any and every hierarch's foolishness in trying to hold power over anyone...just as Tamar revealed the-character-Judah's foolishness...just as Jesus points out to the priestly-hierarchs of his day that their Law is foolish in that the Law cannot contain the wind, YAHWEH.

Keep in mind that it was people dedicated to organized religion who killed Jesus. It doesn't matter what religion they were — Jesus seems to have grown up in the same religion as them, an organized religion which he seems to have left behind, at least much of it. If we trust the historicity of at least some of the stories in the gospels, it seems pretty clear in all of them that Jesus lived outside the Law regarding purity codes, with his disregard for the Sabbath, with his being in relationship with those considered "unclean."

Would Jesus, the crafter of the parables, agree with much of anything Christianity espouses today...with its massive churches and hierarchical-structures of leadership and catechisms and oh so little of the uncomfortable desert that Jesus seemed to prefer as he did sleeping wherever he laid his head and hanging with prostitutes and children and people not on the hierarchical-map of society? Would the 'Jesus' of YAHWEH and the wandering, bordercrossing life of prophets/ecstatics agree with much of anything Christianity teaches as 'the way'?

I'm quite sure most Christians would kill Jesus today.

YAHWEH is the anti-religion. YAHWEH is the ante-religion...which is to say, YAHWEH exists before religion. YAHWEH is the primal experience, the first experience every baby knows through their first inhale. YAHWEH is relationship...something not possible when we try to worship God and mammon/empire.

Prophets point this out — and those who dedicate their lives to religion and to the state feel threatened and kill the messengers, those ecstatically alive with YAHWEH and the profound buzz YAHWEH offers its bliss-filled followers.

It happened to Jeremiah. It happened to Jesus. It's happened over and over and over again since then to people who no longer want to be tied up by priestly, hierarchical ways.

Do you dare leave behind the ways of empire for relationship with YAHWEH? It might be easier with friends...the 'prophet guilds' discussed in 1 & 2 Kings.

The old things done to prophets don't need to be carried into the new age emerging...

The countries known for its wildly imaginative prophets — Israel, India, the United States — are also known for killing them.

Perhaps it was happening during the band of YAH's time too. In the priestly way that the Judah-story is arranged in Genesis — wedged in between the Joseph-saga — what does the character-Judah do with his dream-interpreting prophet-brother Joseph?

While Joseph rots in prison or worse after being sold for some silver, Judah whores around with a prostitute who happens to be his daughter-in-law and only figures it out once he's ready to kill her too.

In the final edition of Joseph-story dampened down by the Levitical priestly editors with their oh-so-very-many-interruptions as they crafted the book of Genesis, the character-Judah one day will make good on his selling his brother into slavery for some silver coins. But not in the original version of the Joseph-saga — I suspect Judah had no place in the original the band of YAH story of Joseph. More on that in a bit.

Like my own nation, one of the greatest sadnesses of the people of Ancient Israel/Judah is that they have a habit of ignoring their prophets — even killing them. Tired of Jeremiah, they kill him. Tired of Jesus, they have the superpower kill him. Perhaps the Judas character in the gospel-stories is created by the gospel-writers to capture that past-reality...Judas, the faithful follower of Jesus who later sells Jesus into jail/death for a handful of silver coins...much like Judah does with Joseph in the Levitical priestly edition of the Joseph story.

The same killing of prophets is quite trendy in my country too...Dr. Martin Luther King, Jr., Malcolm X, Harvey Milk. These are a few famous prophets...add to them the hundreds upon hundreds of people who died for their important witness with civil rights, indigenous rights, LGBTQ+ rights, women's rights....

One of India's own killed Gandhi. Inspired by his own novice reading of the Bible, Gandhi invited Bayard Rustin and Dr. King to look again at the Bible for clever nonviolent strategy in the United States, ushering in great progress for many. Very sadly, we unthinking humans do terrible things to prophets, to people who point out different and co-equal ways of experiencing life.

Prophets as disruptors of economies of exploitation

In the received tradition of the Joseph-story — the final edition crafted by the Levitical priestly editors and the Deuteronomists — we see Judah rallying his bloodthirsty-brothers to sell his brother Joseph off into slavery for a handful of coins. In this case, it's to save Joseph's life. It's also to get him and his dress-wearing and obnoxious, prophetic speech/dreams out of the way.

In the character-Judah's case and for that matter the nation-Judah's case, it's easy to blame the prostitute who was sitting there on the side of the road — whether a common-prostitute or a special-religious-prostitute. How easy it is to blame the prostitute...when the one paying the prostitute made the problem worse...and the local-economy made the woman/man/trans/non-binary sell themselves to eat. Most economies of government and of organized religion fundamentally do not include everyone, even as they protect many. Who lives on the margins in the economy of your nation? Who lives on the margins of the economy of your organized religion?

Note what Judah does in the Judah/Tamar story just when he has some extra income — he pays a prostitute for sex. All the while he has major issues at home, in his family's economy. Judah's whoring around — both as character in the Judah/Tamar story and as nation/tribe — is the problem and the reason that Judah and anyone stuck in the hierarchical royal-slave imagination needs prophets to call him/it back to faithfulness with YAHWEH. The prophet's message is that YAHWEH rules — no one else.

Faithfulness to YAHWEH, after all, is sexy-time with YAHWEH, an erotic relationship of capture...whether by wrestling as Jacob has done or by breathing and witnessing the storm/wind as Samuel invites...check out *The Naked Path of Prophet vol 1* for more on that. There's a reason the prophets are ecstatically running down mountains and through towns in the Samuel-saga. Anyone who has had a whiff of YAHWEH does.

It is not coincidental that much of the prophets' language in their poems through the centuries — Amos, Hosea, the Isaiahs, Jeremiah — is about calling back the bride/Israel to its husband/YAHWEH when the bride was fond of whoring around with its neighbors' gods and goddesses...BAAL, ASHTAROTH, the Jerusalem temple-cult and its beloved ark...an organized religion that gets interwoven with the royal-state and more.

It takes a genderbending imagination to understand what the prophets are doing, an imagination that does not buy into the hierarchical lies that men are better than women, that men-who-have-sex-with-women are better than men-who-have-sex-with-men, that adults are to be valued more than children, that the educated are better than the uneducated, that the non-incarcerated are better than the incarcerated, that the rich are better than the poor, and indeed that some people do not even have a place in the hierarchical order...murderers, people guilty of war crimes, etc.

These are the less-than-truths that prophets cannot

stand. YAHWEH breathes life into each and every human — no matter how 'good' they are. Playing right into the prophetic imagination of equality, Jesus offers: "God lets the sun rise on the good and bad, lets the rain fall on the just and the unjust."

Would that we had the imagination and the courage to lean into this imagination of equality in every encounter!

The layers of the Joseph-saga

It's likely that the Levitical priestly editors want us Bible-readers not to be swept away by this ecstatic feeling of human-equality that comes with knowing YAHWEH in all Its sensuality. And so at every turn they can, the Levitical priestly editors cover it up in the stories that had circled around campfires and in the imaginations of nearly anyone and everyone for centuries. The Levitical priestly editors try to craft a Bible without the prophets...and when that fails, they try to write over the prophets so that their priestly fear-inducing message resounds more than the ecstatic/prophetic invitation to know YAHWEH in all Its sensuality, in real relationship.

Looking at the layers of the Joseph-story can help reveal just how much the Levitical priestly editors were invested in squashing the ecstatic/prophetic imagination.

Scholars today often try to argue that the Joseph-saga might have been a late addition to Genesis, perhaps even placed by there at the last moment by the last round of Deuteronomistic editors before thew whole

Genesis-Exodus-Leviticus-Numbers-Deuteronomy project got minted as The Torah. The Joseph-story indeed might be a late-add...but the interruptions in the story bear the marks of the Levitical priestly imagination, with similar interruptions occurring in the Eden-story and the Jacob-saga. The Levitical priests are intent on covering over anything that has to do with the prophetic/ecstatic imagination — much of their Leviticus was created to do just that, as I will explain through the rest of this book.

In the Joseph-story we have in Genesis, most biblical scholars have argued that there are two layers to the story...an (incorrectly supposed) Yahwist version with Judah as fool-redeemed-as-hero and another storyteller's version with Reuben as hero. In working with this story for the past seven years or more, I suspect that there's an even earlier layer to the story that has neither Judah nor Reuben in it. I'm making an argument that the entire Judah-layer of the story is a much later addition to the fabric of the Joseph-story, perhaps centuries after the band of YAH's tales were first told.

This is not to say that the Judah/Tamar story does not originate with the band of YAH. The Judah/Tamar story very likely originates with the band of YAH. Why? Because it follows a similar storytelling motif to YAH's other tales: another woman-character gets the upper-hand through cleverness. Someone — likely the Levitical priestly editors who likely gave the final shape to the book of Genesis and the larger Torah — stapled the Judah story into the Joseph-saga with all those clever 'add-ons'...when originally, I argue, the Judah story was likely a separate saga in itself.

In the original Joseph-saga of the band of YAH, I argue that Judah is not named...most of the story relates to Joseph and the reactions of 'his brothers'...with the only other character being named is Joseph's full-brother Benjamin and the emotional reunion of the two. Maybe Simeon is named in the original version, the brother kept behind until Benjamin is fetched; maybe not.

In the 'final edition' of the Joseph-saga that we have in the Bible — the so-called "received tradition" of the Torah we have from the Levitical priestly editors and later Deuteronomists — Reuben and Judah vie for attention...but those are much later layers with the Reuben-camp to the North/East and the Judah-camp to the South likely trying to show the heroism of each of their tribes' 'founding fathers'. The biblical editors wisely included both versions of the story to appease the northern Reubenites and the southern Judahites — but note that by including these two versions, they dim down the focus on Joseph and his likely relationship to the prophetic imagination.

If the Tamar story is valuable to the plot of the Joseph-saga about the rise of prophets in Ancient Judah, the character-Judah only gets it right after Judah's wrongs are exposed for what they are...by those who, like Tamar and like the prophets, find clever and nonviolent ways to awaken their oppressors to their foolishness and self-centeredness. Such is Judah's plight — both the character and the nation/tribe. Perhaps this plight is yours and mine too as we negotiate the power in our relationships, within one's own self. As I said earlier, I suspect we all have the ecstatic-freedom of the prophets/ecstatics and the ordered-controlling-ways of the priests/kings with their hierarchical imagination where one is valued more than the other. Which of these two imaginations we live out of determines the course of one's life...and the life of the planet.

Dress-wearing and often-naked Joseph as hero

But even with this clever mastery of editing by the biblical editors in joining the Judah-version and the Reuben-version into a somewhat sensible and cohesive full story of Joseph and his brothers, the true hero is Joseph, who endures the harsh treatment of his brothers and the harsh treatment of the Egyptian empire. Perhaps some of it is Joseph's own fault — he could've kept his dreams to himself...as if any prophet can do such a thing and live an authentic life. And we must note too: those seemingly arrogant dreams do come to fruition in Joseph's case.

But we'd better read the saga before we converse a whole lot more.

Those of us who know the Joseph-saga well know we are soon in for a wild ride...though no one I know notes this wild ride of a Joseph-story has anything to do with prophets. I certainly do! And you can too! Sharpen your senses, friends!

Pay close attention to story and style and the ever-changing wardrobes and I think you too will discover just how much the references in the Ancient Hebrew biblical text play on prophets' style and imagination....

What does this dress-wearing Joseph-character who gets stripped naked by his brothers have to say to all of this?

What does it take for a hierarch like Pharaoh to not only listen to a prisoner from the dungeon but to make that prisoner Pharaoh's Number-Two...a role usually reserved for a queen, right?

And what glimmer does this Joseph-saga have to shed upon our understandings of the biblical prophets?

Come and see.

Genesis 37 - 45

Add-On/Grower & Power-Son

the saga of Joseph
& his long-lost brother Benjamin

<begin at Gen 35.16c>

And Rachel was about to give birth —

she'd been having difficulty in her giving birth.

And so it was —

in her difficulty giving birth
that her midwife said to her,
"Don't fear —
because even this is going to happen
for you —
a son!"

And so it was —

just as all that was alive within her
went out of her
— you see, she died! —

that she called out his name,

"My-Trouble-Son!"

But his father called out for him,

"Power-Son!"

(Rachel calls him BN-AHONY; Jacob calls him BN-YMYN...a rather unusual name for a youngest son... Power-Son...'Son-of-the-Right' in an ancient culture where 'left' was sinister — literally so in Latin — and 'right' was right and powerful. Power-Son might be a better name for the oldest son in an ancient culture with oldest sons having more power than younger sons...and yet Jacob chooses the name for his youngest.

It might seem that the band of YAH — which surely includes women — is dispensing with the women-characters so lightly, without any fanfare. Dinah gets raped; Rachel dies during childbirth, and fast. The insult is abrupt with each woman-character, even going back to Woman in the Pleasure-Orchard/Eden, a woman who had to bear YAHWEH's jealousy and tirade about her embracing Mud-Creature and who then had to watch one of her sons kill the other out of jealousy, maybe even at YAHWEH's prompting. My guess is that this abruptness every time is part of the band of YAH's shocking style — to wake people up to valuing women — and as we'll soon see, people of all genders and gender-expressions — for all they/we are. YAH seeks an awakening, one of huge proportions, all through their clever stories. How big is that awakening...? Just you wait and see!)

<Gen 35.19 - 36.42>

And Jacob was living in the land
after the immigrant-journeying of his father
in the land of the Humble-Traders.

These are Jacob's birthing-stories....

Joseph was a child of seventeen years.

> (In the ancient world, this would be a very old child! Boys and girls would marry at the onset of puberty, usually long before they were 15. It's very likely that ancient audiences would be smirking at "Joseph was a child of seventeen years." It might be a bit like saying today "My teenager is 25 years old."
>
> Recall too that Joseph's name means Add-On....)

And he was shepherding with his brothers the lambs and goats.

And he was a boy
with the sons of Terrified
and the sons of Trickle —
(Terrified and Trickle were) his father's (slave)wives.

And Joseph would go with bad reports and rumors (about his brothers) to their father.

<Gen 37:3a>

And (his father) made for him <u>a flashy dress</u>, the kind that a king's daughter would wear.

(What?! The only other time we get this combination of words — CTNT PSYM — in the Hebrew Bible is in 2 Samuel 13 describing what David's daughter Tamar wore...and in that story we are told this is what "the king's daughters" wore in those days.

Notice the life Jacob is creating as lead-parent of a motherless child...to the old-child who tattles on his brothers, Jacob gives a princess-dress! We might have some significant compassion for this man-boy Joseph and his father Jacob over the early death of their mother and wife Rachel...but giving him a dress?!

What's even stranger is that the word PS, if derived from PSS/PSYM, means 'disappearing.' We'll have to watch for how this whole flashy-dress/disappearing-dress plays out...perhaps quite the punny situation the band of YAH is playing with here...a true 'flash in the pan'....)

And his brothers saw that their father loved him best from among all the brothers.

And they hated him, they couldn't stand to style it out with him peacefully or kindly.

And Joseph, whose name means 'Add-On' —
he dreamed dreams —
and he would tell them to his brothers.
And they would add it all up together and hate him all the more.

And he would say to them,
"Please listen up to this dream that I dreamed:

you see, we were bound-up — tongue-tied, made-to-be-silent! —
we were bound-grain-stalks in the middle of the rolling-field —
and hear this —
my grain-stalk was standing up tall —
you know, like I was standing up dutifully —
and get this —
your grain-stalks were circling around
and bowing down to my grain-stalk!"

And his brothers said to him,
"Do you really think you'll master, master, master us... be king and dictator and rule over us?! Or cleverly master and control us (with such punny style)?!"

And they added it all up together and hated him even more because of his dreams
and his style.

(You see, the brothers catch Joseph's insolence not only in sharing the dream that has them bowing down to him as if he were a king...the brothers also catch his style, his choice of words...the whole 'bound-up' metaphor business. Joseph chooses and repeats the word for 'binding' — first offered as a participle/verb that every other time in the Hebrew Bible means 'speechless/mute' — and then as a noun that every other time in the Hebrew Bible has to do with sheaves or stalks of grain. The brothers catch Joseph's nuance/style and reject him even more.

'Master' was used earlier in the Eden & Cain/Abel stories, and to describe Abraham's slave. 'Master' is MSHL, actually repeated here twice in a row in the Joseph story — a Hebrew style to strengthen its meaning. Here and elsewhere when this doubling-style appears in the biblical text, I've usually tripled the word in the English translation to highlight the Hebrew-style. So here, MSHOL TMSHL I translate as 'master, master, master' and then define that 'be king and dictator and rule over us.' In every instance in the band of YAH's stories, MSHL points to a very unlikely master — here with Joseph, a younger brother ruling over his older brothers. Much later in the Talmudic tradition, MSHL has a sense of rule by cleverness, as in telling a parable or allegory to awaken a new imagination in the hearer. I wonder a bit if that could be the intent here with Joseph's brothers too when they accuse Joseph of this kind of 'mastery.' The prophets are famous — and often hated — for such clever parables and allegories in their well-styled poems and stories that invite an inner mastery once the style unravels the imagination of the story's hearer.

Note too the stylish way the band of YAH narrates the story — with the brothers 'adding it all up together' about their brother 'Add-On'...who could just as well be named 'Add-Up' or 'Grower'...though so far very far from growing in much of any way besides his 'style.'

If indeed this story has anything to do with prophets and the birth of prophets, this whole 'bound/made-to-be-silent' is quite interesting, considering that a prophet/ecstatic is one who has words flying through them...their wild raps and rhymes...style that disturbs a prophet's/ecstatic's hearers, sometimes enough that they and their authorities want to kill the prophet...)

And he dreamed still another dream,
tallied it up for his brothers,
and said,
"Listen up —
I dreamed another dream!
Listen up —
the sun
  and the moon
    and eleven stars
      were bowing themselves down to me!"

And he tallied it all up for his father and his brothers.

<Gen 37. 10b-c>

And his brothers were jealous of him.

And his father protected the style (of his son Joseph).

And his brothers went to shepherd their father's lambs
and goats in Rise-Early-Load-Your-Shoulders-With-Work.

<Gen 37:13>

And (his father) said to him,
"Go! Please!
See how your brothers are getting along —
if all is well, if they're healthy, safe and at peace —
and how the lambs and goats are getting along —
if they're well, if they're healthy, safe and at peace —
and then bring back style for me (about them)."

(Why wasn't Joseph out working with them in the first place?! Beginning to see why his brothers do not like him and are exceedingly jealous of him?! And how their father protects Joseph! And I suspect that if this story has anything to do with the prophets, it teases the nature of the prophets who do not work, who do nothing to further human empires. Prophets were the drop-outs, the misfits, the 'boys,' the slaves or worse, those who did not fit into the empire's hierarchy. Prophets chose not to work — and here we have Joseph pretty clearly not often working, at least not like his brothers work and being protected by his/their father Jacob.)

And he sent him
from the valley of Enchanting-Allies,
and he went toward Rise-Early-Load-Your-Shoulders-With-Work.

And a man found him —listen here — (Joseph) was wandering around lost in the rolling-field!
And the man asked him,
"What do you seek?"

And he said,
"My brothers — I'm seeking them!
Please tell me where they're shepherding!"

And the man said,
"They've pulled up camp and moved on from here.
See, I heard them say,
'Let's go to Rules-and-Regulations.'"

And Joseph went after his brothers,
and he found them in Rules-and-Regulations.

And they saw him from a distance —
and even before he got closer to them —
they acted deviously, shadily toward him —
to kill him.

And each guy said to his brother,
"Look! The BAAL of dreams!
The bossy-god of dreams!
Now let's kill him
and throw him into one of the pits —
we could say that some evil beast ate him —
then we'll see what becomes of his dreams!!"

(In Ancient Israel, the prophetic imagination is often associated with dreaming and dream-interpretation. As we explored earlier, *The Epic of Gilgamesh* has women-characters as dream-interpreters. And if indeed the band of YAH is making associations between dream-interpretation and prophets/ecstatics — especially through this man-child Joseph who wears a princess-dress given to him by his father who wrestled YAHWEH / a god and got groped and penetrated by It — then we'd be wise to take note of the associations that Joseph's brothers make with him/prophets.

Perhaps the band of YAH has these foolish, jealous, bloodthirsty brothers speak out loud what some people thought of the prophets/ecstatics in Ancient Israel...that the prophets/ecstatics appeared so similar to the BAAL-worshippers that they must be done away with. This is certainly the thinking of the Levitical priestly editors who make no mention of any prophet...besides their Moses, who has no prophetic poems associated with him except a few very late adds to Deuteronomy by the Deuteronomists likely trying to rectify the Levitical priests raising up Moses as 'greatest prophet' and the Deuteronomists eventually warming to including the works of the prophets in their growing Bible.

Why were the Levitical priests (and likely the early generations of Deuteronomists) so afraid of the prophets? Perhaps the prophets upset their priests' show and their royal games — much like Gautama did by pointing out that the 'Hindu' priests' rituals were not needed to know enlightenment, much like Jesus did by pointing out that knowing YAHWEH requires no temple and no Caesar. Prophets point out that YAHWEH is immediately accessible and is the best teacher — this wind, this atmosphere in which we all ripen into life — not some special ritual, not some special Law or philosophy that must be memorized, not some special government, not some special place that must be visited.

A prophets' poems and clever sayings try to put the hearers in touch with an experience they already know — their poems are quick reminders to know YAHWEH through one's own senses. Jesus' parables do that too — they help to remove the veils and expose assumptions that prevent us from knowing YAHWEH, giver of life. Even Gautama is said to have crafted riddles/koans designed to unravel one's assumptions and inspire imagination toward knowing the source of life...all on one's own terms.

Priestly-minded people and their royally-minded/ hierarchically-minded adherents cannot handle that. They put such stock in rituals, in doing something to create an experience, that they forget that YAHWEH is being-in-action, being-with-awareness...perhaps even 'consciousness' itself. Itself.

Prophets point out that YAHWEH is accessible by all without a priest or president or king, without any special knowledge, no matter where you are.

Bliss — ecstasy! — is possible for everyone, readily accessible with a single aware breath. That's the very assumption and purpose of the prophets.

Whether it's the priestly rituals involving the ark/temple or the priestly rituals involving BAAL/ASHTAROTH or the priestly rituals of the state/crown, the biblical prophets point out the foolishness and even the problem of ritual — the thinking that someone/anyone can say or do something better or wiser than the wind, than life itself. Itself. To think that we can create bliss/ecstasy — whether by ritual or chocolate or drugs or whatever — is addiction, its own slavery.

Sometimes, as you and I surely know, ecstasy comes through relationship, sexual-relationship. Ecstasy emerges out of nowhere, as if love simply rises up and takes us. For the prophets — at least according to what we see in 1 & 2 Samuel and 1 & 2 Kings — such sexual relationship crossed borders, was not always the default of man-and-woman. The prophets' poems — Amos, Hosea, the three Isaiahs, Jeremiah — often bend gender, with YAHWEH sometimes acting as man, sometimes acting as woman/mother (especially in Second Isaiah), and sometimes acting as the wind...It or more-than-gender. Ancient Israel, in the prophet's poems, sometimes gets referred to as bride, as harlot, as unfaithful wife, as lover, as many things as we'll discover in *The Naked Path of Prophet* series.

And Ancient Israel's hierarchy of priests and kings had a way of doing away with its prophets through the years — for a variety of reasons! I suspect the Levitical priestly editors reacted to the prophets' genderbending and sex-with-YAHWEH-and-anyone ways by crafting a Torah that does not allow the prophets' much of any word in it, and that punishes same-sex love and genderbending ways with death... Leviticus 18 & 20.

Returning immediately to the Joseph-saga with the brothers who call Joseph a "the BAYL/BAAL of dreams"...some might argue that BAYL/BAAL is often used in the scriptures for 'master or rule over someone' or 'to get a husband (who will rule over the wife).' It certainly is used this way — and often by the prophets — but it's always a derogatory use of the verb BAYL. That is to say, BAYL is always used to show how someone is on top of or in charge of a person...the hierarchical imagination. Isaiah and Jeremiah will cleverly and purposefully use the verb BAYL in their poems to show that YAHWEH rules the people — not their human king, and not the ever-addictive god-combo of BAAL/ASHTAROTH with their naked dances where participants could purchase a prostitute for the night for a little hierarchical fun of debauchery...all to make sure the grain grew and that (male) babies would be born to grow one's family. BAAL was about <u>control</u>.

This Genesis passage could be an incredibly important passage through which to understand people's feelings about the prophets and perhaps just how much the prophets were associated with the BAAL-worshippers...I suspect it was the priests who made the quick association of the prophets with the BAAL-worshippers due to both the prophets and the BAAL-worshippers loving the mountaintops and all the sexy-times each separate camp had had on the mountaintops of Ancient Israel/Palestine... though as we'll see through *The Naked Path of Prophet* series, the prophets and the BAAL-worshippers are very, very different...and the freeing imagination and equality-based imagination of the prophets/ ecstatics is far different from both the priests and the BAAL-worshippers whose imaginations were hierarchically-minded, no matter the god/goddess being worshipped.)

<*Gen 37.21-22*>

And so it was —

when Joseph entered — got to his brothers,
they stripped Joseph of his clothes — the flashy princess dress — from him!
And they took him and threw him into the pit —
the pit was empty — there was no water in it.

And they sat down to eat some bread.

And they <u>raised</u> their eyes
and saw — hear this! — a caravan of wanderers —
from The-Gods-and-Goddesses-Hearers —
they were arriving from Pile-of-Protests —
and the camels were carrying

spices whose names have to do with striking and driving someone away

and a balm-resin whose name has to do with cracking with pressure

and myrrh whose name brings to mind covering something up

and they were on their way to going down to Suffering-Egypt.

(NCAHT/'a spice' that gets its name from NCAH/'to smite, to drive away'...such a spice as this —- probably tragacanth gum, as most Hebrew lexicons note — was often used as an herbal medicine for diarrhea or a thick cough...it drove out the illness, perhaps not all that pleasantly

TSRY/'a balm or balsam' that gets its name as *Strong's Exhaustive Concordance* notes TSRY is from an old no-longer-used work having to do with cracking under pressure

LT/'myrrh' getting its name from LUT/'to wrap, cover up, cover over'...just like Abraham's nephew's name

Note all these rather curious products they are carrying to trade also happen to be words to describe what happens to the prophets who speak out — and what's happening here to Joseph because he spoke out his dreams to his bloodthirsty brothers...perhaps another example of the band of YAH's exceedingly clever, storycrafting style.)

<Gen 37. 26 - 28a>

And they drew him up,
climbed up Joseph from the pit,
and sold Joseph to the
The-Gods-and-Goddesses-Hearers
for 20 pieces of silver.

They made Joseph go to Suffering-Egypt.

<Gen 37. 29-30>

And they took Joseph's clothing,
and slaughtered a hairy he-goat — those devilish creatures —
and dipped the clothing in the blood.

> (This type of goat SAYYR recalls the land that Jacob was passing through where fantastical beasts and happenings occurred...Seir, from which we also get the word 'satyr.')

And they sent the flashy princess dress
and made it be brought to their father,
and said,
"We found this.
Please look at it closely —
is it your son's clothing or not?"

And he looked at it closely and said,
"The clothing — it's my son's —
some evil beast ate him —
ripped, ripped, ripped him to pieces!
Joseph!"

And he tore his outer-garment, the one showing his status as head of the family
and as a person of wealth.

And he put on super-itchy sackcloth around his hips and groin
and he mourned his son for many days.

And all of his sons and all of his daughters stood up to comfort him with sighs —
but he refused to be comforted and said,
"I'll go to my son in mourning to Sheol...
down to death's resting place in the underworld!"

His father wept for him!

<Gen 37.36>
<the Judah/Tamar story at Gen 38 was placed here by the biblical editors...I've pulled it out to hear the Joseph story as a whole>
<resuming again at Gen 39.1>

So Joseph had been taken down to Suffering-Egypt.

And Owned-By-Negligence had bought him —

he was Pharaoh-Negligence's eunuch,
he was on-top of — in charge — of the butchers,
a man of Suffering-Egypt —

(he had bought Joseph...)
from The-Gods-and-Goddesses-Hearers who had made (Joseph) go down there.

(Pharaoh was Suffering-Egypt's royal-ruler. A 'eunuch'/SRYS is a man whose testicles had been taken from him to perform his royal-duties, often so that this officer could safely guard the royal-family without any desire for sex with them. And as for the 'butchers' this could mean the executioners or the cooks, who butcher meat not a whole lot differently than executioners do to humans. It's quite ironic and tragically funny, yes, that the person in charge of butchery had been butchered himself, his testicles taken from him? Note the wild style of the story, a hallmark of the prophetic/ecstatic imagination.)

And so it was —

YAHWEH was with Joseph.

And so it was —

he was a man rushed upon, penetrated, pushed forward into goodness.

And so it was —

he was a man in his boss's house, the Suffering-Egyptian.

(Notice the three 'and so it was' clauses...how the band of YAH teases with this trio...each one, perhaps, complicating the other...except for those who know prophets and the prophetic imagination and their wily ways of working with, playing with, complexity!

And yet, isn't that the way it is with anyone, not just

prophets? any creative? any ecstatic who knows something of 'being rushed upon'/TSLCH...this is the same word that the biblical-writer of 1 Samuel uses to indicate YAHWEH rushing upon people into ecstasy...into having visions inspiring the rap-like style of a prophet...the highly erotic relationship of YAHWEH with a human...where YAHWEH's YD/'hand or penis or phallic-control' is upon you and having Its way with you...like the wind does with every breath that penetrates you, every breath that slides into you...as It rushed into Abraham's slave and as it now rushes upon the newly enslaved Joseph....)

And his boss saw that YAHWEH was with him —

and that everything he did
YAHWEH rushed upon, penetrated, pushed forward into goodness
with Its hand/penis/phallic-control.
And Joseph found he measured up in (Owned-By-Negligence's) eyes —

and he served him,
and he took care of him —
put him in charge over — his house,
and all there was to him — all that was his —
he gave into his hand/phallic-control.

(Umm...this is a very strange verb to appear here — PQD. The last time we saw it with the band of YAH's stories was when YAHWEH visited Sarah and Sarah became pregnant. Most translators opt for 'put him in charge' and there are plenty of times PQD is used in that way, but not as often with the preposition AYL/'throughout, upon' that follows it here in the Hebrew text. PQD has such a wide range of meanings...'to visit, to muster, to punish, to appoint.' As a matter of fact, the *NAS Exhaustive Concordance* notes that of the 302 times PQD is used in the Hebrew Bible, 99 times it has to do with 'counting/numbering' as in 'mustering' and 46 times it has to do with 'punishing.' Umm...talk about a confusing verb choice by the band of YAH!

And not only that, the preposition following PQD here is AYL/'throughout, upon'...and one line later PDQ will first take the preposition B/'in' and then AYL again. The word PQD is being massaged here. And who is PQDing whom? Perhaps the band of YAH is purposely making it unclear here...much like they did when YAHWEH's ambassadors were inside Lot's house and when YAHWEH/some god was wrestling Jacob.

Strange things are afoot here...and any ancient hearer's ears would prick up as PQD gets nuanced here in the story. It's a double-entendre, remember, that is the linguistic way — the style — of the prophets...and this could well be another example that would fetch the ears and understandings of any ancient hearer.

In addition to the 'visiting' and 'punishing' and 'putting someone in charge of something' possibilities of PQD, could it be too that PQD as 'numbering/mustering' plays on Joseph's name...Add-On?

In every instance of PQD in the band of YAH's stories,

I've chosen 'take care of' to be the middle-message of the verb and then teased out the nuance in the direction the verb tends to go...hopefully much like an ancient hearer might do.

Note too the genderbending potentials of a eunuch as a character, someone who is 'man' — as I suppose the ancients would place him — and a 'man' without the testicles that guarantee 'manhood' and virility, the ability to give seed/descendants through a woman/wife as is one of the key requirements of adults in the ancient world. How eunuchs complicate the gender-binary...something we see in the language/poems of the prophets who seem to tease the gender-binary and bend society's expectations about gender and gender-roles.)

And so it was —

from then on he took care of him — he visited him? made him in charge of? he punished him? — his house and through — uh, over — all that there was to him — all that was his.

And YAHWEH brought abundance to the Egyptian-Sufferer's house
in rolling around with Joseph — the one whose name means 'Add-On'...Increaser...Grower.

(Another unusual choice of an adverbial-clause BGLL...last time it was used by the band of YAH with Abram telling Sarai that they needed to lie to Pharaoh about their being married. GLL means 'to roll' and it's used idiomatically as 'because of' or 'on account of'...we might say today 'hanging around with' or 'they go together, one flows into the other' as part of our own idiom?)

And so it was —

YAHWEH's abundance was on everything that was
his in the house and in the rolling-field,
and he abandoned/left behind everything that was
his in Joseph's hand/phallic-control —
but he didn't <u>know</u> him — nothing — you see —
except the bread he ate.

And so it was —

Add-On/Grower/Joseph was beautiful in shape and
beautiful in appearance.

And so it was —

following after these kinds of stylings-on that his
boss's wife raised her eyes to Joseph,
and she said,
"Sleep with me!"

But he utterly refused.

(Note...three more 'and so it was' clauses...like before, things that ordinarily might not add up altogether, being added up altogether. And here we have the euphemisms for sex...YDAH/'know' and now SHCB/'sleep'...all but one....)

And he said to his boss's wife,
"Look here, my boss — he doesn't know me —
what's in his house — and all that's his — he's given to
my hand/penis/phallic-control —
there's no one greater in the house than me —
and he hasn't refused anything from me —
you see — except you —
in that you are his wife —
how can I do this awful thing
and terribly offend God-or-the-gods-and-goddesses/
ELOHIM?"

(Note that Joseph says that he's Number 2 in his boss's house — not the boss's wife! One more time where Joseph's big mouth gets him into trouble as it did with his brothers....)

And so it was —

as much as she styled it out to Joseph day after day,
he didn't listen to her to sleep near her —
to be with her.

And so it was —

just at the the time that Joseph entered into the house
to do his work —
and there wasn't a single man from among all the
people there in the house —
and she caught hold of his clothes and said,
"Sleep with me!"

And he left behind his clothes in her hand!
He escaped! He went outside!

(Note the same verb — 'left behind'/AYTSB — used twice here in a matter of a few lines...first, "he left behind/abandoned all that was his in Joseph's hand" and then a few lines later "he left behind his clothes in her hand."

More clever word-play by the band of YAH!

And now we have the trifecta of euphemisms or slang for sex...YDAH/'know' and SHCB/'sleep' and now BOAH/'enter'...and here in the Joseph story, we even get a new one...the verb 'to be' included now too implying sex...this Joseph story is quite punny, quite cleverly in the style of the prophets....

And "there wasn't a single man from among all the people there in the house"...does that include Joseph? the dress-wearing dreamer?)

And so it was —

when she saw that he'd left behind his clothes in her hand/control
and had escaped outside,
she called out to the people of her house
and said to them,
"See here! He <u>entered into</u> us!
The man! The Bordercrosser!
To make a laughingstock out of us!
He <u>entered into</u> me — came into me —
to <u>sleep with</u> me —
so I started calling out with a loud voice —
and so it was — when he heard that I was lifting up my voice —

and I was calling out —
that he left behind his clothes beside me
and fled and went outside!"

And she rested with his clothes near her until his boss entered into his house.

And she styled out to him in this kind of style,
"He entered into me —
the slave!
the Bordercrosser!
the one you made enter into — the one you brought for us —
to make a laughingstock out of me!
And so it was — just as I raised my voice and called out
that he left behind his clothes near me
and fled outside!"

And so it was —
when his boss had heard his wife's stylings-on, which she had styled out to him,
"It was in these styles that he did it to me!
Your slave!"
that his face burned with anger.

And Joseph's boss took him and gave him
to the round-house — the dungeon —
the place where the royal-ruler's prisoners were tied up.

(Curious...'round'/SHR, 'prisoners'/ASYRY, 'tied-up'/ASURYM...all similar-sounding words in Hebrew... enough to tie up your tongue saying it all....)

And so it was —

there he was in the round-house, the dungeon.

And so it was —

YAHWEH was with Joseph,
and It stretched out loyal-love to him.

(This is a very unusual use of this verb with 'loyal-love'/CHSD...and often this verb NTH is used with weaponry, using some implement to demonstrate power. In the Judah/Tamar story, NTH was used twice when Judah had turned into the village to live there and when Judah had 'turned in' to visit the prostitute as if he were 'stretching himself out.' Elsewhere in Genesis, NTH is used to spread out a tent, to pitch a tent. Note the phallic-nature of all of these references, something that an ancient ear would certainly notice and ponder and perhaps prick up.)

And he measured up in the eyes of the guy on-top of the round-house — the dungeon —
and the guy on-top of the round-house gave into Joseph's hand/phallic-control
all the prisoners who were in the round-house — the dungeon —
and all that was done there, it was his doing.

There was nothing the guy on-top of the round-house saw to (concerned himself) with everything in his hand/penis/phallic-control —
in that YAHWEH was with him

and whatever he did, YAHWEH rushed upon it, penetrated it.

> (There's that TSLCH again...the word to describe prophetic-ecstasy in the Samuel-saga and in the band of YAH's story with Abraham's slave.)

And so it was —

after these stylings-on
that they seriously offended —
the drinking-guy (who kept the royal-cup full) for the Egyptian-Sufferer's king
and the baker —
they seriously offended their boss, the Egyptian-Sufferer's king (the Pharaoh).
And Pharaoh-Negligence cracked off — burst into a rage — at his two eunuchs —
men whose testicles had been taken from them to perform their royal-duties —
at the guy on-top of drinking
and at the guy on-top of baking.

And he gave them over to be guarded
by the guy on-top of the butchers/executioners
(remember: same guy who threw Joseph into prison for the antics with his wife...Joseph's old boss),
in the round-house — the dungeon — the same place where Joseph had been imprisoned there.

And the guy on-top of the butchers/executioners took care of Joseph — visited Joseph — with them
and he served them.

(There's that PQD again, the verb used earlier with Sarah being visited by YAHWEH and then soon having a child.

The verb 'to serve'/SHRT sounds very similar to the root for 'on-top'/SRR, especially when conjugated. It's meant to be punny...so stretch out and enjoy it — YAHWEH's loyal-love and all the interesting sex that must be happening among all these slaves of Pharaoh...one prisoner who once wore a flashy/disappearing dress given to him by his father and some eunuchs who have no testicles but who might still like visiting the ever-attractive Joseph tied up in the dungeon and under their guard/control. Note too Joseph's ever-changing wardrobe so far — from dress to nakedness at the hands of his brothers, from slave-clothes to nakedness at the hands of his owner's wife, and now whatever he's wearing or not wearing in the dungeon, the round-house. Remember: whatever happened in the dungeon, it was Joseph's doing!)

And so it was —

they were days upon days under guard.

(Yes. You should be wondering what's going on here. Perhaps the guy in charge of the butchers/executioners just liked Joseph so much that he wanted him around. To serve. And perhaps finally around without his wife trying to get with Joseph too. Remember: this eunuch had abandoned everything in his house to Joseph — even his own wife — and Joseph refused sex with her. But here in the round-house...?)

And they dreamed a dream —
yes, both of them —
each man had a dream one night —
each man had his own way of opening up his dream
for interpretation —
the drinking-guy and the baker —
whom the Egyptian-Sufferer's king had tied up in the
round-house, the dungeon.

And Joseph entered into them in the morning
and saw them and — listen here! —
they were all riled up.
And he asked Pharaoh-Negligence's eunuchs —
these guys whose testicles had been taken from them
to perform their royal-duties —
who were with him under guard in his boss' house,
"What's up with your bad faces today?"

And they said to him,
"A dream!
We've dreamed!
And as for someone to open it up and interpret it —
there isn't anyone!"

And Joseph said to them,
"Isn't it for God-or-the-gods-and-goddesses/ELOHIM
to open up and interpret?
Please tally them up for me!"

(And here we can catch some of the nuance of ELOHIM... if a Hebrew-speaker — especially if influenced by the priestly understanding of ELOHIM being "God" — speaks to a non-Hebrew, the non-Hebrew probably would hear ELOHIM as "gods or goddesses." And thus this clever speaker Joseph communicates and doesn't mis-speak no matter his audience.)

And the guy on-top of drinking tallied up his dream for Joseph, and said to him,
"In my dream — listen to this! —
a vine —
right there in front of my face!
And on the vine — three branches!
and it — when it —
it was growing — budding —
the blossom climbing up and out —
the cluster of grapes boiling up — ripening —
and Pharaoh-Negligence's cup was in my hand —
and I took the grapes —
and I squeezed the juice out of them into Pharaoh-Negligence's cup —
and put the cup
into the palm of Pharaoh-Negligence!"

(Remember...'hand'/YD can be 'penis' and 'palm or hollow'/CP appeared earlier with the Jacob-wrestling-YAHWEH story. And not only this, *Strong's Exhaustive Concordance* notes that the word for 'cluster'/AHSHCLTYH is used for describing grapes and breasts and testicles, as it is in the priest-written Leviticus 21.20. *Strong's* notes too that 'cup'/COS is derived from 'purse, bag'/CYS, which holds things...though I'd expect we'd get a different and more dignified word here than just a simple 'cup' for what Pharaoh drinks from...like a special-drinking-cup-also-used-for-divination as will be referred to later in the story...so perhaps this 'cup' here is slang for something like 'ass'...COS is also used for the 'eye of an owl' or the hole in an owl's skull...as COS is used that way elsewhere in the Torah. Interesting, yes?

The whole dream-fantasy here coming through the guy on-top of drinking is quite ironic in that it is being dreamed by a eunuch, one who has no testicles himself — no grapes to squeeze. This guy on-top of drinking seems to be imagining himself in the dream-fantasy as having testicles and as fucking the Pharaoh...the oppressed dreaming of fucking the oppressor who stole his testicles probably long ago and now has put him in the dungeon.)

And Joseph said to him,
"Here's how it opens up — the interpretation:
Three branches is three days —
that's what they are!
Within three days,
Pharaoh-Negligence'll lift high your head!
He'll make you return to your position!
You'll put Pharaoh-Negligence's cup
into his hand
just like the previous right-way
when you were his drinking-guy —
(I say all of this) because if you remember me —
within yourself — when it all goes well for you —
please do me loyal-love —
make yourself remember me to Pharaoh-Negligence
and make me leave this house —
you see, I was stolen, stolen, stolen away
from the land of the Bordercrossers —
and even here I haven't done anything
that they should put me in the pit!"

(Note...'pit' is how Joseph ended up in Egypt, when his brothers stripped him of his princess-dress and his gifted-status and then sold him into slavery. From this 'dungeon'/HSR, Joseph remembers back to the beginning of his story in the 'pit'/BOR.

Also...ZCR is almost always used to indicate 'remember' but it is also a word to differentiate male from female...with the strange phrasing above with 'if you remember me — within yourself' one might wonder if this is another double-entendre, another punny way of referring not only to what has transpired here in the dungeon — where they took on different roles, male and female — but also what might happen to Joseph in Pharaoh's court....)

And the guy on-top of the bakers saw that the
interpretation was good,
and he said to Joseph,
"Yes, me too!
In my dream — listen here! —
there were three baskets of <u>white</u> —
on my head —
and in the highest basket was all the food Pharaoh-Negligence had made —
he'd been baking —
and the birds were eating them
from the basket on top of my head!"

(Umm...the 'white'/CHRY here is quite an interesting choice. It can mean 'white-bread.' CHR is also simply a word for white — used that way twice in the Esther stories. An ancient hearer of the story — the band of YAH's audience — might have heard that first line with 'the white on his head' as perhaps the breadbaker dreaming of the Pharaoh ejaculating on his head — a much more passive sexual role than the drinking-guy's active-role dream of fucking the Pharaoh.

Note too in the baker's dream that Pharaoh is the baker, the actor...not the acted upon. Quite an unusual dream to have the Pharaoh baking, right?

Note that both the drinking-guy and the baking-guy have both risen to be 'on-top' of their slave-trades... but only one will live....)

And Joseph answered and said,
"Here's how it opens up — the interpretation:
'Three baskets is three days — that's what they are!
Within three days, Pharaoh-Negligence'll lift high
your head from yourself!
He'll hang you from a tree!
And birds'll eat your flesh from you!'"

And so it was —

on the third day given birth by Pharaoh-Negligence
(jokingly said as if Pharaoh-Negligence were in charge
of creation!),
he made a feast with wine for all his slaves.

And he lifted high the head of the guy on-top of
drinking —
and the head of the guy on-top of the bakers in the
midst of his slaves!

And he returned the guy on-top of drinking to his drinking,
and he put the cup
into the palm of Pharaoh-Negligence.

And as for the guy on-top of the bakers —
he hanged —

just as Joseph had opened up and interpreted for them.

But the guy on-top of drinking — he didn't remember Joseph.

He forgot about him.

And so it was —

at the end of two years,
Pharaoh-Negligence dreamed
— and listen here! —

he was taking his stand (as if someone appointed him to do it — the Pharaoh-king!)
by The-Great-Nile-River-That-Was-The-Sufferers'-God —
and — listen to this —
out of The-Great-Nile-River-That-Was-The-Sufferers'-God,
seven young bulls were climbing up —

they were beautiful looking!
and plump & fat fleshed!

and they were grazing on the marshy-reeds —

and — listen to this — seven more young bulls
climbed up after them
from The-Great-Nile-River-That-Was-The-Sufferers'-God —

they were awful looking!
and thin & lean fleshed!

and they were <u>taking their stand</u>
near the young bulls
on the lip of The-Great-Nile-River-That-Was-The-Sufferers'-God —

and the awful looking and lean fleshed young bulls ate
the seven beautiful looking and plump young bulls —

and Pharaoh-Negligence woke up!

(Note that the same verb 'taking one's stand, standing at attention'/AYMD is used for Pharaoh standing and the bulls standing — and it's not the verb-choice of one who 'stands tall'/QUM with some sense of power over/within oneself. Pharaoh stands at attention as if someone ordered him to stand there — just like the bulls do. After all, in the imagination of the band of YAH and anyone who knows YAHWEH, Pharaoh might be lord of the superpower's land and one of the gods/divinities of the land and lord of the Hebrew-slaves/all-slaves but even Pharaoh stands at attention to YAHWEH — or perhaps to the river at which he stands which is far more powerful than any human being, royal or not.

Or taking a hint from the drinking-guy's dream, maybe Pharaoh likes being bossed around, being the submissive? Remember the dream of the drinking-guy...where the punny-version of his dream is that he — a slave! — is fucking the Pharaoh — the highest in the land.... Like all ecstatics/prophets, the band of YAH teases people in power, as they did with the Judah & Tamar story earlier.

Note too that in *The Epic of Gilgamesh*, the Bull of Heaven was famine...perhaps the band of YAH teasing that Babylonian source material.)

And he went to sleep and dreamed a second time —
and listen here! —

seven grain-heads climbed up on one stalk —
fat and good!

and listen here —
seven grain-heads lean and scorched by the east-desert gale
were springing up after them —
and the lean grain-heads swallowed up the seven fat and full grain-heads —

and Pharaoh-Negligence woke up — yikes — it was a dream!

And so it was —

in the morning his breath was beating like a drum —
agitated — a panic —

and he sent for and called out for
every Suffering-Egyptian magician —
those who drew circles and lines to make sense of life —
and every Suffering-Egyptian wise-person.

And Pharaoh-Negligence tallied up his dream for them.

No one would open them up and interpret them for
Pharaoh-Negligence!

And the guy on-top of drinking styled out for
Pharaoh-Negligence,
"Serious offenses — on me —
in remembering the day —
Pharaoh-Negligence had cracked off — burst into a
rage — with his slaves —
and he gave me over to be guarded
in the house of the guy on-top of the butchers/
executioners —
me and the guy on-top of baking —
and we each dreamed one — a dream — one night —
I did and he did —
(and it happened) just as each of us had opened up
and interpreted his own dream that we had dreamed —
and there — with us — a boy — a Bordercrosser —
a slave of the guy on-top of the butchers/executioners —
we tallied it out for him —
and he opened up and interpreted for us our dreams —
each one — his dream — he opened up and interpreted —
and so it was — just as he opened up and interpreted
for us —
just like that it was —
it came to be —
as for me — (you/Pharaoh) made return to my position —
as for him — (you/Pharaoh) hanged!"

And Pharaoh-Negligence sent for
and called out for Joseph
and they hurried him from the pit.

And he shaved
and slid out of his outer-wear
and entered into — umm, arrived —
to Pharaoh-Negligence.

(What was it Joseph shaved? GLCH used here as 'shaved' can also be used for 'baldness' or 'shaved bald.' In 2 Kings 2 we get a story about Elisha being bald and made fun of for his baldness. Perhaps that's a mark of the prophets and the band of YAH is making that clear? Or is it something else?

And 'slid out of his outer-wear'/CHLP?! What indeed is going on here? *Strong's Exhaustive Concordance* has CHLP meaning such seemingly diverse things as sliding, hurrying, passing, springing up/out, piercing, changing...other lexicons agree. There are other stories in Genesis that have Jacob CHLPing this clothes...these are probably priestly-crafted stories. Were those stories added to normalize and dim down this strange use of the verb here by the band of YAH in the Joseph story? It's an ambiguous verb choice for sure — and perhaps more double-entendre that the band of YAH seems often to invite. They choose words that make you lean in and wonder.

Did dream-interpreters wear something special in Pharaoh's court? Anywhere? Is that what Joseph has on?

For that matter, is Joseph standing there naked?

Another hallmark of the prophets we learn through X's 1 & 2 Samuel saga is that the prophets were often naked on the mountaintops. Is that what the band of YAH is getting at here...playing on that assumption that prophets wear nothing or next to nothing...'slid out of his outer-wear'?)

And Pharaoh-Negligence said to Joseph...the one
whose name means Add-On or Grower,
"A dream! I dreamed! And as for opening up and
interpreting it — there's no one to do it.
I — I've heard about you —
heard it said that you listen to a dream to open it up
and interpret it."

And Joseph answered Pharaoh-Negligence saying,
"It's beyond me —
ELOHIM/God-or-the-gods-and-goddesses'll answer
with peace, health for Pharaoh-Negligence!"

And Pharaoh-Negligence styled it out for Joseph,
"In my dream — listen here! —

taking my stand on the lip of The-Great-Nile-River-
That-Is-Our-God —
and listen here —
from The-Great-Nile-River-That-Is-Our-God
seven young bulls climbed up —
plump & fat fleshed! beautifully <u>shaped</u>! —
and they were grazing in the marshy-reeds —

and listen — seven more young bulls climbed up
after them —
<u>dangling</u> and awfully shaped — very much so! —

skinny fleshed! —
never have I seen anything like them in the entire
land of Suffering-Egypt —
so awful —
and the skinny and awful young bulls ate the first
seven plump & fat young bulls —

and when they'd entered into their guts —
no one would've known they'd entered into their guts —
they looked awful —
just like they were at the beginning —

and then I woke up —
and I saw in my dream — listen here! —

seven grain-heads climbing up on one stalk —
full and good! —
and listen — seven grain-heads —
withered — thin — scorched
by the east-desert gale —
springing up after them —
and the thin grain-heads swallowed up the seven
good grain-heads —

I said this to the magicians
but no one would front it for me
— umm — tell me."

(Now note carefully how Pharaoh narrates his dreams here very differently than was said of his dreams earlier...even the subtle change from 'beautiful looking'/YPH MRAHH now becomes 'beautifully shaped'/YPH TAHR ...both of which were used to describe Joseph's beauty earlier in the saga before

Joseph's owner's wife grabbed Joseph and Joseph had to unfurl from his clothes to save his life/reputation.

And then there's this whole business of 'entering into'/BOAH circling back again and Pharaoh's way of describing the repulsiveness of the cows that are 'dangling'/DLOT and 'skinny'/RQOT that were not used earlier in the narration of his dream. *Strong's Exhaustive Concordance* notes, of course, that DLOT often has to do with 'the poor' but can also be used to describe hair, as in hair dangling down...both the poor and hair dangling by a thread.

What had gotten into Pharaoh? Was Pharaoh choosing his very descriptive words to make a point? to inspire Joseph — wearing god-knows-what right there in front of Pharaoh and Pharaoh's court — to offer some clarity about these, um, dreams Pharaoh had been having...? Was Pharaoh encouraging Joseph to plump himself up like the beautiful cows — beautiful in shape and in appearance — for something of Joseph's anatomy to be like a grain-head and fat-fleshed...perhaps Pharaoh here giving Joseph a way out of the dungeon forever?

We might be curious...if indeed Joseph had slid out of his outer-wear and is now standing in front of Pharaoh naked or wearing next to nothing and if indeed Pharaoh was encouraging the young man Joseph to plump himself up with an erection...was this a mark of prophets/ecstatics in their dream-interpretation? Is this what the bordercrossing prophets did? Was their nakedness and their phallic-mindedness key to their being prophets? Was this why the priests wanted them done away and not included in their Torah? The BAAL cults, remember, shaped a piece of wood like a penis and inserted it into the ground and invited dancing around it. Was all this phallic-mindedness — though quite different from the followers of BAAL — what got the prophets in trouble?

It might seem very queer, very strange indeed, until you lay these word choices alongside what happens in 1 & 2 Samuel regarding YAHWEH and the prophets/Samuel and then later to describe some of the very strange stories about the prophets in 1 & 2 Kings. It might very well indeed have been the nature of the prophets to be naked, to be erect on the mountaintops of Ancient Israel, to be titilated — no matter their gender — as YAHWEH touched their skin, breathed life into them, got them up to do some pretty wild things...as the prophets/ecstatics are said to do...like raising the dead to life, like blinding enemies coming to kill, like multiplying bread for friend and enemy alike, like inspiring people with their wild raps and rhymes, their style which comes from YAHWEH alone, the very wind that gave them life in breath.

Whatever it is, Joseph takes Pharaoh's hint to 'front it'/MGYD for him — an interesting choice of words to 'tell.' Pharaoh could have simply said DBR/'style it out' or AMR/'say or speak' but instead chooses the one word about speech that also plays on the word for NGD/'front or tell.' It's an absolutely unusual choice of words here, only perhaps playing on all the other puns from before...and the same word the band of YAH used earlier to describe Eve/Woman in the Pleasure-Orchard/Eden story with AYZR

CNGDO/'talker, complement, similar-but-different.' Woman would be the 'front/talker' for Mud-Creature in front of Snake, and Mud-Creature would one day find himself inside the embrace of Woman's front as they both hid from YAHWEH in their embracing each other/love-making with each other, as was much discussed earlier.)

And Joseph said to Pharaoh-Negligence,
"The dream of Pharaoh-Negligence — it's one —
it's what God-or-the-gods-and-goddesses/ELOHIM
are about to do —
it's being fronted — told to Pharaoh-Negligence —

seven good young bulls are seven years —
they are!
seven good grain-heads are seven years —
they are!
it's one dream —
seven skinny and awful young bulls climbing up after them are seven years —
they are!
seven skinny grain-heads scorched by the east-desert gale are seven years of famine!

That's the style I've styled out
for Pharaoh-Negligence...
what God-or-the-gods-and-goddesses/ELOHIM are about to do...making Pharaoh-Negligence see!

Listen up —
seven years are entering — coming —
a great superabundance through the entire land of Suffering-Egypt —

then seven years of famine will stand tall after them —
all the superabundance in the land of Suffering-Egypt
will be forgotten —
the famine will consume the land —
the superabundance in the land won't be known (from
the ways) this famine shows its faces (reveals itself)
afterwards because it'll be so very heavy —
and the dream was repeated to Pharaoh-Negligence twice
because the style by God-or-the-gods-and-goddesses/
ELOHIM is getting firmed up — standing erect —
and God-or-the-gods-and-goddesses/ELOHIM are
hurrying it up to make it happen —
and now Pharaoh-Negligence sees
a man discerning and wise...
and he's going to set him up
over the land of Suffering-Egypt...
Pharaoh will do this...
counters will take care of everything — they'll count up
everything within the land,
and take a fifth from the land of Suffering-Egypt
during the seven years of superabundance —
they'll gather up all the food of these good years being
entered into —
they'll heap up grain under Pharaoh-Negligence's
hand/phallic-control —
food in the cities — to protect it —
the food'll be taken care of — counted up/stored —
for the seven years of famine which'll be in the land of
Suffering-Egypt —
and the land will not be cut down during the famine!"

(Quite stylish in that 'seven'/SHBAY and 'superabundance'/SBAY are essentially the exact same word except for the placement of one dot before/after the Hebrew characters— audibly, the difference between S and SH.

We have our old unusual friend PQD here again...all the references to 'counting.'

And as for this whole 'getting firmed up, standing erect'/NCON business that Joseph is referring to, perhaps Joseph takes seriously Pharaoh's mention that things 'dangling and skinny' are repulsive to him...so could it be that Joseph firms himself up/gets an erection — the very opposite of 'dangling and skinny' — standing right there in front of Pharaoh?

And with his utter beauty and stylishly charming words and now his erection, Joseph is able to deliver some pretty harsh news that none of Pharaoh's magicians were willing to deliver — that famine is coming and you'd better get ready as Number One/ Pharaoh in the land and make some choices about how we are all to live before the famine comes...you'd better get ready by naming a wise and discerning Number Two...as Joseph seems to be volunteering for the job.)

And the style was good
in the eyes of Pharaoh-Negligence
and in the eyes of all his slaves.

And Pharaoh-Negligence said to his slaves,
"Can a man like this be found —
someone who has ELOHIM/the-gods-and-goddesses'
wind-breath in him?!"

(Note that the slaves/officials in Pharaoh's court do not respond! Perhaps they too are spellbound by the whole scene/style Joseph has cast here — beautiful appearance/shape and maybe his plumped up erection and punny words combined. After all, remember what Joseph's name means...Grower... Increaser...Add-On...the one who adds-it-all-up...and is said to be quite, quite attractive to both women and eunuchs alike — and now perhaps Pharaoh himself.

Note too that Pharaoh recognizes ELOHIM's/the-gods-and-goddesses' RUCH/'wind-breath' in Joseph — prophets/ecstatics being bordercrossing followers of the wind. I'm making an assumption that the character of the Egyptian Pharaoh would be thinking that ELOHIM here means 'the gods-and-goddesses' instead of the Hebrew-speaking priestly assumption of ELOHIM being 'God' or 'the One God.' But the use of ELOHIM in any prophetic text — like the bands of YAH's or X's stories — is probably meant to make us wonder/wander/bordercross.)

And Pharaoh-Negligence said to Joseph,
"Since the-gods-and-goddesses/ELOHIM have made known all this,
there's no one as discerning and wise as you!
You will be over my house —
and upon your mouth all my people will be kissed —
only with the throne will I be greater than you!"

And Pharaoh-Negligence said to Joseph —
the one whose name means Add-On, Grower —
"See here — I'm putting you over the whole land of Suffering-Egypt!"

And Pharaoh-Negligence removed his ring from his hand/penis/phallic-control
and gave it over onto Joseph's hand/penis/phallic-control
and wrapped him in fine clothes
and put a gold chain around his neck
and he rode him in the second chariot that was his —

and they called out before him, "Kneel!"

And Pharaoh-Negligence said to Joseph,
"I am Pharaoh-Negligence —
and besides you,
no man can raise high
his <u>hand/penis</u> or his <u>foot/testicles</u>
in the whole land of Suffering-Egypt!"

(Much more will be said about all of this in the commentary that follows the conclusion to the Joseph story. Suffice it to say, who is ordinarily 'Number 2' to Pharaoh but the Pharaoh's wife? And here Pharaoh gets woo-ed by Joseph — yes, certainly by his interpretation of the dream that wouldn't take a magician to interpret. Perhaps none of Pharaoh's magicians had the courage to tell Pharaoh what must be bound to happen — that tough times might be coming and we Egyptians would be wise to prepare for it — sound advice to store up food for the future no matter what's ahead. But who wants to deliver bad news to a god-guy who's considered to be the Divine Rain for the land? Who would have such courage?

Apparently, Joseph.

But how is it that Pharaoh becomes so enamored by Joseph that Pharaoh could accept such bad news? How does he stand there before Pharaoh at first that then has Pharaoh wrap him in clothes? And not only that, Pharaoh bedecks Joseph as a royal — wearing the ring, the chain, the clothes — and even has him in the second-chariot. This Joseph was just moments before this a prisoner of the dungeon!

Strong's Exhaustive Concordance notes too that RGL is often the word for 'foot,' though it can also mean 'external genitalia.' We already know that YD can mean both 'hand and penis.' The combination of RGL + YD occurs too with the story of Jonathan and his gear-lifter stripping naked as a way to entice and fool the Philistines in 1 Samuel 14, a book full of puns and the prophetic double-entendre imagination. In the story, Jonathan and his gear-lifter climb 'hand and foot'/'dick and balls' up to them. Perhaps so here too with Pharaoh describing how the people will kneel before Joseph with their dick and balls below his.

It's quite interesting that immediately following all of this dressing up of Joseph in royal-garb we get the biblical editors — be they Levitical priests or Deuteronomists — barging into the story to tell us that Joseph married an Egyptian woman and had children. But not in Levitical priestly's version of the story — Joseph does not marry.

All this fuss drummed up the biblical editors to try to distract us from a son/Joseph who once wore a dress that princesses wore, given to him by his father who was impregnated by the wind wind. But now Joseph's not dressed as a princess but as the Pharaoh's queen, his Number 2, who rides in the car behind Pharaoh....)

<*Gen 41.45-52*>

And the seven years of superabundance ended in the land of Suffering-Egypt,
and the seven years of famine pierced —
it entered just as Joseph had said.

(Uhh...this 'pierce' is CHLL...the very unusual verb choice also used when Noah was getting drunk and naked and for the bold act of the people of Babel in building a tower. Again, lexicons note that CHLL has diverse meanings: 'playing the pipe as the life of the party, beginning something new when the old is preferred and tradition is revered, wounding by piercing, doing something offensive.' More pun-play from our band of YAH!)

And so it was —

famine in all the lands —
but in the land of Suffering-Egypt there was bread.

And the whole land of Suffering-Egypt was aching with hunger,
and the people cried out to Pharaoh-Negligence for bread,
and Pharaoh-Negligence said to all the Suffering-Egyptians,
"Go to Joseph!
Whatever he says to you all, do!"

And the famine was over the whole face of the land/
earth —
and Joseph opened everything that was in them (that
had been stored up in the previous seven years of
superabundance) and sold grain to the Egypt-Sufferers.

And the famine in the land of Suffering-Egypt grew in
strength,
and all the lands (countries) entered
into Suffering-Egypt
to buy grain in front of Joseph
because the famine was growing in strength in every land.

And Jacob saw that there was grain for sale in
Suffering-Egypt.

And Jacob said to his sons,
"Why do you stare at each other?!"

And he said,
"Listen up —
I hear that there's grain for sale
in Suffering-Egypt —
go on down there and buy some grain for us from there
so that we'll live and not die!"

And Joseph's brothers — ten of them — went on down
to buy clean, threshed grain from Suffering-Egypt.

But as for Benjamin —
whose name means Power-Son —
Joseph's (full) brother —
Jacob didn't send him with his brothers because,
as he said,
"Otherwise mischief or harm gets called upon ourselves!"

<Gen 42.5>

And Joseph — he was quite potent in the land,
and he was the one selling grain to all the people of the land.

And Joseph's brothers entered into — arrived —
and bowed to him, their faces to the ground.

And Joseph saw his brothers
and recognized them —
but he was unrecognizable to them —
and he styled it out to them harshly,
and said to them,
"From where did you enter?"

And they answered,
"From the land of the Humble-Traders' —
to buy food!"

Joseph recognized his brothers,
but they didn't recognize him.

And Joseph remembered the dreams
he'd dreamt about them,
and said to them,
"From balls/testicles! Spies!
That's what you are!
To see the land's nakedness/genitals —
that's why you've entered!"

(There's RGL/'foot or testicles' again...and it seems he's not only accusing them of being spies but he's cussing them out...RGL here cleverly playing with 'the land's nakedness' and our old friend

BOAH/'entered'...BOAH, again is a euphemism for sex, 'screwing.' Just to be clear and so you know other commentators have noted it too...MRGL/'spies' and M+RGL/'from testicles'...*Strong's Exhaustive Concordance* notes RGL/'foot, or euphemism for testicles or male genitalia'

and it does make a bit of sense this whole stew of RGL-meanings...as in 'those who go on foot' as all lexicons attest...and possibly, as I presume another understanding of M/RGL would then be 'those who put it out there' or 'those who risk it' as spies do... potentially another possibility 'spying' and 'feet' and 'testicles' go together in the Ancient Hebrew language/imagination.

Isaiah 7 talks about Assyria being the razor that will shave the hair from Jerusalem's RGL...certainly not their feet!)

And they said to him,
"No — my boss —
your slaves have entered to buy food —
all of us are sons of one man —
we are true —
we — your slaves — aren't spies!"

And he said to them,
"No! The nakedness/genitals of the land —
that's what you've entered to see!"

And they said,
"Twelve of us slaves — we are brothers —
sons of one man in the Humble-Traders'-Land —

and listen here —
the youngest is with our father today —
and one is no more—"

And Joseph said to them,
"It's just as I styled out to you:
'From balls/testicles! Spies! That's what you are!'

In this you'll be tested —
(I threaten you by) the life of Pharaoh-Negligence —
if you ever leave from here —
it'll be because your youngest brother enters/arrives!

Send away from yourselves only one —
and he'll fetch your brother
and the rest of you'll be imprisoned —
the reliability and confidence of your stylings-on are going to be tested —

or else not —
(I threaten you by) the life of Pharaoh-Negligence! —
because you are from balls/testicles! Spies!"

And he added them all up,
put them under guard for three days.

And Joseph — whose name has to do with Adding —
said to them on the third day,
"Do this and live —
I fear ELOHIM/God-or-the-gods-and-goddesses!
If you are true,
one of your brothers'll be imprisoned in the guard-house you've been in,
and the rest of you, go and take home grain
for the hungry in your houses —

and (as for) the youngest of brothers — make him
come back to me —
and then your stylings-on will be reliable —
and you won't die!"

(Note how the one who added up all of Pharaoh's dreams got himself a job where he added up all the grain into storage for this time when the famine was increasing throughout the land and now he's toying with his brothers — adding to their anxiety — by making them go home and get his younger brother, brother from the same womb, his full brother Benjamin. Such is the story of Joseph... Add-On...Add-It-All-Up...Grower...Increaser...this incredibly complex character with prophetic-style.)

And they would do just that.

Each one said to his brother,
"Truly we're suffering guilt over our brother —
we saw the anguish of his living, breathing body —
in his pleading with us —
and we didn't listen —
that's why this anguish has come to us!"

<Gen 42.22-23>

And (Joseph) turned away from them and wept.

Then he turned back to them
and styled it out with them
and took (their brother) Listening from them
and bound him up right before their eyes.

<Gen 42.25-28>

And they went to their father Jacob — the one whose name means Tricky-Heel-Grabber —
in the land of Humble-Traders
and reported to him all that had befallen them:
"The man of the royal-bosses of the land — he styled it out to us harshly —
he gave it to us like we were spying on the land —
so we said to him,

'We're true/honest!
We're not spies!
We're twelve brothers — sons of our father!
One is no more —
and the youngest is with our father today
in the land of the Humble-Traders!'

And the man of the royal-bosses of the land — he said to us,
'By this I'll know that you're true/honest —
you'll lay up one of your brothers with me
and as for the hungry in your house —
take (grain) and go!
Bring your youngest brother to me
and I'll know that you're not spies
and that you are true/honest
and I'll give your brothers to you —
and you'll be able to travel wherever you want in the land —and even trade and conduct business here!'"

(Note the brothers' style...to sweeten the deal...trying to entice their old father to give over Benjamin/ Power-Son not only to rescue Listening/Simeon but to have trading rights in the land — something Joseph never mentioned, right? The brothers continue in their dishonest ways — just as they did when they stripped their younger brother and threw him into an empty well and lied to their father about his whereabouts by dipping their brother's prized princess-dress in blood when they gave it back to their father.

Note too that the brothers not only fail to recognize that they were speaking to their younger brother Joseph, they also fail to notice that this "man" was the Number Two to Pharaoh...just one more thing to portray the brothers as imperceptive.

And the brothers do not repeat the double-entendre cussing-style they heard from Joseph's mouth — instead to their father they sweeten their recounting of the arrangement with a trade-promise. There's no 'to see the nakedness of the land' and 'entering in' puns in their telling the story to their father. But even with their antics, Tricky-Jacob will see right through to what really matters to him — his sons, especially the ones he no longer has with him and the youngest he's about to lose — with no interest in the potential trading deal. After all, such a deal would be preposterous...a superpower like Ancient Egypt giving trading rights to a small band of people living north of them in the land of wandering, the land of the Humble-Traders...not to mention during a time of famine...not to mention giving trading rights to people Joseph/Pharaoh's Number Two just accused as spies....

'royal-boss' above is ADNY, the word that later will

be the priestly placeholder for YAHWEH when reading the biblical text aloud when the priests feel 'YAHWEH' should not be spoken aloud...ADNY is often translated as 'Lord/lord'

In the Joseph-saga, an ancient person would hear this brothers' speech and Joseph's speech and be able to note the clever differences quite clearly, just as we moderns who listen to our comedians doing stand-up and perceive the subtle shifts in their plays on language to get at seemingly far-fetched connections, all with a matter of a few slightly different words and even syllables. And that's why and how we laugh — we catch the nuances that they invite. It's also how we expand our imaginations...comedians draw us beyond our maps, our assumptions about life. It's the very style of the prophets/ecstatics.)

<Gen 42.35>

And their father Jacob said to them,
"It's me you're miscarrying —
will you leave me with no children?!
Joseph is no more!
Listening is no more!
And Benjamin — (my Power-Son) —
you're going to take him from me!
They're the whole thing!"

<Gen 42.37 - 43.15a>

And they stood up tall
and went down to Suffering-Egypt
and took their stand in front of Joseph's face.
And Joseph saw them with Benjamin...Power-Son.

And he said to the one overseeing his house,
"Bring the men to the house,
butcher the meat and firm things up —
the men will eat with me at midday."

(Here's that verb CUN/'erect, firm up' again...used earlier when Joseph was before Pharaoh.)

And the man did just as Joseph said —
and the man brought the men
toward Joseph's house.

<Gen 43.18 - 23d>

And he made Listening go out to them.

And the man brought the men into Joseph's house
and gave them water,
and they washed their feet,
and he gave them feed for their donkeys.

<Gen 43.25-28a>

(And Joseph arrived at his house.)
And they shriveled
and bowed down.

(Shriveled...the very opposite of 'firming up' and 'standing tall.')

And (Joseph) raised his eyes and saw Power-Son,
his brother, son of his same mother.
And he said,
"Is this your youngest brother about whom you told me?"

And he said,
"God-or-the-gods-and-goddesses/ELOHIM be
gracious to you, my son!"

And Joseph...Add-On hurried out (of the room) —
because they were melting him —
the womb-kindredness for his (full) brother!

And he wanted so badly to weep —
he entered into his inner-room and wept there.

And he washed his face
and went out
and pulled himself together and said,
"Serve the bread!"

<Gen 43.32>

And they (were) sat before him —
the oldest where the oldest sits
and the youngest where the youngest sits —

(and everyone in the correct order in between — he knew their birth order and had them sit at table with him like that!)

the men were astounded —
each one with his friend!
And he carried portions
that were in front of him to them —

and Benjamin's portion was larger
than anyone else's portion —
five times as large!
And they drank and got drunk with him.

And he shouted out orders (in a language his brothers
couldn't understand)
to the one overseeing his house,
"Fill up the men's baggage with food —
as much as they can lift —
and put each man's silver-money
inside the mouth of the baggage —
and as for my special wine goblet —
the valuable, silver one —
put it inside the mouth of the youngest one's baggage
with his silver-money from buying grain."

And (his house's overseer) did it in the style that
Joseph'd styled out.

And it was morning's light,
and the men were sent on — they and their donkeys.

And they'd just left the city —
they hadn't even gotten that far —
and Joseph said to the one overseeing his house,
"Stand yourself up —
chase after the men —
catch them — and say to them,
'Why did you sound out bad instead of good?!
Is this not what my boss drinks from?!
He uses it to hiss like a godly-snake & whisper (like
the wind) —
he reads the signs and tells the future with it —
how could you have done such a bad thing?!'"

And he caught up with them
and styled out these styles to them.
And they said to him,
"Why does my boss style out such styles as these?!
How dare your slaves — us! — do something with such style as this?!!

<*Gen 44.8*>

Whoever is found with it on him —
from among your slaves — us! —
he will die —
and also — we — we'll be slaves for my boss!"

And he said,
"Just as you've styled out — let it be!
'Whoever is found with it will be my slave'
but the rest of you will be innocent."

And they hurried
and brought down — each one of them — his baggage
down onto the ground
and opened his baggage,
one man at a time.

And he searched beginning with the oldest, finishing with the youngest,
and he found the wine-goblet
in Benjamin's baggage.
They were so upset they tore <u>their clothes</u>,
and each man loaded his donkey
and returned toward the city.

(Joseph's recent 'sound out'/SHLMTM and now 'their clothes'/SLMTM are the same consonants except for one little dot...perhaps the band of YAH playfully linking their sounding out by the ripping of their clothes. Clothes-tearing was the ancient sign of showing outwardly the way anyone feels inwardly. There are plenty of other words the band of YAH could have used for clothes, how cleverly they choose this one with such sound-style. More will soon be said about another sound: 'hiss like a godly-snake & whisper (like the wind)'...)

<Gen 44.14a>

And his brothers entered into Joseph's house —
he was still there —
and they fell down on the ground before his face.

And Joseph said to them,
"What's this deed you've done?!
How come you didn't know that I —
a man like me! —
hiss like a godly-snake & whisper (like the wind),
read the signs and tell the future?!"

<Gen 44.16-34>

And Joseph couldn't keep himself together in front of everyone standing-at-attention before him,

and he called out,
"Make everyone leave me!"

Not a single man was stationed there with him
when Joseph made himself known to his brothers.

He gave in, his voice now one of weeping.

The Suffering-Egyptians heard —
Pharaoh-Negligence's house heard!

And Joseph said to his brothers,
"I'm Joseph!
Is he still — my father — is he still alive?"

His brothers weren't able to answer him —
they were trembling, terrified by him, his face!

<Gen 45. 4-11>

"Look here —
your own eyes see —
the eyes of my brother Benjamin —
my mouth, my way of styling it out to you —
tell my father all about my weight —
my respect and honor —
in Suffering-Egypt and all that you've seen —
hurry up —
and go bring down my father here right now!"

And he fell
onto his brother Benjamin's neck and wept,
and Benjamin wept all over his neck —

— the cliffhanger ending
to the band of YAH's stories in Genesis —

<Gen 45.15 - 50.26>

commentary

On Joseph,
His Dress(es),
& His Genital(s)

What gender is Joseph?

Was there a reason Jacob gave a princess-dress to this 17 year old son?

What, umm, genitalia did Joseph have? He's called Jacob's son, so he must have a penis? Or did his dad know — and that's why he gave Joseph a dress — that his son had a vagina, or was XXY and had a penis and vagina? Or did Joseph have some other genitalia as some humans are born differently than most? Or did Joseph identify their genitalia differently...assigned meaning to themself in a different way than most...what today we might call nonbinary...a true bordercrosser? Like a shaman in a lot of cultures, a true shapeshifter — did Jacob sense that power in Joseph?

Or did Jacob just think that his son would be happier wearing a flashy, seemingly disappearing princess-dress? That Jacob knew Joseph was a genderbender and he was just trying to be a good dad — no matter what the rest of the family, especially those bloodthirsty brothers of Joseph's, thought about it? Or did Jacob know that his son Joseph would disappear, be disappeared?

Ah, those siblings of Joseph! Do remember Dinah, and the mad way the brothers enacted Justice for their sister Justice/Dinah? And who was it that led the parade to kill off not just Early-and-Eager Shechem and his Male-Ass of a father? Which two of Jacob's sons led the brothers to kill everyone in the whole entire town for the awful sins of Shechem alone?

> **Levi**...the fictionalized character who will one day be in charge of the bloody Law as priest-leader. And I do mean that quite literally in that the Levitical priests craft the very law meant to kill, meant to punish by death men who have sex with men, perhaps an aspect of these genderbending, bordercrossing prophets/ecstatics. The ancient Levites and their godforsaken Levitical laws bloodied more than 2 millennia of people who mutually reached out to each other — human being to human being, no matter their genitalia — with love or curiosity or passion or whatever, people today identified with the alphabet-soup of LGBTQ+. The Law crafted by the Levitical priests has some beauty to it, for sure, with its care for the poor, etc — and it has some major, major problems that still echo today. Menstruating women need to be sidelined because they are unclean?! Come on.

And who's Levi's fellow bloodthirsty brother and co-leader against Shechem's town?

> **Simeon**...the one whose name quite ironically means 'Listening'...the one eventually locked up by our character Joseph to craftily get the rest of the brothers to fetch Benjamin and bring him to Joseph.

What a family Jacob has, eh? Full of cold-blooded murderers, a dress-wearing 'boy' who dreams of becoming royal and does, a tragically raped young girl, a purchaser of prostitutes, a boy whose birth tragically kills his much-loved mother, and on and on and on.

Life is complex, right?

It's worth noting too in these stories that when Jacob made his way back to Canaan after his stint with Laban, Jacob and his wives brought back a deeper taste of YAHWEH and those idols from Babylon stolen by Rachel from her father...YAHWEH and idolatry, two things that will haunt Ancient Israel in very different ways for centuries...and haunts us all today. The Levitical Law of the Torah haunts as well, though perhaps many of us today are only beginning to realize just how problematic it has been since its creation, especially with its hierarchical priestly prerogatives.

The band of YAH's Genesis stories and the band of X's 1 & 2 Samuel indeed could have been composed to lampoon the Levitical priests' Law, their Torah.

Life is complex....

The Bible is complex....It's like the whole world could find itself in the story of this family of Jacob's, huh? And maybe that's the point, the very clever point, that the band of YAH offers us all if we have the imagination to be with It all.

This is the family-quarrel trying to work itself out for millennia...how priests and prophets can discover ways of getting along...how hierarchically-minded people can recognize the value in circularly-minded people... how lions very well could lie down with lambs, how war-implements very well could be repurposed as tools for growing food.

Back to Joseph and the princess-dress given to him by Jacob, his father who was penetrated by YAHWEH...

Did getting the wind knocked into himself by YAHWEH awaken in Jacob some sense of the future? Of being able to know the future through the present, as prophets do, as ecstatics on drugs or oracles inhaling sulphur from the belly-button of the (Greek)earth or humans high on the wind alone do and have done, it seems, since the beginning of time?

Could it be that Jacob gave Joseph a princess-dress because he knew that one day Joseph would be royalty... that Joseph would be queen...to Pharaoh...and through that rather interesting relationship between Pharaoh and his dress-wearing 'Queen Joseph' that Joseph would save civilization — would save Jacob's family — all by foresight about a coming famine? And if it weren't with foresight, at least with courage to speak up about what seemed so obvious through Pharaoh's dreams that Joseph just had to speak up? knew that he'd be less if he didn't speak up? like prophets/ecstatics clearly feel and have felt for millennia? no matter the cost...

Could that be it?

It's quite a fascinating story, this Joseph-story, yeah?

It's a story that erupts in many directions, and I'm not talking "technicolor."

Such is the prophetic/ecstatic-imagination — far, far different than the hierarchical-imagination (priestly or royal) that cannot seem to handle very well any ambiguity, not to mention any challenge to its god-given authority. You see, gods and goddesses (ELOHIM) give authority to some who inflict their authority onto others with their pecking order, their hierarchies of power and worth; YAHWEH gives authority to all where power is then shared within the equality of all breathers.

That's the substantial difference between the hierarchical-imagination with ELOHIM and the prophetic/ecstatic-imagination with YAHWEH.

Breathe in. For those who know, there is no valid authority other than the wind that gives us all life... YAHWEH.

Eventually everybody realizes that emperors wear no clothes...

There are plenty of intrusions in the Joseph-text, Genesis 37 - 50. What seems like a very long story is actually pretty compact, tight...at least without all those intrusions.

What intrusions? The long speeches by brothers Reuben and Judah throughout the story and Judah's whole story plunked down in the middle of the Joseph story (all of Genesis 38) and Israel's speeches (instead of Jacob's few words) and the Ephraim/Manasseh story and Israel/Jacob's death-story likely added by the biblical editors to harmonize the Jacob and Moses stories. (Remember, Israel is the nickname of Jacob, a name rather strangely preferred by the biblical editors in the Joseph-saga. After all, in the Jacob-stories, the Levitical priestly editors go out of their way to cover-over the YAHWEH-penetrating-Jacob aspect of the wrestling story where Jacob acquires his nickname Israel.)

Sit down with a Bible and read Genesis 37 - 50. It's a long read. It doesn't take a rocket scientist — or a biblical scholar — to note that this text is a mess. Like the Noah story, it has been highly edited, layered, stapled together, added onto. The story moves forward and then portions of the plot are told again but differently. The plot moves on again and this time there's commentary that doesn't move the story forward. And then the text moves back to the plot, and then there's another break in the story. So many intrusions! But beneath all of those intrusions is an original story — a first-telling of the story. Can you imagine, can you listen carefully to Genesis 37 - 50, and hear the first-telling?

Peel away the intrusions in the text and it becomes quite clear that the Joseph-saga is a story about wardrobes. Costumes, if you will.

Leave those intrusions of the biblical editors in the text, and it's easy to miss Joseph's ever-changing wardrobes in the story, and the potential plot-patterning of those wardrobe changes:

A. Joseph's dress-wearing — the flashy-kind princesses wore, perhaps shimmering in such a way that they disappeared, given to him by his father.

B. Joseph being stripped naked from that dress by his jealous brothers.

A. Joseph most likely being dressed as a simple slave in the house of Potiphar/Owned-by-Negligence... Pharaoh's eunuch.

B. Joseph being stripped naked from that slave-ware by Potiphar's wife out of her lust for Joseph.

A. Joseph most likely wearing ancient prison-gear (rags?) in the dungeon/round-house — except perhaps when he's on-top of his eunuch-handlers.

B. Joseph sliding out of that prison-gear and standing before Pharaoh wearing...what? potentially nothing?

A. Joseph being dressed by Pharaoh as a royal official, Pharaoh's queen, Pharaoh's Number Two.

C. Joseph standing before his brothers and wearing the royal-dress and revealing nothing of himself to his brothers — even scheming to capture his full-brother, womb-kindred Benjamin...

B./D. ...and then Joseph standing before his brothers and wearing the royal-dress and weeping and revealing everything of himself to his brothers.

The pattern is quite interesting, isn't it?

And perhaps the pattern helps us to figure out what indeed Joseph was wearing as he stood there in front of Pharaoh and was able to convince him soooo quickly that he himself — Joseph — was the right one for the job as Number Two to Pharaoh. Joseph — the genderbending bordercrosser right out of the Egyptian dungeon!

Just before he first stands before Pharaoh, we are told Joseph 'slipped out of his outer-wear' and that he shaved — what he shaved we're not sure.

But what is it he's wearing there before Pharaoh? We're never told explicitly.

In the pattern of the story, Joseph wears something and then gets stripped naked from it by someone else. If that pattern is trustworthy, then maybe Joseph is indeed standing there before Pharaoh naked.

...and that prophets wear no clothes, maybe no hair too...

Perhaps naked and shaved are signs of a prophet/ecstatic in the ancient world? There's some textual evidence throughout the biblical tradition to support this.

Shaved? In the Joseph story, the verb GLCH is used and it can mean 'to shave, even to shave down to baldness.' In 2 Kings 2, Elisha gets called 'baldy'/QRCH by a pack of children — an insult to him and perhaps his calling/

profession as prophet. QRCH, most lexicons and concordances note, has to do with making oneself bald, perhaps as part of one's mourning ritual, one's public/private grieving. Just after Elijah gets taken up to the heavens in a whirlwind of a raging storm — remember YAHWEH was considered by the ancients as the wind/storm divinity — and Elisha requests and gets a double-dose of Elijah's power, Elisha gets asked to purify a town's drinking water. And Elisha does so with a bowl of salt. And just then some little boys mock Elisha by calling him 'baldy' or 'the fool who made himself bald,' it seems. Elisha curses the children and sicks some she-bears on the children who then are mauled by the bears and die. Forty-two children! Another wild Bible story most people don't like to talk about!

Maybe the prophets were bald, chose baldness over the finery of hair? Maybe being shaved bald was a mark of someone being a prophet? If indeed people would shave their heads bald during their mourning time, it's kind of a sign then that they are dropping out of society for awhile — it's an outward sign revealing their inner turmoil. Maybe that 'dropping out' is what prophets are doing by shaving their heads bald? Or maybe balded-prophets are mourning for "the shipwreck" that is society...as Merton coins the phrase in talking about the desert fathers and mothers who left the shipwreck that was the Roman Empire and its corrupting influences. In 1 Samuel we get a good whiff of such mourning... prophet/ecstatic character Samuel performs funeral and mourning rites for King Saul — while Saul is still alive!

Are you getting the whiff of the playful imagination of the prophets?

It is rather interesting that the Levitical Law recommends men not shave — at least not shave the sides of their hair.

This is all gets even more curious when we lay it all alongside the biblical Nazirite vow — the vow someone takes to not cut their hair as an outward sign of one's dedication to God as crowned-priest. The whole Samson story is about that vow, of course. Rather interestingly, Samuel's mother dedicates her son as a Nazirite, one for whom a razor would never touch his head, before she offers him to the priest Eli to raise as a future-priest. That was Samuel's path until the ark was taken into battle and then lost in battle by Eli's foolish sons. Once those sons are dead and Eli is dead and the ark is gone and the temple-tent is seen as worthless without the ark, Samuel has no role as priest or priest-in-training any more. And he wanders off. We don't hear about him in the story for 20+ years — and even when the ark comes back to Ancient Israel led by some cows, Samuel has no role with the ark even though he's the only one living who had any role with it before it disappeared. The Levites step in to care for the ark...and eventually seem to be in with the powers dedicated to the crown, to Saul and then David.

What happens to Samuel? We don't know, other than 20 years later he shows up and tells people to leave behind their BAALS and ASHTAROTH and be in relationship with YAHWEH alone and then later demonstrates YAHWEH's power with wind and storm. Wind and storm were actually associated with BAAL... BAAL is god of the storm to ancients of the region...but here Samuel is showing the people who really rules the wind, who is the wind, who sails into their nostrils and gives them life...YAHWEH alone. (see 1 Samuel 7)

Whatever happened to Samuel in those 20 years is a mystery — and probably meant to be that way narrative-wise in the Samuel-saga of 1 & 2 Samuel. One thing we know for sure from descriptions after 1 Samuel is that ecstatic Samuel seems to be convening some gatherings of people on the mountaintops of Israel/Palestine — and they are naked and seeming to have some ecstatic experience through YAHWEH. You didn't notice that in your Bible? Well, it's right there in 1 Samuel 19.

As for Samuel's hair, I haven't found yet any references or pun-worthy allusions to it anywhere in the 1 & 2 Samuel text — and will keep looking! Could it be that after he leaves his role as priest-in-training once Eli is dead and the ark is gone that Samuel goes and lives on the mountaintops of Israel/Palestine and no longer has any care about his appearance, including his hair? Maybe through the harsh life of mountain-living and the wild winds that whip everything up and around that Samuel's hair falls out? Or maybe X, the band crafting the wonderful fiction that is 1 & 2 Samuel, thinks this whole hair business is not important?

As for the Levitical priestly editors' hierarchical-feelings and prescriptive-imagination that come through loud and clear in Leviticus, we might do well to notice carefully what happens in Leviticus 18 - 20. In these three chapters we get the prohibitions of men having sex with men under pain and punishment of death and all manner of people and animals with whom sex is not permitted. In Leviticus 19, we get the rather curious promulgations not to wear clothes of mixed-weaves and not to practice divination or future-telling via the word 'NCHSH' — the very same word the character-Joseph uses to describe what he was doing with Pharaoh's goblet. And guess what else...we are told not to 'knock off'/NQP the hair growing at the sides/edges of one's head. It's in these chapters that we also get the prohibition of being near a woman who is menstruating — her blood being seen by the priests as unclean. That's quite a grouping of laws in three quick chapters of Leviticus!

Could much/all of Leviticus 18 - 20 be pushing against the ways of the prophets, of the priests crafting laws that prohibit any of the prophets' ways of life and imagination? Might it also be possible that the Levitical priests were also here rolling together the ways of the prophets (shaving/being bald, wearing mixed up clothes or being naked, plus an openness to welcoming women into their prophetic guilds when menstruating or not) with the ways of BAAL (who had reputations for having orgies around the BAAL-penis-pole...maybe even with family members of all ages, as we see happening in the band of YAH's Sodom and Gomorrah story, Gen 19)?

Are the Levitical priests through Leviticus 18 - 20 essentially prohibiting both the ways of the prophets/ecstatics and the ways of the BAAL/ASHTAROTH-worshippers — lumping them together in a basket prohibiting their very different philosophies?

In 1 Samuel, the character-Samuel makes it very clear that BAAL/ASHTAROTH must be beheaded to follow YAHWEH. The prophets' poems — Amos, the three Isaiahs, Jeremiah, and others — all do the same. Prophets/ecstatics are not the same as BAAL/ASHTAROTH worshippers — not at all!

Maybe the priests do not shave; maybe the prophets

do shave or at least don't care so much about the finery and status of their hair, not to mention their clothes?

This wouldn't be the first time that priests and prophets recommend completely different ways of showing one's faithfulness to the divine, whether conceived by the priests as ELOHIM and by the prophets as YAHWEH. As a matter of fact, priests and prophets seem to be diametrically opposed to one another in just about every way.

Perhaps the Joseph-story is playing on that knowledge and the assumptions about prophets being shaved/bald and naked as Joseph stands before Pharaoh to interpret Pharaoh's dreams?

Which is to say...could it be that every ancient hearer of the Joseph-story would indeed expect Joseph to be standing there naked or not wearing much at all as prophets were known to do...not even a full, healthy head of hair? And that that is why the Pharaoh was wooed so quickly by such bad news as a coming famine that quite possibly could challenge his power if he weren't careful and carefully advised?

A little bit more on naked?

In 1 & 2 Samuel, being naked and YAHWEH's 'self-stripping'/GLH before Its prophets are hallmarks of being a prophet/ecstatic. How many times is GLH used through 1 & 2 Samuel? 21 times, and often to describe what YAHWEH does before human beings.

Even when he was a priest-in-training in 1 Samuel, we are told that the boy Samuel 'had girdled on the special, priestly straggly-yarned underwear.' This special underwear is usually called the "linen ephod" in most translations...but that translation misses much of the nuance of these Hebrew words...Hebrew words that the Levitical priestly editors will clamp down and clarify in Exodus 28 and many places after that.

"Linen ephod" or "ephod made of linen" in 1 Samuel is AHPOD BD. The word BD is 'linen' and comes from the verb BDD/'to be separated, to be alone, to be straggly'...perhaps regarding clothing this would mean 'straggly yarned' as I have opted for in *The Naked Path of Prophet vol 1.* Surely, with something straggly, it would be a bit see-through, or things might come through or even fall out. At the very least, it would allow the breeze to come through. Maybe that's why Samuel's mother Hannah makes for Samuel a little coat — both to keep him warm and to not expose himself to his mother when she came for visits to her son and Eli and the ark, the place where some major poetry leaked from her own lips.

Now it's rather important to note that when it comes time for the Torah's Levitical priestly editors to tell us how the ephod is worn, 'straggly' and 'see-through' are not options. Sure, the under-layer for the priest's Exodus and Leviticus versions of the ephod might be linen, but a whole wardrobe is layered over the linen-underwear: linen-trousers over the linen-underwear, and then an outer breastplate with a robe and a tunic under them and a sash and a turban/head-gear. That whole gear is certainly not see-through! Check it out for yourself in Exodus 28 and Leviticus 16, just for starters. And these Levitical priestly editors' version of the ephod is made from the finest of materials, of course, yarns of different colors: red and blue and purple and scarlet. It's as if the priests had created their own royal-gear, and all of this of course to wear around the big gold-box, the ark containing the Law/Torah crafted by the priests...the Law/Torah eventually finalized with the royally-motivated Deuteronomists that essentially proclaims their power within the hierarchy under ELOHIM/God and, in their priestly/royal minds, ordained by ELOHIM/God...the Law/Torah that mentions absolutely nothing of the prophets and their ecstatic-poems and their wild deeds...the Law/Torah that prescribes death for men having sex with men, that puts women and their menstruation in places away from men, that makes it clear that men are not to lop off the hair at the sides of their heads, and that people should not do what YAHWEH does and the prophets seem to do too in 1 Samuel: to strip naked. Leviticus 18 & 20 also prohibits stripping naked, in a variety of forms, around family members. Maybe the prophets were open to nakedness around family members, as many of my own naturist/nudist friends are too. Nakedness does not imply sex, of course. Nakedness means you take off your clothes and let the breeze and sun lick your skin — not someone else.

Seems that Leviticus 18 - 20 is focused on prohibiting much of what the prophets are associated with, yeah?

...underneath their rich royal-garb, priests and emperors are like everyone else...skin!

No matter what prophets and priests and royals and their Deuteronomistic handlers wear, no matter what their hairstyles are like, underneath it all, we are all alike.

Perhaps that's the message of the prophets — on two fronts:

> Why cover up with fine robes and finely coiffed hair the very things that make us similar? Our skin, our humanity! What was it Jesus invited if someone sued us for our outer-garment, a sign of one's status and wealth in the ancient world? Hand over the outer-garment, Jesus invites, and then hand over the underwear too and stand there naked before all to see...Matthew 5:38-41. Why? Why would Jesus advocate such a thing? Maybe he was onto the prophetic naked-way too? And what would happen in a courtroom if someone were suing you for everything you've got and you gave it to them, including the clothes on your back? And there you were standing naked in the courtroom — with your oppressor holding your clothes! Hmm...what indeed was Jesus up to?

> And if you're naked and the wind blows, what happens for you? It's titilating, yes? Stimulating. Pleasurable. Ecstasy-inducing, perhaps. And if YAHWEH is indeed the wind and the prophets/ecstatics are getting high on YAHWEH on The Heights (Ramah, where Samuel lives...RMH/'high'), then wouldn't you want more and more of your body to be in contact with the wind and not cover it over with cloth upon cloth, no matter how fine?! Wouldn't you want to breathe in more, to let more and more and more of YAHWEH into your every orifice? This is far, far different from just taking off your shoes for God/ELOHIM, as Exodus 3 recommends via Moses. This is far, far different from coming close to the mountain but not touching it, as Exodus 19 recommends, at least until God/ELOHIM blows the shofar/ram's horn-trumpet. And even then,

according to that priestly story, the people are supposed to do a whole purity-ritual with their bodies and their garments before they can even think of approaching the mountain. Touch the mountain too soon and die! Seems that the Levitical priestly editors are intent on killing a lot of people in the name of God/ELOHIM.

Very rarely do the prophets have death on their lips or on their hands. There are a few instances: the Elisha sicking the she-bears on the 42 children, Samuel killing foreign King Agag who was known for his bloodthirsty ways all the while Israel's King Saul wanted to party with him, Elijah in his grudge-match with the prophets of BAAL. But these are just three unusual incidents — and all of them likely fictional. Prophets usually recognize enemies as friends, fellow humans under YAHWEH, and even build their guild-communities near Israel's enemies in 1 Samuel.

Perhaps the prophets/ecstatics of the Bible were the ones who cared little for social-graces, who lived on the mountains and the out-of-the-way places far from the reaches of the empire, perhaps they wore nothing or as little as possible, perhaps they cared little for their hair and even shaved it off...all because YAHWEH mattered more than what society/empire thought of them.

And perhaps as Joseph is standing there before Pharaoh just about to interpret Pharaoh's dreams, every ancient hearer knew what Joseph looked like...naked, shaved and not looking dignified, looking just like a prophet who knows something of dreams, who 'hisses like a snake'/NCHSH, a prophet and dream-interpreter through whom YAHWEH 'whispers'/NAHM...all the things that the Levitical priestly editors reject.

But what if the prophet becomes the emperor, or at least Pharaoh's Number 2?

With Joseph we get an inkling of the problems of someone who has had a whiff of ecstasy beginning to rule as a hierarch.

The fictional characters Saul and David have similar experiences, similar problems.

As far as we know, Joseph is able to handle it — that is to say, he doesn't use his power to get only what he wants, at least doesn't follow through on that initial scheme to trap his brothers. Joseph does hatch a plan to get only Benjamin to live with him and either jail or send home the other brothers...a plan that falls apart very quickly when he is so overcome with emotion that he weeps and must tell his brothers the honest truth, much to their dumbfounded realization. Those dreams he had of them bowing down to him indeed came to reality — and there they are, bowing and kneeling before him. And here is the royal-one now overcome with feeling that he must speak and speak honestly — as prophets/ecstatics often do when they feel something genuine like YAHWEH's touch, through wind or emotion or lingering guitar-string. Just wait until we hear more about such titilating YAHWEH-touches in future books of *The Naked Path of Prophet* series!

Saul and David are a bit different though.

Saul and David both have experiences on the mountaintops of Ancient Israel/Palestine, both of them naked with the prophets and with YAHWEH. Saul and David each get a whiff of YAHWEH's musky scent when their clothes are off and YAHWEH visits them — 'takes care of them'/PQD, as the band of YAH understands it/It — and blows through every orifice and awakens in them the utmost pleasure, ecstasy.

Anyone who just sits and does nothing can feel and know it/It — there's no special training needed, no mediator, just you. Call it whatever you want — but as soon as you name it/It you miss it. Some call it 'meditation' and say that they are choosing to sit and meditate. But that's not it/It either. YAHWEH cannot be directed and ordered. Bliss cannot be ordained to happen at any time, by any special ritual or technique.

Bliss, ecstasy, a feeling of the hum of the planet within the universe, THE ALL...

it/It simply arrives.

That's YAHWEH's musky scent. That's what David and Saul each knew before and during their reigns as Ancient Israel/Ancient Judah's first (fictional) kings, first young royals.

YAHWEH lingers awhile, sticks around, fades, returns. Perhaps it's/It's always there — the atmosphere, life — but only gets noticed when a ripple of wind catches the faintest sheen of sweat that sends a crescendo of oh-my-goodness-Godness through whomever pays attention.

Catch a whiff of that —

— and then try to rule the land and the people and notice all too quickly that it's impossible to continue knowing YAHWEH and rule and not abuse one's power when in charge...corruption is all too easy in any hierarchy. But back on the mountaintops with the prophets/ecstatics, YAHWEH's musky scent is more alluring than engaging in any kind of corruption for one's own benefit, up on the mountaintops where there is no hierarchy among the prophets/ecstatics.

The prophets' mountaintop hangouts with YAHWEH are all a bit different than empire's roles and rules and expectations — no matter if you are king or royalist or slave. An empire's hierarchy puts us all in a place, pigeon-holes us, gives us a role — like it or not, fight against it or not.

But YAHWEH, that musky scent in the breeze, that hum that is always right there but so easy to miss — that's about relationship...a relationship among equals... at one moment, the wind penetrates us...and then we capture it for awhile...and then we let it out. Sure, each of us can foul the flow...breathe in fits and starts, hold it for too long, not breathe deeply enough, whatever. But there's no ruling the wind...and it seems the wind can't rule us completely either. It allows us to capture it/It for a time and then we must let it go for another dollop of capture...the whole give and take of breathing.

That's what YAHWEH is about...relationship.

Can a king have relationship with someone else, with another human? Can genuine love be there in a hierarchical system? Yes...but not really...the power-differential is always there and always on the minds of both king and beloved. The pecking order of hierarchy is always prevalent...that is until you drop out of it like an ecstatic-prophet and get as far away as you can from "the shipwreck" that is hierarchy.

Perhaps Socrates' and Plato's dream and hope for philosopher-kings being the best of all possible rulers is actually not possible — another one of those unachievable ideals. It certainly wasn't possible for the characters Saul and David. Solomon with all his philosophical-wisdom is an even bigger disappointment — especially if you read 1 Kings carefully.

But what about Joseph? Our character Joseph saves the day through the famine. But soon after his death that's all forgotten, as we're reminded, and thus we have the stage set for the story of Exodus. I do wonder what the band of YAH envisioned with the Exodus story, perhaps long before the Levitical priests got to it. The band of YAH's character Moses at the beginning of Exodus is so fun until the Levitical priestly editors get their hands all over the story and set Moses up as priest and prophet par excellence....all without any poetry, without any ecstatic-style. The Deuteronomists, very late in the biblical assembly-game, add Deuteronomy 32-33 probably to try to salvage the Levitical priests' setting up Moses-and-Aaron as pivotal prophet-duo with Moses acting for God and Aaron being the mouth for Moses (Exodus 4). And then the Deuteronomists conclude the five-volume Torah with Moses' death and the proclamation that Moses was the greatest prophet ever (Deuteronomy 34.10). A prophet must have 'style' — ecstatic-style in poetry, pun, cleverness, surprise, ecstasy — to be a prophet, to be a NBYAH/'ecstatic, prophet.' But such ecstatic-style is abhorrent to the Levitical priests — it up-ends their power-game of boosting Moses as the lead in their fiction, in the story they weave to claim as much of the attention and control as possible. At one time when they were the royal-administrators around Ancient Judah's kings, the

Deuteronomists likely did not appreciate the prophets' ecstatic-style either — a style that has no respect for kings or hierarchs other than to remind everyone that emperors are fellow-humans who wear no clothes (or powers) other than those given to them by the people.

Tragically, the Levitical priests' power-grab is a dangerous move that has cost millions (billions?) of lives ever since their Torah was crafted first by them and then edited by their fellow-hierarchically-minded Deuteronomistic collaborators. How many genderbenders like our character Joseph have been stripped naked and thrown in wells by fellow humans, even by their own brothers and sisters? How many genderbenders have been scorned by family, beaten by family with blows and words, and even killed? How many LGBTQ+ folx have done awful things to fellow LGBTQ+ folx with the queerphobia we've all inherited from the Torah and modern religion? How many women have been sidelined from economic life based on the Levitical priests' and Deuteronomists' prejudices-enacted-into-Law?

How might our world be different if genderbenders and women were allowed to offer their gifts without any of these prejudices clouding possibilities?

The ancient Levitical priests and the ancient Deuteronomists and all who are hierarchically-minded and follow in their footsteps have tried through the millennia to enact a biblical tradition for three world religions that have been intent on deciding how people should live, who's in and who's out, who lives and who dies, and then claiming that such decisions are ordained by "God." It's hierarchy, it's fascism, and it's the very thing the biblical prophets and Jesus and Paul and post-biblical prophets push against, often at the cost of their own lives.

The prophets know another way — a way of YAHWEH, of knowing from where life comes, of knowing that the life-breath in me is the same as the life-breath in you, of knowing our equal-value as human beings and creatures on this planet based on the common experience of the atmosphere that surrounds us. And with such an invitation to let go of control comes ecstasy...simply by first knowing the wind and one's own breathing with It.

And such an experience inspires great creativity to unfurl playful tales — fictions — to help us all know better this present-moment experience of YAHWEH... something so easy to miss.

Like the Joseph-saga, the band of X's Samuel-saga is an exceedingly clever fiction where Saul and David catch a whiff of YAHWEH's ecstatic-experience with the prophets but then struggle with what to do about it when the opportunity to rule the new nation of Israel calls to them. Truly, Saul and David screw it up. Royally. Repeatedly. Solomon does even more so.

What's saddest is that moderns and ancients alike read the Saul and David and Solomon stories and think that they are great rulers — heroes. These three fictional kings are the biggest fools — indeed that's the point of 1 & 2 Samuel and 1 & 2 Kings. Samuel warned the people: it's in the nature of a king/royalty to steal the life and livelihood from their own people. Such a hierarchical-system thrives upon it. Royal/slave-imagination — hierarchical-imagination — poisons the well every time.

Perhaps that's the message of the Samuel-saga. In the story, the Philistines have a completely different system of government — essentially a people-led, mayor-directed system of cities working together. While I'm sure that system has its own problems, it seems far wiser than a simple royalty, a simple hierarchy, where power is never checked, where power is not shared, where the whole system is designed to help us forget we all breathe the same air, the same YAHWEH.

The mountaintops and faraway hideouts of the prophets/ecstatics welcomed getting high on YAHWEH without any government, without any priest, without any temple or church, without any ark, without any Law, without anything. YAHWEH is THE ALL. YAHWEH is the atmosphere that surrounds and penetrates us all. From a prophet's perspective, there is no hierarchy of humans...we all breathe the same YAHWEH and thus we all must be equal. Royalty and priests are silly constructs to a prophet/ecstatic who knows the wind and the nature of the wind...any decent prophet allows the poems to come forth, poems that need to be whispered out there so that more and more people realize It...so that more and more people know the nature of YAHWEH, the atmosphere that surrounds us and gives us life, life in all Its abundance.

Saul and David and Solomon and every real/fictional king and queen who comes after them in 1 & 2 Samuel and 1 & 2 Kings royally screw it up until the land and the nation are no more thanks to the Assyrians and then the Babylonians who swoop in and exile everyone. And while all that is happening, the prophets are on the mountaintops having their wild experiences of the wind, of YAHWEH. Ecstasy. And all seem to be invited to join them — even King Saul who chases young David with intent to kill him.

Indeed, Ancient Israel's prophets seem to feel safer living closer to the Philistines — Ancient Israel's enemies — than the royal-government of their own nation. Note that well in 1 Samuel.

In the Samuel-saga, we are led to wonder what would have happened to Ancient Israel/Judah had Saul and David stayed a little longer on the mountaintops of Israel/Palestine with YAHWEH, with the prophets. Instead Saul and David come down from that ecstatic-high and repeatedly use their power for their own ends, for their own advancement, for their own making trophies to honor themselves, and for their own pleasure.

It's the story of nearly every leader of any hierarchically-minded institution, isn't it? Presidents, kings/queens, emperors, prime ministers, CEOs, popes, bishops, high priests...on and on and on.

Prophets herald a new way...if anyone wants to accept It/YAHWEH

Maybe a new imagination is needed instead — an imagination that does not get stuck in the hierarchical default — an imagination that allows the wind to bring forward something new. Like a circle of deciders, a true democracy among equals — something Paul envisions for the early Jesus-interested communities — something Peter's camp tried to trounce. And did.

It's time for some new imagination, some new way to

be born...something that will allow our grandchildren to have a future before the planet swallows us all whole. The hierarchical imagination — in its many manifestations in government, in organized religion, in universities, in corporations, in families — is killing us and trying to kill the planet. The planet, of course, will live on without humans on it.

Hierarchical imagination has become the default and has been maybe since the almost-beginning of human time — how quickly we look at people to decide if they are better than us or worth less than us. How quickly we do that with all creatures of the Earth. How quickly we do that with the Earth itself, this amazing planet on which we move and live and breathe. And how foolish we are in thinking that those choices made out of hierarchical-imagination — a pecking-ordered imagination — do not have long-term consequences.

Maybe a new imagination is sitting right there if we have the courage to do nothing for awhile, let the breeze blow awhile. In the Samuel-saga, we meet Samuel who could have fallen right in line with the hierarchical-camps of temple-cult and state-cult...but once the ark is stolen and the temple-tent is then no more, the character Samuel disappears for 20+ years and only re-emerges to warn people to know YAHWEH alone, not BAAL/ASHTAROTH.

The wind is powerful, Samuel reveals. The wind wants you and me to take off our clothes and feels Its full message, Its full sensation, on and within every pore of our being. Ecstasy-by-wind awaits anyone and everyone. All are called, so few choose themselves. The lure of power (à la Saul and David and the Deuteronomists) and the lure of crafting Law/catechism (à la the priestly editors/hierarchy or any organized religion) and the lure of trying to be good boys and girls who follow the Law (à la everyone who fears Law/priestly-authority/royal-authority more than the wind)...the lures are very real, aren't they?

But all the while Ancient Israel/Judah is being built and very soon after crumbling, the prophets are high on the wind on the mountaintops of Israel/Palestine, having no enemies, even feeding their enemies, multiplying bread and oil to save widows and their children from debtors' prison, raising the dead to life through some very strange means, purifying poisoned water and poisoned food, curing leprosy and awful diseases so that people can live fully and wholly again, waiting for the next clever word to come to them so that YAHWEH's style becomes more and more evident, more and more known.

What is it that prophets do? A whole bunch of helpful nothing!

Sometimes all we need is a friend to invite us to sit awhile and feel the wind.

And that's what the prophets do.

That's what Gautama did too before people clobbered him with the title 'Buddha' (in Sanskrit, 'the one who woke up') and changed the dynamic oh so quickly... enough that all the chants and aphorisms and bows and statues and shrines take us into paying more attention to him/Buddha than the wind moving into and out of one's body and oh so subtly vibrating it...the vibration of life.

Gautama found enlightenment under a tree, for crying out loud — not in a shrine.

That's what Jesus did too — what on earth do you think he was doing out there in the desert?! — before people put him on a pedestal as Christ and Savior and Redeemer and built monuments to him instead of paying attention to the experiences he was inviting. "Take nothing with you for the journey" into the desert, into an enemy-city, into anywhere!

It's the wind — YAHWEH — who redeems. YAHWEH alone.

There's a reason the biblical band of X in the Samuel-saga has YAHWEH repeatedly strip Itself of clothes like a slave or exile is forced to do by Its captor. The Hebrew verb is GLH. Most Bibles translate GLH as "revealed"... as in God's revelation to the prophets. Sounds quite important, yes? But "revelation" misses the nakedness of YAHWEH, the sexy and alluring and sensual nature of YAHWEH wanting inside of you and me...YAHWEH wanting to ravish you and me...YAHWEH wanting sexual-ravishment with you and me.

It's what we do when we breathe, right? We let YAHWEH in.

Can you conceive an intimacy such as this? Of YAHWEH moving in and out of you, giving you life with each breath, giving you the opportunity to feel, to sense, to know the ripple of life that induces ecstasy?

Intimacy with YAHWEH! Yes!

How our world would be so different if we did a lot more of that feeling, that sensing what is...what IS... YAHWEH...from the Hebrew verb 'to be.'

A call for honest exegesis — reading meanings out of the biblical stories

Why don't more Bible translations tell us that the Hebrew verb there in 1 & 2 Samuel is GLH/'to strip naked before a captor' and not simply the verb 'to show'/YRAH? The band of X certainly knew what they were doing...the fiction they craft is wild, funny, and tragic. It's one of the best stories of all time. When I was teaching high school freshmen, even kids who hadn't read a thing yet started reading the band of YAH's stories in Genesis and the band of X's stories in 1 & 2 Samuel. Those bands of storycrafters knew what they were doing. They were that good, that captivating. How foolish that most people do not even read these stories — or worse, catch a few snippets in their congregation's lectionary cycle and think they know the whole of it and even think David was a good king.

How foolish biblical scholars and translators run from the 'original' Hebrew texts and the wild verb choices there in YAH & X's stories. Why do they do it? Those verbs are sitting there for all to see, for all to hear, for all to experience. Why do scholars run so quickly from what's there in the Bible?

I suspect it's because most scholars and translators who read the Hebrew biblical texts think, "This can't possibly mean this! God is not sexy like this!" But God is this way — you and I can both know It through our own experience, right? And if we're careful readers who read what's there in the Hebrew texts and not insert what we think should be there, we'll come to know a YAHWEH who is funny, refreshing, wild...in the biblical texts and in life. And in knowing this aspect of the divine — of YAHWEH — we might have a chance for human beings to continue to live on this amazing planet. A different imagination informed by the sensual wind — YAHWEH — just might give us a chance and our grandchildren a chance...to live...to learn to love.

There are so many layers built up by the priestly & Deuteronomist traditions of centuries gone by trying to take us away from what's sitting right there in the biblical texts. *The Naked Path of Prophet* series, I hope, invites curious readers to take a second look — and to try to read the prophetic-texts without the lens of the priestly/royal hierarchical-imagination that has forever tried to obscure the prophetic/ecstatic circularly-inspired-imagination. My great hope is that more Hebrew readers will sit with the texts and wonder a bit more about them — and I hope more people will want to learn Hebrew to uncover — 'to denude'/GLH — what is sitting right there in the biblical texts. *Exegesis*, after all, is a commitment to read out what is there in the text...not reading onto the text what we think should be there (*eisegesis*).

And I suspect that getting to what is there in these biblical texts will welcome a new world in which our grandchildren can have a future that is possible and hopefully even joyful on this amazing planet. How? The answer, as someone in every generation notes, is in the wind.

There's a lot more to riddle out of the Joseph-saga... for those who want to pay attention...

Maybe we learn something about Joseph based on who finds him attractive, who falls in love with him, naked or clothed....

His brothers certainly can't stand him — everyone except his younger brother Benjamin it seems.

A woman likes Joseph — Potiphar's wife.

And Potiphar likes Joseph, enough to give control of his house to Joseph — and Potiphar is a eunuch, a man with no testicles anymore.

And the guys in prison like Joseph — and they don't have any testicles either, all of them seeming to be eunuchs like Potiphar.

And Pharaoh likes Joseph — enough to make Joseph his Number 2 within minutes of meeting him. (Perhaps that's the band of YAH showing just how much prophets break up the hierarchical assumptions...Joseph gets promoted from prisoner to Pharaoh's Number 2 in a matter of minutes.)

Pharaoh says that Joseph will kiss every person of Egypt — what an unusual thing to say! Joseph will rank only behind Pharaoh, ride in the second car, have all the rights and rank as Pharaoh except the title of Pharaoh itself. Was Pharaoh tired of all the eunuchs and finally found a man who could get it up...something a eunuch is said to have trouble doing (at least based on a few internet searches)?

Pharaoh doesn't seem to have a wife, a Queen. Are we to assume that by making Joseph his Number 2 that Joseph was Pharaoh's queen, riding in the second chariot?

And what was Joseph wearing there before Pharaoh? Did Joseph take Pharaoh's hints offered in Pharaoh's descriptions of his dreams — descriptions that are much more graphic in his own words than what had been narrated earlier about his dreams?

> — that Pharaoh doesn't like skinny and dangling things as they are 'the most awful I've ever seen'
>
> — that Pharaoh likes them big, growing in fact — just like the very name of Joseph/YSOP which could be translated as 'Add-On' or, in fact, 'Grower.'

And maybe Joseph had somehow come to know through the dungeon-banter what had happened to the two eunuchs who had had those two very graphic dreams —

and that the one who dreamt of fucking Pharaoh and squeezing his grapes into Pharaoh's ass lived

and that the one who dreamt of Pharaoh cumming on his head was hanged and died.

Did Joseph then take the hint and give Pharaoh what he wanted...that Pharaoh wanted to be dominated and not dominant?

Is that what this is all (comedically) about?

Or is it truly that Joseph — loved by women and eunuchs and Pharaoh himself — has some alluring power, that he truly is a snake-charmer, 'hisses and enchants like a snake'/NCHSH (the quote from Joseph at the end of the tale), whispers and hisses like the prophets were said to do (in Hebrew: NAHM)...to understand the whispers of the wind, of YAHWEH's clever whispers in the wind? The prophets always have YAHWEH whispering... NAHM...as we can see in 1 Samuel 2 and throughout the prophets' poems...376 times in the Hebrew Bible!

Is that it? That prophets are mesmerizers and can put a spell on anyone as they imitate the wind and that's why a woman and eunuchs and Pharaoh all love Joseph.

If that's the case, a lot gets resolved here.

But that princess-dress — given to him by his father, his same father who got groped and sexually-ravished by YAHWEH and who fathered a bunch of kids — boys and at least one girl — and he gives a princess-dress to Joseph, the first-born of the wife he loves the most. And that princess-dress was said to be flashy, glimmering, so much so that at times it seems disappearing...and in fact is disappeared from Joseph by his bloodthirsty brothers.

That princess-dress messes up the whole mesmerizing-prophet thing in that it's not just that Joseph can put a spell on people. In fact, it's not a spell. We're told that YAHWEH rushed upon Joseph and all that Joseph touched...in Potiphar's house, in the dungeon of Pharaoh's prison, in Pharaoh's court. Did YAHWEH's rushing upon Joseph change him? help him to 'Grow'... as in affirming Joseph in his name and identity as prophet?

And those dreams he has when he's a man-boy of 17 years old — they do indeed come to be when his brothers are kneeling before him begging for grain and then later their lives.

Prophets are known for their dreams, for their abilities to interpret dreams — we see that in the prophets' poems, we see that in the stories about the prophets in the Samuel-saga and the Kings-saga.

But the band of YAH might be doing a clever little thing here...especially when the interpreters of dreams in *The Epic of Gilgamesh* are most certainly and always women. And the ISHTAR-shamans in *Gilgamesh* appear to be women.

But in the band of YAH's Joseph story, Joseph and eunuchs and Pharaoh all have dreams and Joseph is interpreter of dreams for all of them (except maybe his own dreams).

Joseph...our princess-dress wearing son of Jacob, the man who got groped and sexually-ravished by YAHWEH, top of the gods and goddesses.

In the band of YAH's primal version of the story, Joseph has no wife and no children. The Levitical priestly editors make it clear in their final version of Genesis that Joseph marries, like a good boy. But the Levitical priestly editors ascribe no mention of Joseph in the 12 tribes of Israel. That's a rather significant slap in the face considering every other son of Jacob — even the ones with foolish actions like Judah and bloodthirsty actions like Simeon and Levi — gets a tribe named for them. But Joseph does not.

Of course, neither does Dinah/Justice — and perhaps that's the band of YAH being crafty and clever too, as in 'there is no Justice in Ancient Israel's 12 tribes.' The Levitical priestly editors resolve the no-tribe-named-Joseph issue, in their minds, by naming Joseph's supposed sons Ephraim and Manasseh as half-tribes of Ancient Israel instead of naming any territory after Joseph. The ancient Levitical priests do nothing to memorialize Dinah into the tradition besides carry forward the story.

From the prophetic-imaginers' viewpoint, not only is there no Justice in Ancient Israel's royal-government and ark/temple/hierarchical ways, there's no Growth (Joseph) either.

Rather strangely, the 'half-tribe' of Manasseh actually has two enormous tracts of land; Ephraim's half-tribe will one day be a nickname for the entire Northern Kingdom of Israel, with its well-known city of Shiloh.

But Joseph — enormous character that he is with nearly as much story-material about him as Abraham and Jacob — gets no namesake in the 12 tribes of Israel. As a matter of fact, he gets nothing except the very unusual story about him. Is this another slam by the Levitical priestly editors in dissing the prophets? Or did the priests simply have no room in their imagination for a princess-dress wearing boy who keeps getting naked in the story? As you might be able to tell from the <*Gen x.xx*> margin-notes in the Joseph story, the Joseph-story is heavily edited by the Levitical priests and perhaps the Deuteronomists. Heavily. They could have simply left the entire Joseph-story out of the Torah if it was so unpalatable for them. Perhaps the Levitical priestly editors and Deuteronomists felt compelled to include the Joseph story in the Torah because the story was so popular among all the people — but the priests could not stand to have it in their Torah as it was.

Was that because the priests rejected all ideas of the bordercrossing prophets? Or was it because the priests rejected Joseph's unusual sexuality and, what we might call today, Joseph's bordercrossing gender-identity? Or both?
Of course, the Levitical priests outlaw men sleeping with men, having sex with men in their version of the Law, Leviticus. Men who sleep with men must be punished with death, the Levitical priests tell us in Leviticus 18-20.

The Deuteronomists prohibit crossdressing in Deuteronomy 22.5 — 'men who wear women's clothes are morally disgusting to YAHWEH.' What would the Deuteronomists do with Joseph who once wore a dress given to him by his father who is one of the three great patriarchs...and not only that, YAHWEH rushes upon Joseph and makes everything Joseph does become good?

Are you catching the complexities of the Bible?

The Eden story, the Jacob getting groped and penetrated by God story, the primal version of the Joseph story — they're all quite entertaining and meaning-rich, aren't they? And the Levitical priests and the Deuteronomists likely knew that their growing Bible was worthless without these stories — that the people would always reject a Bible without these key YAHWEH stories. So what do the Levitical priests and Deuteronomists do? They include the stories, heavily edit them by placing all kinds of distractions and interpretations around them, and make clear that genderbending of any sort is morally offensive.

But the prophets know YAHWEH better...
as freely as the wind...
the very nature of the wind
that topples borders and laws....

We've wondered a lot here about Joseph's gender...

but what gender is YAHWEH?

As you know, I've translated YAHWEH's masculine pronoun as 'It.'

With a language like Ancient Hebrew that has masculine and feminine grammatical-gender and no third neuter grammatical-gender, some things that get a masculine pronoun in Hebrew would receive the pronoun 'it' in English...a few examples would be 'house' and 'river' and 'field.' They all are masculine grammatical-gender in Hebrew; in English they are usually considered neuter grammatical-gender.

A word like 'road' (DRC) is used both as both masculine grammatical-gender and feminine grammatical-gender in Hebrew. Rather unusual to us moderns, yes? Rather interestingly, so too is the word for 'wind, spirit, breath' in Hebrew...RUCH is both masculine grammatical-gender and feminine grammatical-gender.

My Sanskrit teacher would remind me now not to put too much stock in grammatical-gender having much to do with something being more masculine or more feminine in nature — no matter the language. And I think she's right, for sure.

But it is more than a little interesting, isn't it, that the Hebrew word for 'wind'/RUCH is both masculine-grammatical gender and feminine grammatical-gender?

My God!

EL, ELOHIM, YAHWEH. What to make of all of this?

Recall that EL is the Canaanite word for 'godhead' — their conception of Zeus, head of the pantheon of gods and goddesses like BAAL and ASHTAROTH. 'EL' and its Babylonian version 'IL' existed in ancient imaginations long before the band of YAH was crafting their tales.

The band of YAH uses the plural of EL — ELOHIM — to refer to 'all the gods and goddesses' and then shares stories where YAHWEH is the 'godhead'...as in YAHWEH is the God of all gods and goddesses. This would have been quite controversial, to say the least.

The Levitical priestly editors pluralize EL with the ordinary masculine-grammatical endings to make singular-EL into plural-ELOHIM as a name for God. The Levitical priestly editors' use of ELOHIM/'God' is far different from the band of YAH's usual use of ELOHIM/'the gods and goddesses.' Why do the Levitical priestly editors settle on the pluralized EL for their name of 'God'...pluralized out of respect for 'God'? Maybe. Or maybe to try to harmonize their priestly-tales and priestly-lens with the band of YAH's stories and their very different use of ELOHIM? Or was it to create their own form of monotheism far different from the prophets' all-encompassing YAHWEH-as-atmosphere, as It ALL.

Most scholars and priests and rabbis and imams today assume that ELOHIM used by the band of YAH and ELOHIM used by the priestly editors means the same thing. But translating ELOHIM as 'God' in the band of YAH's stories simply does not work. Take for example the story of Jacob and his dream of the gods and goddesses climbing up and down on the earth-mound (ladder, probably a ziggurat) with YAHWEH at the top. It's very clear in that story that ELOHIM — as in the one 'God' — is not climbing up and down the earth-mound with YAHWEH above it. Instead, Jacob dreams that all the Powers on earth and in the heavens — THE ALL — are under YAHWEH and take their direction from YAHWEH. Indeed, if YAHWEH is the wind and the atmosphere, every being on earth needs the wind/atmosphere of life to live, right?

With our heavily-influenced priestly-imagination that comes to us through organized religions like Judaism and Christianity and Islam, we moderns often lump ELOHIM and YAHWEH together as one being...as a quick reading of the Bible translated into English seems to do just that. How many sermons and lectures have you heard that 'God is out there and we need to get in touch with Him and we need guidance from a well-studied mediator like a rabbi or priest or pastor or imam who knows well God's laws.' And yet how very uncareful these so-called well-studied leaders have been for millennia.

With the prophetic/ecstatic-imagination, there is

no 'getting closer' to YAHWEH when YAHWEH is inescapable — like the atmosphere that surrounds everything...like the wind. We are alive and swimming through life in this atmosphere that sustains us, that penetrates us with every breath.

In the band of YAH's Genesis stories, YAHWEH breathes into Mud-Creature and Mud-Creature comes to life, YAHWEH walks in the afternoon breeze in Eden/Pleasure before finding Mud-Creature and Woman hiding themselves in their love-making with one another — indeed, breathing their sexual pants and breaths into one another. YAHWEH rushes onto and busts onto people's paths, something that the band of YAH's characters pray will happen to make their lives/journeys whole and good.

YAHWEH as It, as all-gender, seems best to me... as it seems to be the case with RUCH in Hebrew... both masculine grammatical-gender and feminine grammatical-gender. YAHWEH is the breeze, the breath of life, in the band of YAH's stories. YAHWEH will wrestle Its beloveds to the ground, will penetrate Its beloveds, will let Its beloveds get on top too. YAHWEH rushes onto and busts onto the paths of slave and son-wearing-a-dress and royal alike, as It did for Abraham's slave and for Joseph both as non-royal and royal. YAHWEH visits and takes care of women who seem to not be able to have children and gives them seed, life — as It did with Sarah, laughter and all.

Talk about a bordercrossing YAHWEH!

A Sensual, Sexy YAHWEH

As close as the atmosphere, YAHWEH — it/It seems — longs for each one of us, longs to be inside each one of us, slips into you and me and everyone no matter if they/we are 'good' or 'bad.'

YAHWEH awaits Its own style of sex with you and me on our next breath...

such...incredible...intimacy....

YAHWEH comes into me...It goes out of me...It goes into you...It goes out of you...It enters into and out of another human...and another human...and another creature...and on and on and on....

YAHWEH doesn't seem to care what genitalia you have. YAHWEH doesn't seem to care how you like your sexual intimacy — in/with your genitalia, in your ass, with your skin or breasts or ribs, in your mouth, or even in your nose as Mud-Creature first gets It in Eden/Pleasure.

People are far more than their genitals — though their genitals are wonderful, no matter what they have and no matter if they use them or not. People are far more than their genders too, perhaps a key tenet to the prophets'/ecstatics' identities gleaned from the Joseph-saga.

And so is YAHWEH far more than Its gender and genitals...wonderfully sensuous, sensual, sexy, alluring, ravish-worthy.

What would happen to our human-world, our human-nature, and our planet if we all allowed ourselves a little more of this sensual, sexy YAHWEH into us...

...indeed, if we realized that we're all swimming in this One YAHWEH that swims into and out of and constantly between you and me and every creature...this YAHWEH providing life and pleasure and abundance with every breath?

May the winds of life — YAHWEH — teach us.

May we grow to be adaptable, flexible and strong as bone, through our whole lifetimes, for as long as the wind feeds us.

May we be bordercrossers, inspired by the wind.

May we have the courage to be who we are — whomever we choose to be, whenever, however, whyever.

May we grow in our comfort in our own skin, comfortable enough to be naked or clothed on our own, in any crowd. And if we find ourselves aroused, comfortable enough to discover those feelings can change, can grow stronger and if mutual can be a gift and at the same time can be reversible just as much as any move we make...as Moshe Feldenkrais reminded us. May we be so potent. May we be like the wind that is constantly changing, is Itself.

May we be people who no longer give our power away, but claim it for ourselves, and invite that power to be shared in a circle that all may live and grow.

May we become people who tell stories with love and playfulness to topple pyramids of authoritarian-power — that's what nonviolence is, telling those kinds of stories with the hopes of laying bare the foolish uses of power in hopes that the hierarchical powerholder realizes their foolishness and grows out of it in renewed friendship with the storycrafter as an equal — that's what the band of YAH was doing — that's what we'll see the band of X doing in 1 & 2 Samuel in *The Naked Path of Prophet volumes 1 + 2* — that's what Jesus was doing with his parables, like the prophets before and after him.

May we even be able to laugh at and with ourselves when we discover ourselves using hierarchically-minded motivations — that we might be wise and grow with the wind that will always be more powerful than anything we can ever scrounge or build together.

May we be happy.

May we be.

May we.

Come, let's see...

Resources for Further Discovery

the band of YAH's Stories in Genesis
(traditional chapter & verse markings)

The Ins & Outs of Pleasure

Eden, Cain & Abel,
Noah & his sons, the Tower of Babel

Genesis 2.4b - 2.9
2.16 - 2.23
2.25 - 3.19
3.21 - 4.16
6.3
6.5 - 6.8
7.1 - 7.5
7.7
7.16b - 7.23
8.2 - 8.3a
8.6
8.8 - 8.12
8.20 - 8.22
9.18
9.20 - 9.27
11.1 - 11.9

From Slackers to Prosperers

Abram & Sarai become Abraham & Sarah in a land far, far away from the old prosperous metropolis of Ur[uk] and its hierarchical imagination

Genesis 12.1 - 12.4a
12.5 - 13.18
15.1 - 15.15
15.17 - 15.18
16.1 - 16.13
16.15
18.1 - 19.28
19.30 - 19.38

Laughingstock

the stories of Isaac & Rebekah

Genesis 21.1 - 21.2b
21.3
22.1 - 22.13
24.1 - 24.67
25.21 - 25.26b
25.27 - 25.34

Gruff-Squeeze(s) & Tricky-Heel-Grabber

the brothers Esau & Jacob
and Jacob's Clever Wives

Genesis 27.1 - 27.45
28.10 - 28.16
29.1 - 29.23
29.25 - 29.28
29.30 - 29.35
30.14 - 30.16
30.24 - 30.30
31.1 - 31.7
31.17 - 31.36a
32.4 - 32.32
33.1 - 33.17
34.1 - 34.31

Throw-Up-Your-Hands-In-Praise & Erect-Palm-Tree

the interlude story
of Judah & Tamar

Genesis 38

Add-On/Grower & Power-Son

the saga of Joseph
& his long-lost brother Benjamin

Genesis 35.16c - 35.18
37.1 - 37.2d
37.3b - 37.10a
37.11 - 37.12
37.14 - 37.20
37.23 - 37.25
37.28b-e
37.31 - 37.35
39.1 -- 41.44
41.53 - 42.4
42.6 - 42.21
42.24
42.29 - 42.34
42.36
43.15b - 43.17
43.23e-24
43.28b - 31
43.33 - 44.7
44.9 - 44.13
44.14b - 44.15
45.1 - 45.3
45.12 - 45.14

It should be noted, of course, that the standard chapter & verse markings that we have grown accustomed to in the modern world are actually very new (13th century & 16th centuries CE) in the history of the biblical tradition. The band of YAH was telling their stories thousands of years before the chapter and verse markings came about. The original assemblers of the Bible, of course, were not interested in what we moderns would see as handy ways to look things up — their concerns were much different from ours.

Hebrew Alphabet - transliterated

It would be fair to say that my rendering below of the Hebrew (Aramaic) characters/sounds into English letters is far from perfect. I do hope it is useful, and easier than most renderings. Many Hebrew letters have multiple sounds, depending on if the letter is doubled or depending on the vowel with which it might be associated. I have let a lot of that go for simplicity's sake.

The Hebrew 'alphabet' (*aleph-bet*) itself has no vowels — they are assumed, in a sense. For clarity, between the 6th - 10th centuries CE, a group of biblical scholars called the Masoretes added vowels below the Hebrew consonants to clarify the sounds and even meanings of the written Hebrew language. In some ways, the Masoretes' work clarified meanings of Hebrew words; in some ways, the Masoretes' work flattened the meanings, especially of the ecstatic-prophets' poems and 1 & 2 Samuel and the band of YAH's stories — all of which rely on the pun-richness of the Ancient Hebrew language...the ways words expand and explode with multiple meanings and possibilities.

The work of the Masoretes is still in use today in Hebrew Bibles used to translate the Bible into other modern languages like English.

My only hope with this simplified system of transliterating Ancient Hebrew sounds into English approximated-sounds is to encourage more people to study Ancient Hebrew...to dig deeply in the sandbox of language and understanding to discover our roots and to make better choices in our present moment.

		my transliteration
א	*aleph*	AH
ב	*bet*	B
ג	*gimmel*	G
ד	*dalet*	D
ה	*hey*	H
ו	*vav*	V or U
ז	*zayin*	Z
ח	*chet*	CH
ט	*tet*	T
י	*yod*	Y
ך/כ	*kaf*	K or hard C

ל	*lamed*	L
ם/מ	*mem*	M
ן/נ	*nun*	N
ס	*samech*	S
ע	*ayin*	AY
ף/פ	*pey*	P
ץ/צ	*tsade*	TS
ק	*qof*	Q
ר	*resh*	R
ש	*shin*	S/SH
ת	*tav*	T

Major Characters

(the ordinary English Bible translation...Hebrew transliterated letters...my translation with explanation)

The First Family in Our Epic-Story

Adam...AHDM...mud-creature...AHDMH = 'mud' so the AHDM must be 'creature made from mud'...also the word to describe not just one character but a classification of characters (humans)

Eve...CHUH...Life...CHYH = 'to live'...through most of the Eden story, though, the mud-creature and the narrator refer to 'Eve' as 'Woman' based on the mud-creature naming her when YAHWEH presented the new creation to the mud-creature

Cain...QYN...Spear-Getter...QYN = 'spear' and QNH = 'to get, acquire'...and Eve's/Life's exclamation after Spear-Getter's birth plays on both of these meanings

Abel...HBL...Wasted-Breath...HBL = 'vapor, breath, vanity, empty'...quite tragically ironic in that Wasted-Breath doesn't last too long

* * *

Yahweh/Lord...YHWH...YAHWEH...from the verb 'to be'...say 'yahweh' out loud a few times and what does it sound like? the breeze? one's breath? what any ancient and hopefully modern person knows sustains life...the air...the atmosphere that pervades everything and every opening, no matter how much we try to keep It out

either **God** or **'the gods and goddesses'...AHLHYM... ELOHIM**...a plural word that could refer either to the regional gods, the region from which Ancient Israel emerged, or by the Levitical priestly editors as 'God'...EL was the chief god of the Canaanite pantheon of gods and goddesses...everyone in the region would have referred to their gods and goddesses as EL or ELOHIM...north of Canaan in Ancient Babylon — the land between the two great rivers named Tigris and Euphrates/Mesopotamia — they refer to god as IL....note the similarity between EL and IL, especially in sound

* * *

Noah's family

Noah...NCH...Tranquilizer...from NOCH 'to be restful, to be in a trance'

Noah's sons:
Shem...SHM...Renowned...SHM = 'name, fame, renowned'

Ham...CHM...Hot...CHM = 'hot' (and plays on the previous lines from YAHWEH in the story)

Japheth...YPT...Handsome...YPH = 'beautiful, handsome, pleasing' (YPT is the construct-state of YPH) and PTH = 'alluring, open, spacious'...a combination of which gets played out in the tragi-comedic punny words from Tranquilizer/Noah

Noah's grandson:
Canaan...CNAYN...Humble-Trader...CNAY = 'humbled, humiliated, subdued' and also the Canaanites have the reputation for being merchants or traders in the region, and they lend their identity (or vice versa) to words for luggage (CNAYH) and traders (CNAYNY)...Hot's/Ham's son

* * *

Abram...AHBRM...Patriarch-Helps-or-Hurts...from AB = 'father, patriarch' and RM(H) has three immediate potential meanings...'throw, shoot' and 'to deceive someone, leave someone in the lurch' and 'to be high, lofty'...and I suspect that's what the biblical band of YAH is playing with here...an ancient person would hear 'Abram' and begin to wonder which meaning is being invited here...more of YAH's mastery as a storyteller...and in his early days as a character in the story, Abram is quite the undependable, uncommitted slacker...a Slack-Daddy

> **Abraham...AHBRHM...Patriarch-Prospers**...from AB = 'father, patriarch' and the insertion of H between RM probably rules out the 'throw, shoot' and 'deception' possibilities that could potentially be heard and wondered about in Abram via the verb-root RMH...now we're closer to the verb-root RUM — with some uses of that verb RHM — and RUM = 'to be high up, to exalt and be exalted'

Note also:

RAHM / RAYM = 'wild ox' (which would be valuable when caught and tamed for work or making babies/ wealth)

RAHM = 'to tower high' (not the same word as used in the Babel story but has resonances...don't make towers but be great and stand tall like towers...to proudly proclaim he's a bordercrossing wanderer)

RUM = 'to be exalted, high up, lifted high'...which would be a surprising thing in the ancient world for this wondering Aramean with little to no stake on a land — though promised to him by YAHWEH — to be considered great

As was mentioned earlier, it should be noted too that Abram/Abraham — AHBRM/AHBRHM — both sound very similar to AYBRYM...'bordercrosser/bordercrossing.' Curious, yes?

* Why have I usually chosen 'Patriarch/Patriarchy' throughout instead of simply 'Father'? Because fatherhood in the ancient world wasn't simply the progenitor of a child but a whole system of hierarchy... husband over wives over children who weren't considered human until puberty when they were suddenly valuable for more work and for marriage/marrying off.

Sarai...SRAY...On-Top...from SR = 'chief, ruler, prince(ss)'... which must go back to the verb-'root' SRH 'to contend/strive/prevail against/be on top'...which is what any ancient leader must do to assert supremacy over their own people or against an enemy to remain free...SRH is where we get Israel (see below)

> **Sarah...SRH...Clearly-On-Top**...still from SR and SRH as noted just above, though this time even clearer... as a noun, SRY is the construct-state of the feminine-grammatical noun SRH, which means it needs to join with something, something must follow it in that construct-state...SRH can stand on its own, in a sense... would an ancient person have detected the change in sound by ear and this subtle meaning? Perhaps.

Abram's 'son' bought/acquired & fear by Abram to be his only heir:
Eliezer...AHLYAYTSR...My-EL-God-Helps...AHLY = 'My EL' & AYTSR = 'to help'

Sarai's slave-woman & son with Abram:
Hagar...HGR...The-Immigrant...H = 'the' & GR = 'immigrant, foreigner'

Ishmael...YSHMAYAHL...EL-Listens / Divinity-Listens...YSHMAY is from the verb SHMAY 'to listen, hear' & AHL = EL / head of the gods and goddesses of the Canaanite region

Abram's nephew Lot and Lot's grandsons — who are also his sons!
Lot...LOT...Cover-Up...LOT = 'to wrap, envelope, cover'

Moab...MOAHB...From-My-Father...M = 'from' and AHB = 'father, patriarch(y)'

(Son/s of) Ammon...(BNY) AYMON...Inbreds / Sons-of-My-Kin...BNY = 'sons, children' and AYM = 'tribe, kin'

Abraham's & Sarah's son:
Isaac...YTSCHQ...Laughingstock...TSCHQ = 'he laughs, mocks'

Abraham's relative from his home-land...brother:
Nahor...NCHOR...Snort...from NCHR 'to snore, to snort'

* * *

Isaac's & Rebekah's family

Isaac...YTSCHQ...Laughingstock...TSCHQ = 'he laughs, mocks'

Rebekah...RBQH...Well-Fed...RBQ is perhaps the verbal-root of the participle/noun MRBQ 'cattle-stall' where animals would have been well-fed and not-so-exercised... to 21st century ears this sounds like a great insult...to ancient ears, a larger, rounder woman was considered more attractive for a lot of reasons, especially child-bearing as larger hips were thought to bring more ease to child-bearing, which was one of the great dangers of the ancient world for women...RBQH and her size could also be a play upon the possibility that she did not have to work much living with her brother Laban, both of them hailing from the rich, big city life of Babylon, very different from the bordercrossing lifestyle of Sarah and, later, Rachel.

Esau...AYSO...Gruff-Squeeze...from AYSH 'to squeeze, press in a rough way'

> **Edom...AHDOM...Mud-Red**...AHDM = 'red' and those same consonants are also 'mud-creature' (Esau's nickname)

Jacob...YAYQB...(Tricky-)Heel-Grabber...AYQB = 'to swell out/up, to take someone by the heel (literally or figuratively), to trick, supplant, go around'...a wonderfully punny name

> **Israel...ISRAHL...On-Top-of-God**...from SRH (same word as our character Sarah, Jacob's grandmother) 'to be on top, to be in charge, to be prince(ss)...as in having power, prevailing over other people as more powerful' and AHL = EL, chief god

Rebekah's family:
Bethuel...BTUAHL...EL's-Virgin...perhaps from BTH 'an end of something, destruction' and AHL = EL/God (Bethuel is Rebekah's brother)...*Strong's Exhaustive Concordance* notes that BTUL shares the same root as 'virgin'

Milcah...MLCH...Queen...MLCH = 'queen' (Bethuel's mom; Nahor's wife)

Nahor...NCHOR...Snort...from NCHR 'to snore, to snort' (Abraham's brother; Milcah's husband)

Laban...LBN...Harden-Bricks...LBN = 'to make bricks' and 'whiten' which is what bricks did in the ancient world when hardened in the fire/ash...same word as used in the Tower of Babel story

* * *

Jacob's & Rachel's family

Jacob...YAYQB...(Tricky-)Heel-Grabber...AYQB = 'to swell out/up, to take someone by the heel (literally or figuratively), to trick, supplant, go around'...a wonderfully punny name

> **Israel...ISRAHL...On-Top-of-God**...from SRH (same word as our character Sarah, Jacob's grandmother) 'to be on top, to be in charge, to be prince(ss)...as in having power, prevailing over other people as more powerful' and AHL = EL, chief god

Rachel...RCHL...Little-Lamb...RCHL = 'ewe, little lamb'

<u>*their children:*</u>
Joseph...YOSP...Add-On...from YSP = 'to add, increase'

Benjamin...BNYMYN...Power-Son...BN = 'son' and YMYN = 'right hand'...and in the ancient world, the right hand is the hand of power, of making deals, of eating, of fighting (left being 'sinister' — even Latin preserves this — and with the left-hand only such socially-hidden / socially-acceptable things as wiping one's rear end and holding the cup at meals)...this whole business of left and right is vital to understanding the world from which the Bible comes, and is the key to understanding the pivotal saying of Jesus about turning the other cheek (Matthew 5. 38-41)

> **Ben-oni...BN AHONY...My-Trouble-Son**...BN = 'son, child' and AHNOY from AHON = 'trouble, distress, sorrow' and the Y adds a first-person singular pronoun to it (the name Rachel gives Benjamin just as he was born and she was dying)...quite ironic in that Benjamin becomes 'trouble' for his father Jacob in Joseph's scheme to see his long-lost brother who didn't seem to be there when Joseph was stripped and thrown into the pit before being sold into slavery in Egypt

* * *

Jacob's & Leah's family

Leah...LAHH...Tiring-and-Dreadful...LAHH = 'to be weary, tiring, loathsome'

their children:
Reuben...RAHUBN...Looky-Here-a-Son...RAHU is an imperative form of RAHH = 'to see, look' and BN = 'son'

Simeon...SHMAYON...Listening...from SHMAY = 'to listen, to hear'

Levi...LUY...He's-Attached...from LUH = 'to be attached, joined'...and quite appropriate as Levi's seed/descendants will one day be the ones attached to — in service to — the ark of the covenant, the priests

Judah...YHODH...Throw-Up-Your-Hands/Penis-In-Praise...YD = 'hand...also a euphemism for penis' and the verb-form in Judah's name means 'to throw (with one's hands)'...in the story with Tamar, Judah certainly has a way of putting his penis out there too!

Dinah...DYNH...Justice...from DN = 'to judge, to administer justice...literally at its root: to sail directly to your destination'

* * *

Jacob's slave-wives

Bilhah...BLHH...Terrified...from BLH = 'to be troubled, frightened, terrified'

Zilpah...ZLPH...Trickle...*Strong's Exhaustive Concordance* suggests that Zilpah has something to do with fragrant trickle as in myrrh pouring from a bottle

* * *

Judah...YHODH...Throw-Up-Your-Hands/Penis-In-Praise...YD = 'hand...also a euphemism for penis' and the verb-form in Judah's name means 'to throw (with one's hands)'...and quite punny in that his penis does get him into quite a pickle!

Hirah the Adullamite...CHYRH AYDLMY...Pale-with-Shame from Retreat-in-the-Hill-Country...from CHOR 'to turn pale (with shame)' and AYDLM is an old Canaanite city that often has to do with retreat/refuge (Judah's new friend)

Shua...SHUAY...Cry-for-Help...SHUAY = 'cry for help' (Judah falls in love with this man's daughter and marries her...a Canaanite/Humble-Trader)

Er...AYR...Wake-Up...from AYUR = 'to wake up, to rouse oneself' (Judah's first son)

Onan...AHONN...Vigorous...from AHON = 'vigor, strength, wealth' (Judah's second son)

Shelah...SHLH...Ask...perhaps from SHAHL = 'ask'...and SHLH could playfully be heard as 'Ask-Her' later in the story (Judah's third son)

Tamar...TMR...Erect-Palm-Tree...TMR = 'palm-tree or date-palm-tree' and *Strong's Exhaustive Concordance* reports that TMR is from an unused root that means 'erect'...as a palm tree is...tall and strong and long...as Judah and his sons are when they encounter Tamar (first-wife of Judah's son Er/Wake-Up)

Perez...PRTS...Break-Out...PRTS = 'break out, breach' (Tamar & Judah's first-son)

Zerach...ZRCH...Dawn-Rising...ZRCH = 'rising light, dawn' (Tamar & Judah's second-son)

Other Characters

Pharaoh...PRAYH...Pharaoh-Negligence...this Egyptian royal-title sounds like the Hebrew verb PRAY 'to let someone/something hang loose, run wild, to neglect, to be negligent'...now surely the Egyptians haven't named their god-leader after the Hebrew verb, but we can only guess what the Hebrews heard in their mind every time they heard the word 'Pharaoh,' who was indeed negligent toward everyone except Joseph, at least as the story goes

Shechem, son of Hamor, the Hivite...SHCM BN CHMOR HCHUY...Early-and-Eager, son of Male-Ass, one of the villagers...SHCM = 'to rise early' (verb) & 'ridge of a mountain, shoulder/neck for carrying burdens' (noun)... BN = 'son, child'...CHMOR = 'donkey, male-ass'...HCHUY from CHUH = 'tent-village'

Potiphar...POTYPR...Owned-by-Negligence...from PUT = 'Libya' and PR or PRAY = 'Pharaoh' and that Egyptian title sounds like the word 'Negligence' in Hebrew... and why 'owned' for Libya? Well, through some way or another, this human being is under the hierarchy of Egypt...whether by conquest, slavery, acquisition, domination...after all, his testicles had been taken from him...men/boys were made eunuchs often as a royal-prerogative to ensure that such a man would have no desire for the royal-family as these eunuchs perform their royal-duties

* * *

a most important descriptor

Hebrew...AYBRY...Bordercrosser...from AYBR = 'to cross over...as in a river or a border' and sometimes this word also has to do with 'alienating' as anyone who crosses borders might do to someone who holds borders as sacred or important...echoing the nomadic lifestyle of Abraham & Sarah, Isaac & Rebekah, Jacob & Leah &

Rachel and their families...quite ironic and clever too in that Abram/Abraham's name sounds like AYBR/Bordercrosser when spoken aloud...in Genesis, the first Bordercrosser is Bordercrosser....

Often Named Cities/Places

Ai...AYY...Heap-of-Ruins...AY = 'heap of ruins, overturned'

Aram Naharyim...AHRM NRHYM...The-Highland-Palaces-by-the-Two-Rivers...AHRM/Aram is Syria, the northern country, and may derive from AHRMON 'citadel, towers, highlands...as in mountains that create the effect of towers' and NRHYM is the dual-form of 'rivers'...as in 'two rivers'

Babylon/Shinar...SHNAYR...Ancient Babylon...Shinar is probably derived from Sumer, another more ancient name for Babylon

Beer-Lahai-Roi...BAHR LCHY RAHY...Well-for-the-Living-Who-Sees-Me...BAHR = 'well' and L = 'for' and CHY = 'living' and RAHY = the verb 'to see' plus a pronoun attached 'me'

Beer-Sheba...BAHR SHBAY...Seven-Wells...BAHR = 'well, pit' and SHBAY = 'seven'...in the southern desert, on the way to Egypt

Bethel...BYT-AHL...House-of-EL-God-of-the-Land... BYT = 'house' and AHL = EL, the name of the head god of the Canaanite region

Canaan...CNAYN...Humble-Traders'-Land...the land named after the character Canaan, Noah's grandson whom he bitterly cursed in Noah's drunken, naked stupor after being covered up by his sons...Canaan from

CNAY = 'humbled, humiliated/subdued' and also the Canaanites have the reputation for being merchants or traders in the region and lend their name to commerce

Chezib...CZYB...Land-of-Liars...from CZB = 'to lie, to be false'

Dothan...DTN...Rules-and-Regulations...maybe from DT = 'regulations, laws'

Eden...AYDN...Pleasure...AYDN = 'pleasure, delight'

Edom...AHDOM...Red-Land...from AHDM = 'to be red, like mud'

Egypt...MTSRYM...Suffering-Egypt, same consonants as a singular word in Hebrew that means 'suffering'... who knows what an ancient Hebrew would first think of when they heard MTSRYM? To any Hebrew person though, it was a place of suffering as the story says they were slaves there. Egypt, of course, did not call itself "suffering"...that combination of sounds surely produced different meanings in the many languages used in Egypt but to Hebrew ears it was "suffering"; Egypt referred to itself by many names, Masur being one name. (Notice the similarity between Masur and MTSR). In any case, the great irony is that Ancient Israel chooses a similar system as their legendary enslavers — the Egyptians — for the form of government they would most like for themselves, a government led by a king/queen, a royal-ruler.

Euphrates...NHR-PRT...Fruitful-River...NHR = 'river' & PRT is most likely a Babylonian name though might sound to an ancient Hebrew speaker like some conjugations of PRH 'to bear fruit, make fruitful'...and the river-valley was certainly known for being fruitful and fertile

Gilead...GLAYD...Pile-of-Protests...from GL = 'pile (of

rocks)' and AYD from AYUD 'to protest, to say again and again, witness'

Gomorrah...AYMRH...Bind-Abundant-Harvest... perhaps from AYMR 'to bind sheaves (at harvest time)... insinuating abundance'...harvest-time was festival-time as so much work yielded (hopefully) quick currency/ wealth

Haran...CHRN...Scorched-and-Glowing-Land...from CHRR = 'to glow, burn, dry out'

Hebron...CHBRON...Enchanting-Allies...from CHBR = 'to unite, tie a magic knot, to cast a spell'

Jabbok...YBQ...Devastate-and-Demoralize...from a form of the verb BQQ 'to devastate, demoralize, pour out, take over in some wild and uncontrollable way'

Jordan...YRDN...Going-Down-River...from YRD 'to go down'

Moriah...MORAYH...YAHWEH's-Gonna-See... participle-form of RAHH 'to see' and YH = YAH, an abbreviated form of YAHWEH

Oaks of Mamre...AHLNY MMRAH...The-Trees-Where-You-Can-Get-Drunk-&-See-Things-&-Do-Wild-Things...from AHLON = 'great oak, terebinth tree, turpentine tree,' used to create strong drink/liquor and many delicacies in the ancient world (perhaps descended from AHYL = 'strong, a ram')...AHLNY is the plural & MMRAH could be from the verb MRAH 'to flap wings, to whip, to be lusty' or could also hearken back to a participle-form of RAHH 'to see' (in the Abram story just after Lot departs, YAHWEH tells Abram multiple times 'See!')

Padan Aram...PDN AHRM...The-Highland-Palaces-on-the-Plateau...AHRM/Aram is Syria, the northern country near Babylon and sometimes controlled by it, and may derive from AHRMON 'citadel, towers, highlands...as in mountains that create the effect of towers'...and *Strong's Exhaustive Concordance* suggests that PDN means 'plateau' and seems to have cognates in Arabic+ that have to do with oxen and herds...animals that graze on plateaus and rolling fields

Peniel/Penuel...PNYAHL/PNUAHL...Face-of-Divinity...PN = 'face' and AHL = EL, chief god/divinity... singular in the word itself but rather unusually in the words immediately following the first instance of the name at 32.30 is 'faces to faces'...a double plural...and as for the variance of Y vs. U in the name, it doesn't change the meaning much, if at all, and perhaps even could be a scribal copying error as U is basically a longer Y in orthography...that is to say that Y is kind of like half a U in length of ink-stroke

Seir...SAYYR...The-Rugged-Land-That-Will-Make-Your-Hair-Stand-On-End...from SAYR = 'hair' and *Strong's Exhaustive Concordance* notes that it's very similar to the similar word SAYYR (same consonants, different vowels) which is 'devil, hairy goat, faun, satyr' (say <u>SYYR</u> and <u>satyr</u> out loud...very similar-sounding!) and a number of other similar-sounding words have to do with being 'horribly afraid'...whirlwinds and storms coming out of nowhere, and the like

Shechem...SHCM...Rise-Early-Load-Your-Shoulders-With-Work...SHCM = 'shoulders' (noun) and SHCM = 'to rise early for work, to be eager'...note this is also a name for a character (Early-and-Eager, who defiled Dinah) though it's a place-name in the story before the character, it seems...going back to Abram

Sheol...SHAHL ...'down to death's resting place in the underworld'...interestingly, related to the verb SHAHL 'to ask about, to inquire'...at the time when these biblical stories were told, Sheol was the place of the dead, the place where the dead went as long as they had a decent burial...someone like Lot's wife who became a salt-pillar and then blew away in the wind would have no place in Sheol...only the people who had a decent burial would make it to Sheol in the ancient imagination

Sodom...SDM...Their-Bondage...although this city name is probably from a foreign derivation, an ancient Hebrew might have heard SDM as 'their bondage, shackles' as SD = 'bonds, chains' and adding an M at the end is the plural-possessive form. The great irony is that in their dancing around and sexual licentiousness they thought they were so free...but in the Hebrew mind, it's bondage. And later even worse...the city has the reputation of being 'scorched'

Succoth...SCOT...Hut...from SCH = 'hut, booth'

Terebinth of Moreh...AHLON MORH...Drunk-Tree-Gets-You-Flowing-Like-Arrows...AHLON = 'great oak, terebinth tree, turpentine tree,' used to create strong drink liquor and many delicacies in the ancient world (perhaps descended from AHYL = 'strong, a ram') & MORH = participle-form of YRAH 'to throw, shoot arrows' and at its root 'to be in the flow, like water'

Timnah...TMNH...Count-It-Up...a form of the verb MNH 'to count, to number'...appropriate name for a city where sheep are shorn and wool needs to be weighed and sold/traded in the Judah story

Ur of the Chaldeans...AHUR CSDYM...the Flaming Light, the Ancient Babylonian Land of the Wise-Ones... AHUR = 'flame/light' & CSDYM = name for region of Southern Babylon, sometimes associated with astrology, ancient ways of wisdom

Zoar...TSOAYR...Little-Place...from ZAYR = 'to become insignificant'

Bibliography

On the deep past of the Ancient Near East from which the Bible springs...most important to understanding anything of the Bible as the storycrafting bands of YAH and X weren't creating out of thin air...they were creating out of the basement-stories of the deep past... just as we do today:

Michael David Coogan. *Stories from Ancient Canaan.* Louisville, KY: Westminster, 1978.

Nicola Crüsemann, Margarete Van Ess, Markus Hilgert, and Beate Salje. *Uruk: First City of the Ancient World.* Los Angeles: J. Paul Getty Museum, 2013. This beautiful book took me back to memories of Berlin and an afternoon at the *Pergamonmuseum* and being amazed at the Uruk exhibit...but as I viewed the exhibit I did not yet realize Uruk's profound importance to the Genesis stories... perhaps the entire imagination against which the bands of YAH and X and the prophets are pushing, instead seeking the nomadic life, the freedom of the wind.

Stephanie Dailey. *Myths of Mesopotamia: Creation, the Flood, Gilgamesh, and Others.* Oxford: Oxford University Press, 1989. Fascinating translation in that Dailey translates the *Gilgamesh* passage about Enkidu and the temple-prostitute as "love-making"...and then in the notes makes the clear connection that this kind of sex is from the rear, her fleshy rear — and that such a sexual position is well attested in Mesopotamian art, etc. While I salute Dailey's forthrightness in her notes 71 pages after the story/translation, we need more scholars who come right out and include that information in the text/ translation itself — whether that translation is of ancient myths from Babylon or Canaan or Israel, like the Bible itself. The time for hiding is over — the pain it has wreaked for millennia for those who "live by every word of God" in their Bible translations is not small, especially the pain inflicted on those not seen as pure by the biblical priestly purity/holiness codes written, in all likelihood, to smother the prophets/ecstatics and their wild ways of knowing and being known by YAHWEH.

John Gardner and John Maier. *Gilgamesh*. New York: Vintage, 1985. This translation says — in the translation itself — that Enkidu "lay" and then "fucked" the temple-prostitute. No information about sexual positions though a much clearer image than just "lay" which is used at first.

Alexander Heidel. *The Babylonian Genesis: The Story of Creation*. Chicago: University of Chicago Press, 1951.

On the ancient world from which these scriptures — the band of YAH's and X's stories and later biblical writings — emerged:

Robert Alter. *The Art of Biblical Narrative*. New York: Basic Books, 2011 (revised and updated edition).

Israel Finkelstein. "A Great United Monarchy? Archeological and Historical Perspectives." (I read it via academia.edu...originally published in *One God - One Cult - One Nation*. ed. by Reinhard G. Kratz and Hermann Spieckermann. Berlin: De Gruyter, 2010.)

Israel Finkelstein and Neil Asher Silberman. *The Bible Unearthed: Archaeology's New Vision of Ancient Israel and the Origin of Its Sacred Texts.* New York: Touchstone, 2002.

Jennifer A. Glancy. *Slavery in Early Christianity*. Minneapolis: Fortress, 2006.

Theodore W. Jennings, Jr. *Jacob's Wound: Homoerotic Narrative in the Literature of Ancient Israel*. New York: Continuum, 2005. This book flipped my world up-side down. I found a used copy at Strand Bookstore in New

York City three years ago while there for Feldenkrais training. For the past year or so before that, I had been working on a book about the prophets and was flailing around with it. There were strange things in the Ancient Hebrew texts that I didn't think were palatable for modern audiences. I wondered if I had the courage and resolve to say out loud — or in writing — what was there. Dr. Jenning's book gave me the nudge to go with it, to let those ancient writings say now what they were trying to say then...hopefully with some ears in this 21st century that might wish to listen and ponder a YAHWEH that wants intimate relationship with you and me. Irony of ironies, a high school religion colleague took graduate school classes with Dr. Jennings at Chicago Theological Seminary! My only sadness is that Dr. Jennings died before I could meet him. My condolences and love to his wife and family and many students.

Bruce J. Malina. *The New Testament World: Insights from Cultural Anthropology*. Louisville, KY: Westminster/John Knox, 1993.

Herbert G. May. *Oxford Bible Atlas*. New York: Oxford, 1984.

Walter J. Ong. *Orality and Literacy: The Technologizing of the Word*. New York: Routledge, 2012.

Thomas Römer, editor. *The Future of the Deuteronomistic History*. Leuven: Leuven University Press / Peeters, 2000.

Thomas Römer. *L'Ancien Testament*. Paris: Que sais-je? / Humensis, 2019.

Thomas Römer and Loyse Bonjour. *L'homosexualité dans le Proche-Orient ancien et la Bible*. Geneva: Editions Labor et Fides, 2016.

Thomas Römer. *The Invention of God*. (trans Raymond Geuss). Cambridge, MA: Harvard University Press, 2015.

Thorkil Vanggaard. *Phallos: A Symbol and Its History in the Male World.* New York: International Universities Press, 1972.

On the imagination of the prophets:

Walter Brueggemann. *The Prophetic Imagination.* Minneapolis: Fortress Press, 1978.

Arthur J. Dewey, Roy W. Hoover, Lane C. McGaughy, Daryl D. Schmidt. *The Authentic Letters of Paul: A New Reading of Paul's Rhetoric and Meaning.* Salem, OR: Polebridge, 2010.

Robert W. Funk, Arthur J. Dewey, & the Jesus Seminar. *The Gospel of Jesus: According to the Jesus Seminar.* Salem, OR: Polebridge, 2015.

Robert J. Miller, editor. *The Complete Gospels.* Salem, OR: Polebridge, 2010.

J. Andrew Overman. *Matthew's Gospel and Formative Judaism: The Social World of the Matthew Community.* Minneapolis: Fortress, 1990.

Bernard Brandon Scott. *Hear Then the Parable: A Commentary on the Parables of Jesus.* Minneapolis: Augsburg, 1989.

Indries Shah. *The Sufis.* New York: Anchor, 1971.

Amos Niven Wilder. *Theopoetic: Theology and the Religious Imagination.* Minneapolis: Fortress, 1976.

Walter Wink. *Engaging the Powers: Discernment and Resistance in a World of Domination.* Minneapolis: Fortress, 1992.

On the later desert fathers and mothers who emerged during the Roman Empire, perhaps following the prophets before them

Sayings from the Desert Fathers. Translation & art by Yushi Nomura. Maryknoll, NY: Orbis, 2001. Check out the excellent Epilogue by Henri Nouwen where he refers to Thomas Merton's understanding of the desert fathers and mothers feeling the need to swim away from "the shipwreck" of life in the Roman Empire, or any empire. (We get a glimpse of why in Glancy's *Slavery in Early Christianity* noted above.)

On the kind of language that is the wind...

David Abram. *The Spell of the Sensuous: Perception and Language in a More-Than-Human-World*. New York: Vintage, 1996.

Moshe Feldenkrais. *The Potent Self: A Study of Spontaneity and Compulsion.* Berkeley, CA: North Atlantic Books, 2002.

Used for translating the 'original' Hebrew texts of the Bible:

Biblia Hebraica Stuttgartensia. Stuttgart: Deutsche Bibelgesellschaft, 1990.

F. Brown, S. Driver, and C. Briggs. *The Brown-Driver-Briggs Hebrew and English Lexicon*. Peabody, MA: Hendrickson, 1996.

William L. Holladay. *A Concise Hebrew and Aramaic Lexicon of the Old Testament*. Grand Rapids, MI: William B. Eerdmans Publishing Co, 1988.

biblehub.com was very useful as well in helping to compare verb-form possibilities and its excellent clickable concordances, especially *Strong's Exhaustive Concordance*.

One invites love and flexibility...

today...groups who are curious about the deeper roots and who seek to mine the gifts of the present moment and all present...circles of deciders

the writer of the Gospel of Thomas, wisdom through personal experience and 'study-through-play' of past wisdom to create new wisdom

Paul and his all-are-equal-before-God imagination...Paul is the first imaginer ever of democratic communities without slavery

Jesus and his clever, funny wisdom sayings and actions inviting conversion within and love of enemies and relying on God alone (not priests or kings or authorities)

wildly clever poems of the prophets...
Amos, the Isaiahs, Jeremiah, and others

the band of X, authors of 1 & 2 Samuel and (perhaps) 1 & 2 Kings and the inspiring stories about the prophets and the foolishness of kings & priests

the band of YAH's Genesis stories that upset the hierarchical & patriarchal apple-cart of Ancient Babylon

ecstatics' (prophets') mountaintop experiences of YAHWEH, the wind...the playful, clever, spiraling, poetic imagination reacting to Ancient Babylon's and Ancient Egypt's royal/slave superpower imaginations today…groups who still think one human being is worth more than another (hierarchical, priestly, royal/slave fascist imagination)

the writer of the Gospel of John and "belief" as all you need (makes Thomas look like a fool)

Peter and his hierarchical camp that rejected Paul's vision of equality and perhaps wrote Acts of the Apostles to reduce Paul's power/prestige (they also change Paul's letters years later)

the military/royal title "**Christ**" and the king/redeemer mythology inflicted upon Jesus, an imagination cementing over Jesus' wisdom and lifestyle

Ezekiel, Nehemiah, Ezra and I/II Chronicles...
the priestly efforts to craft a priest-led religious tradition and subvert the prophets

priestly imagination that assembled the **Torah** and the character **Moses** as greatest of everything, even greatest prophet…though he has little to no ecstatic poetry/action like the prophets

the **Deuteronomist** "political party" who enabled the royals and began the first written Bible during King Josiah's reign

Ancient Babylon & its towers and metropolises like Uruk…and **the hierarchical, royal/slave imagination** required to build such things… where one human is thought to be better than another…the imagination of slavery/royalty

…one does not.

about the author

Author of **The Naked Path of Prophet** series, Brian J. Shircliff is one of the original founding members of VITALITY Cincinnati in 2010. He is fascinated by the impossible and incredibly important opportunity of trying to imagine or even guess at the human experiences that gave rise to ancient stories and traditions by reading the ancient texts and artifacts we have inherited...the inner basements within us ALL. As a somatic explorer and meditator, he directs programs at VITALITY and is excited to see VITAL-friends beginning their own small businesses through yoga, meditation, gardening/ farming, sustainability, Movement Intelligence®, Healing Touch and more that they go on to invent with the big wind of life.

about the artists

Katherine Colborn...*interior image of a member of the band of YAH (dedication)*

Katherine is an artist and instructor working in Cincinnati, OH. Her work has been published internationally in *ArtMaze Magazine* and she has exhibited her work around the United States. Recent exhibitions include a solo show at the Kansas City Artist Coalition, as well as group shows with the Bolivar Gallery at the University of Kentucky and the Weatherspoon Art Museum, and nationally juried exhibitions at Site: Brooklyn in New York City, Manifest Gallery in Cincinnati, OH, and Durham Art Guild in Raleigh, NC. Her work engages primarily with themes of sanctuary and threshold, exploring the place of painting in a culture saturated with speed and an abundance of imagery.

Julie Lucas...*other interior images, cover design, VITALITY's logos*

Julie is a graphic designer, illustrator and meditator whose creative process draws from inquiry and deep listening into the heart of it all. See more of her work at *withinwonder.com.*

Frances N Malone, HTCP...*front cover images*

Healer. Intuitive. Artist. Married. Three daughters; 10 grandchildren; 1 great-grandchild. Gardener of all things; tame and wild. Reads many different genres. Owned by a dog and cat. Fed by nature. Loves to knit. Walks for fun. Has an inquisitive mind. Deep love of all the Madonnas. Grateful for the places I have lived and the people whom I have met. Other art on Instagram at *francesmalone72.*

Tom Payne graciously and wonderfully photographed Fran's cover painting and Katherine's sketch. Thank you!

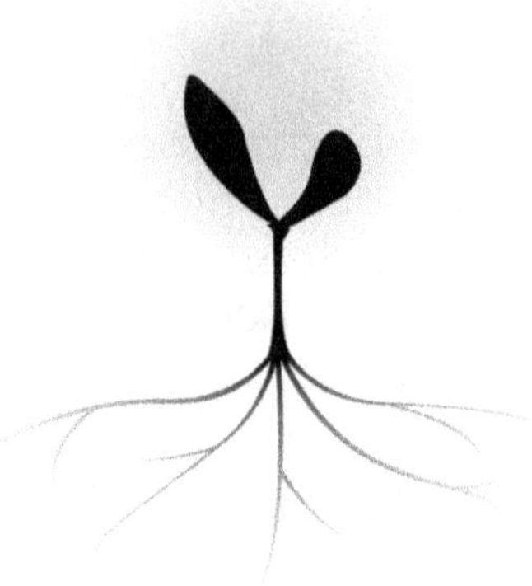

VITALITY buzz, bliss + books LLC

publishing books created by VITALITY's circle of friends who inspire love, creativity, possibility...

vitalitybuzz.org

In addition to **The Naked Path of Prophet** series and the graphic-novel **YAHWEH IS THE WIND!** authored by Brian J. Shircliff and illustrated by Sean K. Long...

A New Setting of the Spiritual Exercises: Hearing, Seeing, Feeling Old Stories in New Ways
the Companions of VITALITY Cincinnati

Selected Homilies: allowing life experience to open up the ways and the Word of God
Richard Bollman, S.J.

yoga is THE ALL: an invitation to sensational life
the Companions of VITALITY Cincinnati

With You in Our Dreams...a reading & coloring book for all ages by Mike Eck (poet) & Claire Long (artist)

Midlife Calm: An Alternative to Midlife Crisis
Krista M. Powers

Milford: A poet's life in spiritual retreat
Evan R. Underbrink

Now Is Love, poem & paintings
Cooper Hayes Simmons

Adventures of Hope: A New Family for Hopi
Shannon M. Petree, True J. Knowles, & Jessi Journey

Rodney the Rhino Just Can't Win
Kyle Powers (author) & Katie Brobst (illustrator)

a final poem

YAHWEH as experienced
by the biblical prophets/ecstatics is...

the anti-religion and the ante-religion

no ritual
no creed
no code
no cult
open group...

for all who are open themselves to the wind instead of the cruel demands of hierarchy (government, politics, organized religion).

Only misfits may apply — all who no longer fit into the hierarchy or who never fit into it in the first place.

God tops our tricky misfit Jacob,
even gropes and penetrates Jacob's hollow-hole —

Jacob's prophetic/ecstatic sweet-talking style tops God
and everyone in his family —

but YAHWEH tops all humans
and all conceptions of 'God' — ancient or modern —

YAHWEH...Life...Breath...Atmosphere of THE ALL!

Unfurl from your clothes, feel the wind on your skin...let every orifice and pore welcome YAHWEH...know and be known...YAHWEH...call upon It, call upon Its name...

the deep love-making pants that erupt from you... the love-rushes...let YAHWEH ravish you in your wild love-making life together...all of us being breathed by YAHWEH...

It's bliss...ecstasy...whispering for you, for ALL...

www.ingramcontent.com/pod-product-compliance
Lightning Source LLC
Chambersburg PA
CBHW070856120626
46546CB00001B/26
* 9 7 8 1 9 5 4 6 8 8 0 4 9 *